Problem Solving with the Private Sector

"An essential work comprising an objective and comprehensive analysis of modern public sector management instruments to lead to effective and efficient service delivery."
Christopher H. Bovis, *University of Hull, UK*

Problem Solving with the Private Sector presents advice and solutions for fruitful government–business alliances from the perspective of everyday public management. With a focus on job training, economic development, regulation, and finance and innovation, each chapter discusses a traditional tool of government, presented in a practical and applied manner, as well as the implementation of the tools with clear examples. Content-rich case studies on a wide range of policy issues, including regulatory policy, natural resources, manufacturing, financial services, and health care highlight opportunities for government and business to collaborate to pursue the public good.

This book offers current and future public managers possible solutions to complex problems for effective government–business alliances in a range of settings. It is essential reading for all those studying public management, public administration, and public policy.

Daniel E. Bromberg is Assistant Professor of Public Administration and the MPA Director at the University of New Hampshire, USA.

MARC HOLZER, SERIES EDITOR

MARC HOLZER, SERIES EDITOR

Problem Solving with the Private Sector

A PUBLIC SOLUTIONS HANDBOOK

Edited by
Daniel E. Bromberg

Routledge
Taylor & Francis Group

NEW YORK AND LONDON

First published 2016
by Routledge
711 Third Avenue, New York, NY 10017

and by Routledge
2 Park Square, Milton Park, Abingdon, Oxon OX14 4RN

Routledge is an imprint of the Taylor & Francis Group, an informa business

Library of Congress Cataloging-in-Publication Data
Names: Bromberg, Daniel E., editor.
Title: Problem solving with the private sector : a public solutions handbook / edited by Daniel E. Bromberg.
Description: First Edition. | New York : Routledge, 2016. | Series: The public solution handbook series ; 7 | Includes bibliographical references and index.
Identifiers: LCCN 2015041314 | ISBN 9781138920798 (hardback : alk. paper) | ISBN 9780765644060 (pbk. : alk. paper) | ISBN 9781315686820 (ebook)
Subjects: LCSH: Public-private sector cooperation—United States.
Classification: LCC HD3872.U6 P76 2016 | DDC 658.4/03—dc23
LC record available at http://lccn.loc.gov/2015041314

ISBN: 978-1-138-92079-8 (hbk)
ISBN: 978-0-7656-4406-0 (pbk)
ISBN: 978-1-315-68682-0 (ebk)

Typeset in Times
by Apex CoVantage, LLC

Contents

Figures

Tables

Series Editor's Introduction

I am proud to announce the sixth volume in the Public Solutions Handbook series: *Problem Solving with the Private Sector*, edited by Daniel E. Bromberg. For centuries, governments and private businesses have been balancing the needs of societies. Some argue that where markets fail, governments can succeed, and in situations where governments fail, markets may offer compelling solutions. It seems we are well beyond the perspective that the public and private sectors are separated by some illusory wall in which functions of one can be isolated from the other. Rather, we frequently view government and business as mutually dependent when it comes to dealing with society's most complex problems. Certainly, we recognize that government and business play different roles in these solutions; nonetheless, a collaborative effort is often the most productive.

This book makes no attempt to argue the proper role of government and or business. Instead, the book provides a series of chapters offering possible solutions to complex problems. While many of the cases highlighted in this volume provide successful examples, we caution readers to thoughtfully pursue these collaborative efforts with their eyes wide open.

This volume is divided into four sections: Job Training, Regulation, Economic Development, and Finance and Innovation. Each section offers chapters with specific case studies to highlight opportunities.

In Chapter 1 Lauren Bock Mullins, Alexander C. Henderson, and Linda L. Vila focus on public–private partnerships supporting workforce development in public education. The chapter provides a broad overview of these relationships and explores partnerships as tools for retaining an existing workforce, connecting unique or focused private-sector needs with specifically tailored programs in public educational institutions, and providing early access to educational opportunities for children. The key takeaways offer thoughts about scalability, addressing specific needs of the population and how such partnerships might offer solutions to complex problems.

In Chapter 2 Brian Robert Calfano, Joumana Silyan-Saba, and Sheldon Cruz provide a very specific example of a public–private collaborative effort taking place in the City of Los Angeles. The chapter focuses on the collaboration between the City of Los Angeles Human Relations Commission, the Youth Ambassador's Program, and Google's Los Angeles office. The collaborative effort seeks to engage high school students on a number of fronts, including an introduction to government, a historical perspective of the city, civic engagement, human relations, social justice and organization, and professional and personal development. The broad goals of the program create opportunities for both government and business to engage with constituents and to create better relations with youth in the community.

In Part 2 the book shifts focus to collaboration in environmental regulation. In Chapter 3 Ian C. Graig describes a collaborative effort in the rulemaking process concerning the automotive industry. Specifically, the chapter examines the rulemaking process for automotive carbon emissions. Ultimately, Graig concludes that early collaboration is essential to avoid some of the typical pitfalls that government, industry, and citizen groups frequently experience in the regulatory context. The goal of these collaborative efforts should be to find solutions that work for all parties involved, increasing the likelihood of successful efforts.

In Chapter 4 Jian Cui offers insight on engaging the community in decisions about hydraulic fracturing or "fracking." She introduces "smart engagement," a strategic tool to help both citizens and public leaders move forward through these challenging decisions. The framework offered in this chapter will help communities find common ground, which can lead to more sustainable solutions.

In Chapter 5 Katharine A. Owens explores the balance between business and environmental needs by examining a case from the Netherlands. As Owens writes, this is a case that needs to balance those who "support nature for its own sake, whereas others view nature's value only in its capacity to support human activity." These two different perspectives make for a complex, yet very common, policy environment. Ultimately, the solution is one in which compromise shines through, in which neither side is completely satisfied but the policy moves forward.

In Section 3 the book shifts to business–government collaborations in economic development. In Chapter 6 Jonathan Q. Morgan looks at collaboration among government, business, and the university. He focuses on how a collaborative model among these three partners, known as "the Triple Helix," can leverage knowledge and technology to increase economic development in the region. Morgan's chapter explores how communities can strategically align goals across sectors, building on the skill set of each partner. Although these partnerships are often complex and challenging to sustain, the benefits are great in terms of economic development.

In Chapter 7 Carrie Blanchard Bush and Karen Jumonville focus on an economic development effort that took place in Tallahassee, Florida. The case demonstrates how collaborative efforts between government and business can enhance economic development. One of the major results of the collaborative effort was the "Fast Tracking" system created by both government and business to help manage new development in Tallahassee. Tallahassee, like many communities, tries to balance a number of needs, including community identity, land use issues, and development. This case is instructive on many of the challenges that communities wrestle with.

In Section 4 the book focuses on areas of finance and innovation in business–government relations. In Chapter 8 Joshua Franzel and Ryan Gregory provide a range of cases that cover important responsibilities, from (1) generating funding for higher education to (2) investing assets to cover pension and retiree health benefits to (3) pooling and investing assets for local governments. These cases are illustrative examples of public–private arrangements that have been established to manage important public trust funds.

In Chapter 9 Quintus Jett and Arturo E. Osorio explore the idea of a benefit corporation. Benefit corporations offer private companies the flexibility of pursuing dual roles of profit seeking and social benefit by providing them with a unique tax status. A number of recent trends make this new legal status an effective solution to solve public problems. First, as government continues to shift responsibility for service provision to private businesses, a benefit corporation offers government an option to contract with a group of companies that have legally committed to pursuing the public good—similar to nonprofit organizations. Second, the benefit corporation model caters to the ideals of millennials, who in multiple surveys say that they think businesses should pursue positive social impacts along with profit (see for example the 2015 Deloitte Millennial Survey).

The last chapter of the book, written by Daniel E. Bromberg and Jonathan B. Justice, focuses on Social Impact Bonds. Social Impact Bonds leverage private investment to pursue a public initiative. These arrangements typically provide a service through a nonprofit provider and are managed by a third-party intermediary. While highlighting some of the opportunities that might exist, Bromberg and Justice caution against being overly optimistic about Social Impact Bonds.

Overall this book provides a wide range of opportunities for government and business to collaborate to pursue the public good. Many of the opportunities, while effective, have a number of challenges that must be overcome. The goal of this book is to highlight some examples of the opportunities so that both students and practitioners may learn from these experiences while pursuing effective partnerships. We hope that both the successes and challenges of the cases communicates across the U.S. will aid managers in future pursuits.

The impetus for this series of public management handbooks is simply that public managers must have ready access to the best practices and lessons learned. That knowledge base is surprisingly extensive and rich, including insights from rigorous academic studies, internal government reports and publications, and foundation-supported research. Access to that knowledge, however, is limited by substantial barriers: expensive books and academic journals, "thick" academic language and hard to decipher jargon, and the sheer volume of information available. Our objectives in initiating this series are to identify insight based in practice, to build competencies from that knowledge base, to deliver them at an affordable price point, and to communicate that guidance in clear terms.

GROUNDED INSIGHTS

Each volume in the series incorporates case-based research. Each volume will draw helpful insights and guidelines from academe, government, and foundation sources, focusing on an emerging opportunity or issue in the field. The initial volume, for example, addresses shared services for municipalities and counties, e-government and websites, generational differences, government counter-corruption strategies, public-sector innovation, and performance measurement and improvement.

COMPETENCIES

We initiated this Public Solutions Handbook series to help build the competencies necessary to empower dedicated, busy public servants—many of whom have no formal training in the management process for the public offices and agencies they have been selected to lead—to respond to emerging issues, to deliver services that policymakers have promised to the public, to carry out their missions efficiently and effectively, and to work in partnership with their stakeholders. Enabling practitioners to access and apply evidence-based insights will begin to restore trust in governments through high-performing public, nonprofit, and contracting organizations.

Just as important, students in graduate-degree programs, many of whom are already working in public and nonprofit organizations, are seeking succinct, pragmatic, grounded guidance that will help them succeed far into the future as they rise to positions of greater responsibility and leadership. This includes students in master of public administration (MPA), master of public policy (MPP), master of nonprofit management (MNPM), and even some master of business administration (MBA) and doctor of law (LLD) programs.

AFFORDABILITY

Handbook prices are often unrealistically high. The marketplace is not serving the full range of public managers who need guidance on practices. When faced with the need for creative solutions to cut budgets, educate for ethics, tap the problem-solving expertise of managers and employees, or report progress clearly and transparently, a grasp of such practices is essential. Many handbooks are priced in the hundreds of dollars, beyond the purchasing power of an individual or an agency. Journals are similarly priced out of reach of practitioners. In contrast, each volume in the Public Solutions Handbook series is modestly priced.

CLEAR WRITING

Although the practice of public administration and public management should be informed by published research, the books that are now marketed to practitioners and students in the field are often overly abstract and theoretical, failing to distill published research into clear and necessary applications. There is substantial valuable literature in the academic journals, but necessarily, it is written to standards that do not easily connect with practitioner audiences. Even in instances when practitioners receive peer-reviewed journals as a benefit of association membership, they clearly prefer magazines or newsletters that present information in a straightforward, journalistic style. Too often, readers set the academic journals aside.

Marc Holzer

Part I

Job Training

1

Public–Private Collaboration in Workforce Development

Examining the Intersection of Public Education Programs and Private-Sector Employer Needs

Lauren Bock Mullins, Alexander C. Henderson, and Linda L. Vila

Workforce skills and the nurturing of individual capacity are gaining increasing attention as an area of cooperative activity for public and private organizations. Though much attention has focused on capacity building within organizations and on workforce development programs as a means of supporting the unemployed, another specific focus is on the creation and development of innovative educational and job training programs. In many instances these new programs are taking place at local schools, community colleges, and state universities. The benefits of these activities accrue to both sectors: public-sector organizations provide training and development more directly tied to the needs of employers; by taking part in the training, private organizations ensure that they are able to hire people with the requisite skills and abilities. To explore these issues, this chapter provides an overview of the literature regarding public–private partnerships and collaborative activities.

These types of intersectoral collaborations are often referred to as "public–private partnerships" (PPPs), "public–private cooperation" (PPC), or other related forms, such as "business improvement districts" (BIDs) or "community improvement districts" (CIDs). These partnerships are, however, not without attendant conceptual difficulties. Although American socio-political and legal foundations may encourage us to adhere to a separation of the public and private sectors, the interrelationships between these sectors are instead becoming more and more prominent. Businesses are experiencing varying amounts of stress as they hire and retain employees in the midst of pressures from the organization's environment, whereas governments work to both improve economic development opportunities for businesses and become more efficient during exceedingly challenging financial times.

These challenges are especially important when considering the shifts in demand for and consumption of goods and services, and the necessary skills and training related to these shifts. Recently, Alperovitz discussed a "New-Economy Movement," noting that ". . . the movement seeks an economy that is increasingly green and socially responsible, and one that is based on rethinking the nature of ownership and the growth paradigm that guides conventional policies" (Alperovitz, 2011, para. 2). This movement to the "New Economy" produces concomitant pressures on both the public and private sectors to provide talented and skilled workers who fit production and service needs. These economic challenges seem far beyond the capacity of the current economic and political system, suggesting a greater need for innovation and substantial changes in systems. Furthermore, the moving target of what the new economy actually is or should be remains a quandary. The initial expectation was that information technology would create a new economy; instead the new economy seems to have begun in the 1990s with increasing innovation in management and creating more competition among businesses, as opposed to the emergence of the Internet (Farrell, 2003).

The need for workforce development is not a new trend for the public sector, which has long developed and supported workforce development programs, with a number of these initiatives stemming from the highest levels of government. Presidential initiatives for public–private partnerships began as early as 1933, when President Franklin Delano Roosevelt commissioned the Tennessee Valley Authority (Roosevelt, 1933). Over the past 80 years, public and private organizations have become increasingly interested in partnerships to develop workforce skills and individual capacity, and to produce mutually beneficial outcomes. President Barack Obama announced in February 2014 the launch of a public–private program to promote economic and educational opportunities for black and Latino disadvantaged youth; the program will have $200 million in support from foundations, public officials, and leaders in business (Lee, 2014).

Private-sector organizations are taking notice of the benefits of collaboration in providing employee development and ensuring a sufficient supply of workers in the immediate geographic region. A survey of private-sector executives found substantial concern for training and development amid the recovery after the Great Recessions, with more than two-thirds of CEOs planning to further invest in the nation's talent pipeline (PricewaterhouseCoopers, 2013). Such investment allows for some amount of influence in the process of defining and shaping the local available workforce without the risk or loss of profits that could come with the full assumption of providing internal training or education.

Businesses are, in many cases, struggling to recruit appropriately educated and skilled staff. Winthrop, Bulloch, Bhatt, and Wood (2013) noted, "[t]he inability to secure future talent with the right skills and to manage talent-related costs keeps firms from being able to quickly scale up their operations to meet demand in new locations and to launch new products and services" (p. 2). Firms are reacting by launching efforts to build sustainable talent pipelines and purposefully seeking out and engaging in public–private partnerships.

The educational focus of public–private collaboration to build these talent pipelines is a relatively new trend, with many public schools and universities engaged in workforce training programs that have the potential to increase both development and enrollment. An influx of capital to support new programs is necessary and significant, as cuts in funding for public education are becoming deeper and more pervasive. Private educational institutions are not far behind their public counterparts, exhausting long-held techniques to lower operating budgets, keep tuition down, increase enrollment, and enhance reputation.

A number of questions arise as to the appropriateness of such partnerships in relation to public education. For example, does it make sense for public education institutions to knowingly educate students based on the surrounding job market, or does this, in essence, constitute a process of catering to business preferences? This also raises potential questions about the structure of higher education. If pipeline programs are successful, does it make sense to move toward further privatization in which private educational institutions would compete with public institutions?

Public–private collaborations in education also raise questions of concern for businesses as to whether it is worth investing in the local talent or better to contract out to ready-to-go staff in other more economically favorable regions where workforce costs and the regulatory environment are less intensive. One needs to look no further than debates about minimum wage and fair compensation to understand how outsourcing can wreak havoc on a local economy. However, with advancements in technology and globalization, it could be argued that outsourcing may be a more effective and efficient way of handling staffing needs.

Though compelling questions exist from the perspectives of both the public and private sectors, the focus of this chapter is more preliminary and broad: In essence, why are public–private partnerships appropriate in providing workforce training, and are they effective? This chapter begins with an overview of public–private partnerships. This is followed by an introduction to current examples of public–private partnerships aimed at the development of workforce training programs in public educational institutions. Examining the current state of public–private partnerships in theory and practice will provide a more nuanced understanding of program implementation, an opportunity for further robust theory building, and future creation of best practices for such collaboration. This will contribute substantively to the base of knowledge available to students and practitioners interested in collaborative activities.

EXAMINING THE PUBLIC–PRIVATE DISTINCTION AND COLLABORATION

Developing an understanding of the characteristics, distinctiveness, and compatibility of the public and private sectors is an important first step in framing a discussion of the collaborative process. Identifying similarities and differences across sectors allows for making distinctions and determining areas of intersection in which these partnerships can be established. Scholars and practitioners from both the public and private sectors have grappled with these topics and have provided answers steeped in theory and observation.

A number of key distinctions between sectors exist. Allison (1992) explores Sayre's precept that management of public and private sectors are not alike, but for insignificant similarities such as planning strategy, managing internal components, and managing external constituencies (p. 490). Perry and Rainey (1988) outline and explore the varying ways that scholars have differentiated the sectors, and offer a typology for understanding and unpacking the differences in three arenas: *ownership* of the organization, as determined by the legal status of the entity as a publicly or privately held body; *funding* of the organization by public or private entities (or a combination); and *mode of social control*, which differentiates between the influence of market forces and the "polyarchical" control of a public-sector bureaucracy (p. 195) (see Table 1.1).

Boyne (2002) finds evidence in the literature that public organizations are more bureaucratic and that managers in the public sector have less organizational commitment and seem to be less focused on materialism than those in the private sector. In essence, sectoral differences exist and are a key consideration in how we think about these collaborative activities.

Collaboration is, however, possible and important. Osbourne and Gabler (1992) focus on the promise of integrating private-sector practices into public-sector agencies. They promise renewal of the public sector and a rethinking of government through a shift in focus to become more "market-oriented," "mission-driven," and "customer-driven" (Osbourne & Gabler, 1992). A natural extension of this package of public-sector reforms, entitled the "New Public Management" (NPM), encourages mutually beneficial cooperation between the public and private sectors given the decentralization, flexibility, and performance-based nature of these relationships.

Table 1.1

Differentiation of Sectors

Concept	Description
Ownership	Ownership of the organization is one factor that creates distinctions between the public and private sectors. Organizations can be *publicly owned* (e.g., governments, government corporations, or enterprises) or *privately owned* (e.g., private enterprises, government-sponsored enterprises, or government-regulated enterprises). Hybrid models may share authority in leadership positions in collaborative activities.
Funding	The primary sources of funding for organizations are important in differentiating sectors. *Public organizations* are generally funded with the proceeds of taxing activities. **Private organizations** are generally funded by the proceeds of market-based activities. Hybrid organizations may be publicly or privately owned, but may derive funding from public sources or market activities.
Mode of Social Control	Organizations may be shaped or controlled by a number of external controls. These may be the aggregate decisions of individuals participating in the market (*private organizations*) or the pluralistic values and interests of individuals and groups acting to influence governmental agencies (*public organizations*).

Note: Adapted from Perry and Rainey (1988).

Both the public and private sectors offer unique attributes to public–private partnerships that may prove beneficial. Public organizations are well versed in navigating regulation, meeting accountability expectations, and ensuring transparency. They are skilled in resource planning, due to stringent annual budgets and acute resource dependencies (Johnson & Scholes, 2001), and in managing project risks associated with strategy and political volatility (Baldry, 1998). Public managers are more oriented to social goals and public interest (Perry, 1996, 1997) and, thus, are able to balance a multitude of internal and external stakeholder interests and agendas, often with contradictory demands and complex obstacles, while assuring stakeholder participation and collaboration in the decision-making process (Behn, 2003; Halachmi & Bovaird, 1997; Llewellyn & Tappin, 2003; Thong, Yap, & Seah, 2000). Public organizations are successful in retaining employees and have less employee turnover than private organizations do; as a result, public servants often have a better understanding of public-sector culture, services, and process than outside experts do (Scholl, 2004). The public sector values equity as an important goal and has a great commitment to providing access to services for all citizens regardless of their ability to pay (Berman, 1998).

Private organizations offer greater variance than public organizations in the actions management can implement, and they must follow fewer restrictions and regulations governing structure and organizational form. They have more discretion in dealing with employees, particularly in offering monetary incentives and in undertaking and imposing employment actions without repercussions (Meier & O'Toole, 2011; Rainey, 2003). Similarly, they have more discretion in fulfilling customers' needs and generating customer satisfaction (Jurisch, Ikas, Wolf, & Krcmar, 2014). This sector possesses the malleability to change procurement processes, products, services, and market position (Meier & O'Toole, 2011) and, as a result, has greater in mobility among different markets, creativity, innovation, and entrepreneurship (O'Toole & Meier, 2003). Private entities are especially successful in the areas of project management, change management, and resource management (Abdolvand, Albadvi, & Ferdowsi, 2008; Halachmi & Boviard, 1997), and they value and promote investing in development and research.

There are important differences between public and private organizations. The two sectors complement one other and, by leveraging the expertise of each, a "best of both worlds objective can be achieved: blending the public purpose of creating needed, socially and economically beneficial infrastructures with the efficacy and cost-conscious management capability and financing power of profit-driven corporations" (Riccio, 2014, p. 50).

EMERGING PUBLIC–PRIVATE PARTNERSHIPS

A number of different types of public–private partnerships have emerged in recent years under different names and with different purposes. Wettenhall (2003), in suggesting a classification system for distinguishing different types of public–private partnerships, focuses on consistency in protecting public values across the types. He notes that "[p]ublic service legitimacy, public service ethics, and public service motivation must all be defended and strengthened, so that the public sector can hold its own in all its new intersections with the private sector" (Wettenhall, 2003, p. 99).

Wettenhall presents public–private partnerships as "mixes," noting that the term "partnership" could be misleading, because often public–private partnerships are not what one would think of as a typical partnership. Types of "mixes" he discusses include *mixed enterprises* (public–private owned mix); *outsourcing* or *contracting out* (public has control over the arrangement or policy); and *subsidization, controlled competition,* and *regulation,* in which there are varying levels of interaction between public and private sectors (Wettenhall, 2003, pp. 91–92) (see Table 1.2). According to Wettenhall, these mixes can contain horizontal and vertical relationships, but there is disagreement about whether vertical relationships that involve contracting out are less likely to resemble traditional partnerships.

Thus, aside from studying cases, it is difficult to come to terms with a particular typology for public–private partnerships and/or mixes.

As Flinders (2005) suggests, public–private partnerships are a trade-off in some respects; in return for efficiency and better services, there will be costs in terms of democracy and politics. Bloomfield (2006) draws lessons from local government case studies to show that governments engaging in long-term contracts should be aware of the necessity of contract management, strong governance structure, and expert specialization in order to minimize risk, local resource limitations, and transparency issues. Bloomfield warns that the partnership model is not a good fit for many commercial transactions. Miraftab (2004) warns that public–private partnerships in disadvantaged communities

Table 1.2

Mixing Public and Private Elements

Concept	Description
Mixed Enterprises	Mixed enterprises may include organizations in which ownership is shared between public and private sources. Government organizations may initiate such services and then sell portions of the organization (while remaining majority or minority stockholder).
Outsourcing or Contracting Out	Public organizations may retain authority over the function and policies related to the provision of a key public function, but may engage private organizations to directly provide those services.
Subsidization, Regulation, or Controlled Competition	Public entities may provide subsidies for private organizations to provide services that the public sector cannot provide, may create regulations in such a way that private organizations are favored or supported, or may control the competitive processes by which organizations can assume the authority to provide a service.

Note: Adapted from Wettenhall (2003, pp. 91–92).

could further private interests, while leaving out the public sector and poor communities they are meant to serve. As these authors suggest, such collaborations are not a one-size-fits-all undertaking and should not be taken for granted as such.

Levin (1999) explores public–private partnerships in light of school vouchers and points out that the nature of education is that it serves both public and private interests. He notes that this duplicity can cause some difficulty when these interests are at odds with one another, specifically in terms of education policy. This concern is more recently echoed in higher education as discussed by Belkin and Porter (2014). They note the possibility of private capture of university curricula, something that may prove damaging to academic integrity. In short, such partnerships are not free of extraordinary challenges and potentially harmful effects on the public sector.

Despite the evidence of the limitations of public–private partnerships of all kinds, we must also consider the remarkable and unprecedented benefits that can arise from such arrangements. Kettl (1993) finds that although governments have relied on public–private partnerships since World War II, many have not properly judged the markets, thus reducing the benefit to public organizations. Schaeffer and Loveridge (2002) discuss public–private cooperation in light of characteristics that encourage or inhibit cooperation, and define such dimensions as goals, coordination, and resources. They discuss how cooperation between public and private entities is unique for various reasons, including how public activities are more limited by laws and geography, whereas the private sector is mostly limited by revenue, the ability of the organization to change, and a limited scope of law (patent, antitrust, and employment). However, it is in the differences that are inherent between the public and privates sectors that "opportunities for mutually beneficial cooperation arise" (Schaeffer & Loveridge, 2002, p. 175). Where one sector falls short, the other can lead, and vice versa.

Hodge and Greve (2007) focus on the long-term infrastructure contract and warn that they find mixed results as to whether or not partnerships are effective, illustrating the importance of examining what types of partnerships exist and how classifying them could be useful in future planning of such arrangements. Devising prescriptive models of "if/thens" could be helpful not only in planning, but also in evaluation of performance, because this would encourage comparisons and perhaps establish a ranking system.

BUSINESS IMPROVEMENT DISTRICTS

A brief discussion of business improvement districts (BIDs) is warranted here due to their similarity in function and structure to public–private partnerships. Becker (2010) discusses BIDs as quasi-governmental bodies that have both private and public features, that may be authorized by the public but managed entirely by a private entity. BIDs have been known to accomplish major tasks and have been responsible for mainstream projects, such as the transformation of a suburban business district by a public–private partnership among private developers and Montgomery County, Maryland (Houston, 2003), as well as notable projects like the revitalization of New York City's Times Square (Mitchell, 2008).

A substantial body of research has examined BIDs in varying contexts. Grossman (2010) indicates that BIDs can be conceptualized as public–private partnerships and that they can enhance governance processes and capacity. Caruso and Weber (2008) review performance measurement efforts in BIDs, noting their increased adaptability and tailoring to fit substantive goals. MacDonald, Stokes, and Blumenthal (2010) found that BIDs in Los Angeles appear to mirror the diverse interests of the community in terms of budgeting activities and setting priorities, and that they are aligned to the community's purpose and environments. Ellen, Schwartz, and Voicu (2007) suggest BIDs can generate a positive impact on commercial property values.

However, not all BIDs are equal. Reenstra-Bryant (2010) suggests that in order to increase transparency and accountability of BIDS, performance evaluations need to be customized to fit each set of circumstances, must be more frequent, and must be of better quality and rigor. Likewise, challenges of accountability and management exist (Morcöl & Wolf, 2010), and concepts of accountability to public interest emerge as central to the conversation (Morcöl & Zimmerman, 2006).

Regardless of the name we affix to such partnerships, whether business improvement districts or public–private partnerships, existing research suggests the importance of handling them with care so as to best achieve the goals and objectives of these organizations. Their purpose—the creation of new structures, activities, and capacities—must contribute to optimizing gains and minimizing harm for all parties while introducing pragmatic solutions.

UNPACKING PAST SUCCESSES: RESEARCHING WORKFORCE DEVELOPMENT PROGRAMS

One functional area characterized by mutually beneficial public–private cooperation is that of workforce training programs, particularly those developed within public educational institutions. Pantazis (2002) suggests, ". . . cross-sector partnerships assure the proper level of investment in, and attention to, promoting new learning strategies, taking successful practices to scale, and accelerating the speed of needed changes" (p. 23). These collaborative activities exist both to meet broad educational needs and to create some amount of real and tangible economic benefit.

A number of these partnerships in education have focused on improved diversity and representativeness in specific service sectors. Watson and Froyd (2007), examining pipelines in engineering education, suggest ways in which the education system can help improve diversity by increasing the extent to which the workforce reflects general population demographics. Bailit, Formicola, Herbert, Stavisky, and Zamora (2005) examined a program funded by The Robert Wood Johnson Foundation, the California Endowment, and the W.K. Kellogg Foundation aimed intently at providing better preparation for dental students to serve their communities, practice serving underserved populations, and recruit underserved and minority students to become dentists (Bailit et al., 2005). Though founded by private foundations, officials from public universities and public health care programs were central to the development and implementation of the program. Faculty members and administrators from the University of California, University of Texas, University of Oklahoma, University of Medicine and Dentistry of New Jersey, and National Institutes of Health, as well as administrators from state health agencies, were involved in the advisory board of the joint effort, and dental schools in a number of public universities were involved in program implementation. Extending and deepening representativeness can be a boon for both the private and public sectors as cultural, social, and informational diversity can benefit any field.

Pipelines are also necessary in other fields, such as teacher education. A number of efforts have been successful in recruiting high school students into programs through community colleges, which then lead to baccalaureate degrees and staffing of critical teaching positions from kindergarten through grade 12 classrooms (Bragg, 2007). Such pipelines in teacher education are especially important in times of teacher shortages and in order to improve performance so as to meet and surpass global competition.

Workforce training and educational pipelines have been particularly crucial in the field of health care, where workforce diversity is related to health disparities that continue to plague the health care system (Smith, Nsiah-Kumi, Jones, & Pamies, 2009). Smith et al. (2009) identify ways in which programs can avoid critiques associated with affirmative action law and yet still provide opportunities for minority advancement:

- Expand the number of academic partnerships with local public school districts to increase enrollment in pipeline programs for URM [underrepresented minority] students—Sustained partnerships between local school districts, community-based organizations, and health professions schools provide curricula and experiences that make science exciting and relevant to students. Early exposure to rigorous science programs will prepare students to be competitive for undergraduate and medical school.
- Increase the number of undergraduate and postbaccalaureate programs that seek to increase enrolment in medical education for traditional and nontraditional URMs—Pipeline programs for URM college students and individuals with bachelor's degrees have been successful in preparing URMs for the rigors of medical school.
- Proactively recruit URMs and develop "holistic" admissions strategies in medical school admissions—The selection of well-qualified future health care professionals should be based both upon academic indicators, such as MCAT scores and grade point average, as well as nonacademic factors, including talents, interests, and ability to overcome adversity. Admissions criteria should also focus on an applicant's commitment to working in underserved areas and with vulnerable populations.

(Smith et al., 2009, pp. 844–845)

Existing literature on more general public–private partnerships is also applicable to talent pipeline development. For example, Huxham and Vaugen (2000) point out the importance of establishing trust in collaboration, which is a primary consideration to any successful partnership and something that must be nurtured over time. Trust is important here in that it also works to reduce perceived risk by parties to a partnership. Lowndes and Skelcher (1998) identified and defined four stages of the partnership lifecycle, and highlight the fine line between competition and collaboration at each stage. They note that a key consideration in ensuring the success of partnering is how to manage the ongoing interactions of different governance types and, in the process, be prepared to tackle unexpected problems with pragmatic solutions in a responsive manner. Being prepared to expect the unexpected and pragmatic enough to adjust to changes each step of the way are essential to implementing successful intersectoral partnerships.

EXAMINING INNOVATION, WORKFORCE TRAINING PROGRAMS, AND PUBLIC EDUCATIONAL INSTITUTIONS

Public and private organizations are currently collaborating on a number of workforce training programs that can be of benefit to both sectors. These include programs aimed at the developing and retaining an existing workforce, at connecting unique or focused private-sector needs with specifically tailored programs in public educational institutions, and at providing early access to educational opportunities for children. Understanding the structure and conditions necessary for creating a successful talent pipeline is central to this discussion. In this section, several cases outline the basis of the structure, mission, and key services provided.

Developing the skills of an incumbent workforce and retaining employees is a key consideration for both public officials seeking to provide employment opportunities for residents and private-sector employers attempting to fill positions and retain employees within reach of the organization's operations. These two goals are central to the Ohio Incumbent Workforce Training Voucher Program (Ohio Development Services Agency, 2014). This program, structured as a collaborative effort of the State of Ohio, the Ohio Development Services Agency, and a private Ohio-based jobs website (itself a cooperative activity of the National Federation of Independent Businesses and the State of Ohio), has a mission to provide vouchers of up to $250,000 per fiscal year to private-sector firms to promote employees' skill development while enhancing organizational competitiveness. The program works by ". . . offset[ting] a portion of the employer's costs to upgrade the skills of its incumbent workforce and will provide reimbursement to eligible employers for specific training costs accrued during training. The program's funding will be used in conjunction with private contributions to fund skill-upgrade training" (Ohio Development Services Agency, 2014, para. 2). Employers can choose public institutions, contracted private agencies, or an in-house entity to conduct training programs. The funding for these partnership programs, which itself comes from a partnership, is intently focused on providing services that will benefit the public and private sectors while doing so in a flexible manner that can be tailored to the needs of the organizations involved. A success of this case is the program's built-in flexibility to the needs of each organization, instead of simply providing one type of standard service or training.

Programs tailored to develop a specifically trained population of employees have also become increasingly prevalent. One such collaboration is happening at Clemson University's International Center for Automotive Research (CU-ICAR, Clemson University, 2014), a center for automotive innovation and collaboration in Greenville, South Carolina. CU-ICAR houses educational programs created and facilitated with $250 million dollars in capital costs raised from 18 industry leaders that have partnered with the university to create a hub of automotive innovation, a fantastically unique structure. CU-ICAR houses five dedicated areas for different programmatic activities. One area, Innovation Place, was created to connect faculty members at Clemson University with automotive companies for research purposes. A second area houses the BMW Information Technology Research Center, where BMW collaborates with the IT industry and universities to develop information technology for vehicles tailored to customers. The Center for Emerging Technologies is a multi-purpose facility housing various private-sector organizations that expand or develop technologies that coincide with Clemson faculty and student research.

The Clemson campus also includes a Graduate Engineering Center that conducts vehicle testing and the KOYO/JTEKT Group, an $11 billion company that houses the primary research and development center for needle bearing design and technology development. All together, these graduate programs and connected activities in automotive engineering engage about 200 students pursuing their graduate degrees and provide hands-on industry experience through the programs. The benefits of these distinct service areas under the umbrella of Clemson accrue to individuals and organizations in all sectors. Students benefit from applied projects, while the automotive industry benefits from targeted education, early access to talented students, and a direct connection to innovative faculty members. This case serves as a premiere example of what a university–private partnership can accomplish on such a large scale, both in terms of high-level private funding and significant numbers of students gaining specialized skills.

Similarly, Greenville Works (2014) is a public–private partnership created by the City of Greenville, the county schools and workforce investment board, the local chamber of commerce, the state employment commission, the United Way, and 11 universities in the Greenville, South Carolina, area. Greenville Works' mission is to identify the specific targeted needs of local businesses for employees and provide assistance in recruitment, selection, and hiring; customized pre-employment training and new and specifically tailored training programs for new businesses; data collection and analysis in workforce development; local networking and consulting on improving efficiency and effectiveness; and direct capital investment for expansion and job creation. For example, an aerospace maintenance facility in Greenville needed new staff to meet its needs for a series of new projects. Greenville Works created a six-week program to recruit, screen, and train potential new employees. At the conclusion of the program, the company could select newly trained applicants to fill its open positions. The outstanding element of this case is how the partnership is able to create remote human resources support to help local organizations recruit and hire employees.

Together these three cases—workforce development vouchers in Ohio, ICAR at Clemson University, and Greenville Works—point to the potential benefits of targeting collaborative workforce programs to the needs of local private-sector organizations. However, there are other public–private collaborations that may work toward similar goals through less direct mechanisms. One example focuses on research, education, and the creation of substantive connections among health care providers to improve public health, workforce preparation, and overall economic performance. This collaborative, Health Sciences South Carolina (HSSC, 2014a), is a statewide biomedical research collaborative funded by the Duke Endowment. HSSC began as a state-based program created by the South Carolina General Assembly in 2002, titled "SmartState Programs," which was then expanded into a cooperative activity for universities and health systems (State of North Carolina, 2014). The goal of HSSC is to connect with private and public partners to engage in medical research, public health improvement, health care quality, and innovation. It has also launched the first state clinical data warehouse, where electronic patient records are linked and matched so providers and researchers can follow this large population in real time for better health outcomes and research opportunities. This program highlights the ability of partnerships to tackle complex and potentially overwhelming public challenges (such as the management of health data) and to formulate related goals in an innovative manner (HSSC, 2014b).

Other public–private educational partnerships take a longer-term perspective on necessary programs. The Generation Next Partnership (2014a), located in Minneapolis and St. Paul, Minnesota, is a cooperation of various stakeholders from public, non-profit, and private organizations working to narrow the educational achievement gap using a cradle-to-career framework modeled after the National Strive Network (2014). Key leadership council members include local kindergarten through grade 12 teachers and school superintendents, union representatives, educational interest groups, charter school representatives, municipal elected officials, administrators from local public and private colleges and universities, representatives from local and national foundations, and private-sector corporations from the area (Generation Next Partnership, 2014b). This project seeks to correct a number of deficiencies identified from data collected in the Twin Cities. Key goals include improved kindergarten readiness, increased scores on grade 3 reading benchmarks, increased attainment of grade 8 math benchmarks, 100% high school graduation rate on time, and completion of a postsecondary degree or certificate within six years of graduation (Generation Next Partnership, 2014a). The program is noteworthy in its focus on the complexities and temporal considerations of workforce preparation, as well as its ability to create an inclusive and comprehensive program to encourage progress at multiple points along the trajectory from early childhood through initiating and maintaining employment.

Taken together, these cases point to the substantive and focused development of public–private partnerships in education and workforce from a variety of goal-oriented and temporal perspectives. The development of public–private partnerships in education is important and requires significant discussion, collaborative activities, and tailoring of program design to meet the needs of participating organizations and the sectors they serve (see Figure 1.1).

Figure 1.1   **Development of Educational Public–Private Partnerships**

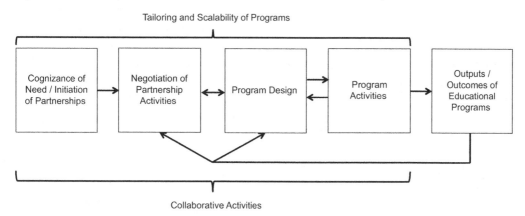

Tailoring and Scalability of Programs

| Cognizance of Need / Initiation of Partnerships | Negotiation of Partnership Activities | Program Design | Program Activities | Outputs / Outcomes of Educational Programs |

Collaborative Activities

These partnerships contribute to improved access to education and support for young children, development of a focused workforce with the skills necessary to meet demands of local employers, improved retention of the current workforce and decreased drain on talent in specific geographic centers, and the creation and implementation of research and innovation centers for faculty and private-sector organizations.

CONCLUSION

The cases described in this chapter illustrate the applicability of public–private partnerships to accomplish a wide variety of collaborative goals in education: training an incumbent workforce, developing specialized skills for a future workforce, identifying and meeting the needs of local businesses, integrating a broad health services community through research, providing early childhood education, and a establishing a cradle-to-career framework. Each case uniquely involves education and incorporates local stakeholders in a substantive way, and each contributes lessons learned to the broader picture. These types of activities continue to be laboratories for innovation and experimentation in education and intersectoral collaboration.

The variety of cases presented here points to the necessary specificity of these programs. Creating a single program model or "ideal" partnership that can be translated from one situation to the next is not entirely possible given the intrinsic variety found in resources, capabilities, and local needs. Thus, we cannot make concrete and universally applicable recommendations for programmatic structures or goals. However, it behooves us to be attentive to these partnerships' performance and to gather information about successes and failures as these partnerships continue to operate, which allows for a more complete understanding of their creation and management. The accomplishments of these programs are representative of the successes of collaborative activities in which sectors may provide support to or compensate for the weaknesses of the other.

By tracking the performance of such cases over time, future practice and scholarly inquiry stands to gain information about the highly contextualized nature of what may and may not work. For example, it could be useful to consider such collaborations as vehicles of upward career mobility, especially in the case of minorities or individuals from disadvantaged backgrounds. Such studies could inform how public–private partnerships could extend to sustaining individuals' professional growth and mobility, while staying current on their skills. Tracking the progress of such cases also provides insight into the best ways to blend or mix various elements and functions of the private and public sectors, on an experimental basis.

Several key takeaways can also be extracted from the literature and examples reviewed here. It becomes apparent that there is a need for a more streamlined language with which to discuss public–private partnerships so that generalizations and comparisons can be more easily made. However, based on the work of Wettenhall and others, it is very apparent that discovering or developing patterns and typologies is akin to finding a needle in a haystack or trying to fit a square peg into a round hole. With so many possible variations and combinations of structure and purpose, classifications and even common terminology are more elusive than ever, despite the pressing need for such structure to be established.

There is also much work to be done in developing best practices for the process of creating and implementing public–private partnerships. Although performance measurement is an important factor in successful implementation and sustainability of public–private partnerships, we have more to learn, such as an expansion and refinement of the application of comprehensive and inclusive measurement techniques such as the balanced scorecard (Kaplan & Norton, 1992) to public–private partnerships (see, for example, Forrer, Kee, Newcomer, & Boyer, 2010). Further, in considering what public–private partnerships of the future may look like, it will be interesting to see how the structures and dynamics of such partnerships will change over time. Programs of the future may be based more or less within specific sectors as a response to past successes or lack thereof. These programmatic decisions contain, at their very essence, cost–benefit evaluations that should necessarily focus on both public-sector values and economic impact. Public–private partnerships of all kinds will continue to be created and implemented, especially in the realms of workforce training and public educational institutions, which have the potential to meet societal needs and build communities while enhancing economic performance and improving both public- and private-sector performance.

KEY POINTS

- Public–private partnerships can provide tailored services that are flexible in responding to the needs of the recipients, as opposed to providing one standardized and inflexible service.
- Public–private partnerships are scalable, and large-scale university–private collaborations have demonstrated that a significant investment of resources and dedicated personnel can train significant numbers of students in specialized skills.

- Public–private partnerships can provide essential and specialized services in a cost-effective manner that may not have otherwise been possible, including basic human resources functions, such as recruiting, selecting, and hiring employees trained by the public–private partnership.
- Multiple public–private partnerships can address complex challenges in an even more effective manner and over a longer period of time, with collaborative work in education beginning early in a student's educational experiences.

REFERENCES

Abdolvand, N., Albadvi, A., & Ferdowski, Z. (2008). Assessing readiness for business process reengineering. *Business Process Management Journal, 14*(4), 497–511.

Allison, G. T. (1992). Public and private management: Are they fundamentally alike in all unimportant respects? In G. M. Shafritz & A. C. Hyde (Eds.), *Classics of public administration* (pp. 457–474). Belmont, CA: Wadsworth.

Alperovitz, G. (2011, May 25). The New-Economy Movement. A growing group of activists and socially responsible companies are rethinking business as usual. *The Nation.* Retrieved July 20, 2014, from www.thenation.com/article/160949/new-economy-movement#

Bailit, H. L., Formicola, A. J., Herbert, K. D., Stavisky, J. S., & Zamora, G. (2005). The origins and design of the dental pipeline program. *Journal of Dental Education, 69*(2), 232–238.

Baldry, D. (1998). The evaluation of risk management in public sector capital projects. *International Journal of Project Management, 16*(1), 35–41.

Becker, C. (2010). Self-determination, accountability mechanisms, and quasi-governmental status. *Public Performance & Management Review, 33*(3), 413–435.

Behn, R. D. (2003). Why measure performance? Different purposes require different measures. *Public Administration Review, 63*(5), 586–606.

Belkin, D., & Porter, C. (2014, April 7). Corporate cash alters university curricula. *The Wall Street Journal.* Retrieved April 7, 2014, from http://online.wsj.com/news/article_email/SB1000142405270230 38478045794815004979963552-lMyQjAxMTA0MDAwODEwNDgyWj

Berman, E. M. (1998). *Productivity in public and non profit organizations: Strategies and techniques.* Thousand Oaks, CA: Sage Publications.

Bloomfield, P. (2006). The challenging business of long-term public–private partnerships: Reflections on local experience. *Public Administration Review, 66*(3), 400–411.

Boyne, G. A. (2002). Public and private management: What's the difference? *Journal of Management Studies, 39*(1), 97–122.

Bragg, D. D. (2007). Teacher pipelines: Career pathways extending from high school to community college to university. *Community College Review, 35*(1), 10–29.

Caruso, G., & Weber, R. (2008). Getting the max for the tax: An examination of BID performance measures. In G. Morcöl, L. Hoyt, J. W. Meek, & U. Zimmermann (Eds.), *Business improvement districts: Research, theories, and controversies* (pp. 319–348). New York, NY: CRC Press.

Clemson University-International Center for Automotive Research. (2014). *About.* Retrieved from http://cuicar.com

Ellen, I. G., Schwartz, A. E., & Voicu, I. (2007). *The benefits of business improvement districts: Evidence from New York City.* New York: Furman Institute for Real Estate and Urban Policy, New York University.

Farrell, D. (2003, October). The real new economy. *Harvard Business Review - The Magazine.* Retrieved July 20, 2014, from http://hbr.org/2003/10/the-real-new-economy/ar/1

Flinders, M. (2005). The politics of public–private partnerships. *The British Journal of Politics & International Relations, 7*(2), 215–239.

Forrer, J., Kee, J. E., Newcomer, K. E., & Boyer, E. (2010). Public–private partnerships and the public accountability question. *Public Administration Review*, *70*(3), 475–484.

Generation Next Partnership. (2014a). *About*. Retrieved from www.tcgennext.org/about/

Generation Next Partnership. (2014b). *Leadership council*. Retrieved from www.tcgennext.org/about/board/

Greenville Works. (2014). *About*. Retrieved from www.greenvilleworks.com

Grossman, S. A. (2010). Reconceptualizing the public management and performance of business improvement districts. *Public Performance & Management Review*, *33*(3), 361–394.

Halachmi, A., & Bovaird, T. (1997). Process reengineering in the public sector: Learning some private sector lessons. *Technovation*, *17*(5), 227–235.

Health Sciences South Carolina. (2014a). *About HSSC*. Retrieved from www.healthsciencessc.org/about.asp

Health Sciences South Carolina. (2014b). *Strategic plan 2012–2016*. Retrieved from www.healthsciencessc.org/upload/index_9_1830648586.pdf

Hodge, G. A., & Greve, C. (2007). Public–private partnerships: An international performance review. *Public Administration Review*, *67*(3), 545–558.

Houston, Jr., L. O. (2003). *BIDs: Business improvement districts*. Washington, DC: The Urban Land Institute.

Huxham, C., & Vaugen, S. (2000). Ambiguity, complexity and dynamics in the membership of collaboration. *Human Relations*, *53*(6), 771–805.

Johnson, G., & Scholes, K. (2001). *Exploring public sector strategy*. Essex, England: Pearson Education Ltd.

Jurisch, M. C., Ikas, C., Wolf, P., & Krcmar, H. (2014). Key differences of public and private sector business process change. *E-Service Journal*, *9*(1), 3–27.

Kaplan, R. S., & Norton, D. P. (1992). The balanced scorecard—measures that drive performance. *Harvard Business Review*, *70*(1): 71–79.

Kettl, D. (1993). *Sharing power: Public governance and private markets*. Washington, DC: Brookings Institution Press.

Lee, C. E. (2014, February 27). Obama launches program for disadvantaged minority youth. *The Wall Street Journal*. Retrieved February 27, 2014, from http://online.wsj.com/news/article_email/SB10001424052702304071004579407992832670628-lMyQjAxMTA0MDIwNzEyNDcyWj

Levin, H. M. (1999). The public-private nexus in education. *American Behavioral Scientist*, *43*(1), 124–137.

Llewellyn, S., & Tappin, E. (2003). Strategy in the public sector: Management in the wilderness. *Journal of Management Studies*, *40*(4), 955–981.

Lowndes, V., & Skelcher, C. (1998). The dynamics of multi-organizational partnerships: An analysis of changing modes of governance. *Public Administration*, *76*(2), 313–333.

MacDonald, J. M., Stokes, R., & Blumenthal, R. (2010). The role of community context in business district revitalization strategies. *Public Performance & Management Review*, *33*(3), 439–458.

Meier, K. J., & O'Toole Jr., L. J. (2011). Comparing public and private management: Theoretical expectations. *Journal of Public Administration Research & Theory*, *21*(Suppl. 3), 283–299.

Miraftab, F. (2004). Public-private partnerships: The Trojan Horse of neoliberal development? *Journal of Planning Education and Research*, *24*(1), 89–101.

Mitchell, J. (2008). *Business improvement districts and the shape of American cities*. Albany, NY: State University of New York Press.

Morcöl, G., & Wolf, J. F. (2010). Understanding business improvement districts: A new governance framework. *Public Administration Review*, *70*(6), 906–913.

Morcöl, G., & Zimmerman, U. (2006). Metropolitan governance and business improvement districts. *International Journal of Public Administration*, *29*(1–3), 5–29.

National Strive Network. (2014). *Strive together story*. Retrieved from www.strivetogether.org/vision-roadmap/strivetogether-story

Ohio Development Services Agency. (2014). *Ohio incumbent workforce training voucher program.* Retrieved from http://development.ohio.gov/bs/bs_wtvp.htm

Osbourne, D., & Gabler, T. (1992). *Reinventing government.* Reading, MA: Addison-Wesley Publishing Co.

O'Toole Jr., L. J., & Meier, K. J. (2003). Bureaucracy & uncertainty. In B. Burder (Ed.), *Uncertainty in American politics* (pp. 98–117). Cambridge: Cambridge University Press.

Pantazis, C. M. (2002). Maximizing e-learning to train the 21st century workforce. *Public Personnel Management, 31*(1), 21–26.

Perry, J. L. (1996). Measuring public service motivation: An assessment of concepts and measures. *Journal of Public Administration Research and Theory, 12*(4), 533–580.

Perry, J. L. (1997). Antecedents of public service motivation. *Journal of Public Administration Research and Theory, 7*(2), 181–197.

Perry, J. L., & Rainey, H. G. (1988). The public-private distinction in organization theory: A critique and research strategy. *Academy of Management Review, 13*(2), 182–201.

PricewaterhouseCoopers. (2013). *16th annual global CEO survey.* Retrieved from www.pwc.com/gx/en/ceo-survey/2013/index.jhtml

Rainey, H. G. (2003). *Understanding and managing public organizations* (3rd ed.). San Francisco: Jossey-Bass.

Reenstra-Bryant, R. (2010). Evaluations of business improvement districts. *Public Performance & Management Review, 33*(3), 509–523.

Riccio, L. J. (2014). Public-private partnerships: Pitfalls and possibilities. *Public Administration Review, 74*(1), 50–51.

Roosevelt, F. D. (1933). *Presidential address.* Tennessee Valley Authority, TN.

Schaeffer, P., & Loveridge, S. (2002). Toward an understanding of public-private cooperation. *Public Performance & Management Review, 26*(2), 169–189.

Scholl, H. J. (2004). Current Practices in e-government-induced business process change. *Proceedings of the 2004 Annual National Conference on Digital Government Research* (p. 10). Digital Government Society of North America.

Smith, S. G., Nsiah-Kumi, P. A., Jones, P. R., & Pamies, R. J. (2009). Pipeline programs in the health professions: Part 1: Preserving diversity and reducing health disparities. *Journal of the National Medical Association, 101*(9), 836–840.

State of North Carolina. (2014). *SmartState programs.* Retrieved from http://smartstatesc.org/enabling-legislation

Thong, J. Y. L., Yap, C.-s., & Seah, K.-L. (2000). Business process reengineering in the public sector: The case of the Housing Development Board in Singapore. *Journal of Management Information Systems, 17*(1), 245–270.

Watson, K., & Froyd, J. (2007). Diversifying the U.S. engineering workforce: A new model. *Journal of Engineering Education, 96*(1), 19–32.

Wettenhall, R. (2003). The rhetoric and reality of public-private partnerships. *Public Organization Review 3*(1), 77–107.

Winthrop, R., Bulloch, G., Bhatt, P., & Wood, A. (2013). *Investment in global education: A strategic imperative for business. Executive summary.* Retrieved February 27, 2014, from www.brookings.edu/research/reports/2013/09/investment-in-global-education

2

Pathways to Partnership

The City of Los Angeles Human Relations Commission and Google LA Coproduction of Youth Capacity

Brian Robert Calfano, Joumana Silyan-Saba, and Sheldon Cruz

CITY OF LOS ANGELES HUMAN RELATIONS COMMISSION

One of the primary goals of human relations programs at the local government level is building capacity among underserved and underrepresented populations. Capacity building is especially important for groups with the potential to make substantial impacts on the government and business sectors over the long term. Given their age, high school youth are arguably the most deserving of focus for programmatic efforts that give voice to countless new participants by providing them with the skills and perspectives necessary for improved governance and business operations. Furthermore, the matching of city human relations programming with business community partnerships can facilitate learning opportunities that open new vistas for students by not only providing facilitator-directed models for growth in personal efficacy and engagement, but also encouraging youth to take a co-producing role in their own development. In this chapter, we examine the cross-sector government–business partnership found in the collaboration between the City of Los Angeles Human Relations Commission (City HRC) Youth Ambassador's (YA) program and Google's Los Angeles office (Google LA).

The human relations emphasis in local government in Los Angeles is unique in that it is not widely practiced across municipalities. Given its experience with the 1965 Watts Uprising, Los Angeles developed its Human Relations Commission to address systematic injustices and intergroup distrust (see Fogelson, 1967). Today, City HRC is involved in an array of initiatives that support the improvement of group relations among Los Angeles's diverse constituencies. These efforts include training community members in conflict management, increasing civic engagement across neighborhoods, promoting interfaith dialogue, and fostering community and youth opportunities. City HRC, therefore, is a key public-sector contact point for developing programs that draw on private-sector resources.

Cross-sector or public–private partnerships, or more informal relationships like the City HRC/Google LA arrangement discussed in this chapter, are becoming more common (Googins & Rochlin, 2000). This is due to a variety of factors, including the weakening of nongovernmental organizations (NGOs) and growing sensitivity within the business sector

20

reasons

about the need to promote sustainability initiatives in the economic, social, and environmental domains (Burke, 1999; Sullivan & Skelcher, 2002). The scope of constituencies
affected by these initiatives clearly recommends a programmatic focus beyond the business
community as a voluntary driver of community improvements. Although certain political
ideologies tend to favor the market or the state as a wholesale solution to entrenched social
and economic challenges, the reality that neither sector has produced broad-based resolu-
tions to common social problems has spurred a focus on the potentials of the public–private
hybrid (Wettenhall, 2003). At the heart of the hybrid is the realization that this partnership
creates opportunities extending beyond what either the public or private domain might
individually achieve, especially in terms of service delivery and urban renewal (Logsdon,
1991; Moore & Pierre, 1988). We would add to this list of achievements the fostering of
youth capacity and engagement as a way of bolstering the future workforce.

This leads us to the consideration of just how the pairing of the sectors might
function collectively. In many cases, "partnerships" are construed as the active resources
from a business to a nonprofit or NGO. These one-way transfers are also made from
government to business. Of course, businesses were long characterized by one-sided
transfers to government in the form of taxes paid. However, in a true partnership, each sector provides a specific set of contributions that meets the needs of its partner (see Waddell,
1999). According to Smith, Mathur, and Skelcher (2006), these partnerships include reciprocal exchange (typical transactional format), developmental value creation (joint work
and rewards, but also independent avenues for success), and symbiotic value creation
(interdependent exchange of ideas, resources, and efforts to set and achieve goals).

We suggest that the City HRC/Google LA collaborative functions as a version of
the developmental value creation partnership model in that the collaboration provided
by the pairing offers a variety of rewarding outcomes for participants, but both entities maintain the inherent flexibility to set their own courses for continued creation of
outcomes supporting their core missions.

Figure 2.1   **Sector Partners in the Co-production of Services**

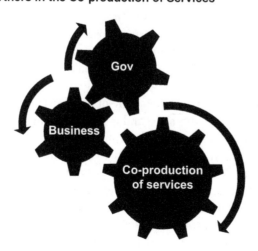

Part of the importance of focusing on developmental value creation and the co-production of youth capacity and engagement in an urban context is that the academic literature consistently shows that minorities and individuals of low socio-economic status bear the brunt of developmental risk factors (Bowen, 2001; Freudenberg, Pastor, & Israel, 2011; Wright, Bryant, & Bullard, 1994). Lack of development opportunities and infrastructure usually leads to a diminishment of civic and political efficacy, particularly where disadvantaged populations are concentrated. This serves to reinforce the vulnerable positions in which minorities are often situated and presents challenges to business and economic development for municipalities.

The stated policy goal of government departments working in human relations is to mitigate the risk factors confronting these communities while developing opportunities to identify and handle challenges in an increasingly independent manner. Though community development may lead to new and increased economic investment locally, the strength of correlation between these two is not consistent and may depend on a litany of factors unrelated to the core human relations challenges that a community confronts. Hence, there is a clear role for government to foster partnerships with entities that provide a variety of direct and indirect impacts. Capacity is a clear example of the latter (Chaskin, 2001).

Community capacity is defined as a "set of dynamic community traits, resources, and associational patterns that can be brought to bear for community building and community health improvement" (Norton et al., 2002, p. 205). There are three dimensions of community capacity building: (1) the role of assets and empowerment (vs. disease and deficiency), (2) the role of bottom-up, community-determined processes and agendas (vs. top-down/externally determined ones), and (3) the processes for developing community competence to protect community well-being (Raeburn et al., 2006).

The building of community capacity around the augmentation of social and political skills for youth leaders can significantly bolster collective efficacy. Collective efficacy—social cohesion among neighbors and a willingness to intervene in neighborhoods in a community—is associated with reductions in violent crime (Saegert, 1993; Sampson et al., 1997). In Taylor's (1996) estimation, neighborhoods with crime problems may actually have greater cohesion, even as crime poses a threat to social organization and human well-being at the individual, group, and societal levels (Perkins, Hughley, & Speer, 2002) (different from social capital; see Putnam, 2001).

We view the City HRC/Google LA developmental value partnership as existing within the New Public Governance/Management (NPG/M) paradigm, in which public management functions as a collaborative and is projected outside the hierarchical structure of individual public/government organizations. Under this arrangement, different actors are connected vertically and horizontally to co-produce public services (Alford & Hughes, 2008; Osborne, 2010). According to Osborne (2006, p. 377), "The time of NPM has been relatively brief and transitory between the statist and bureaucratic tradition of public administration and the embryonic plural and pluralist tradition of NPG."

Emerson et al. (2012, p. 2) provide a broad definition of "collaboration" as "the processes and structures of public policy decision making and management that engage

Figure 2.2 **Determinants of Community Capacity**

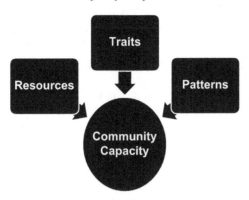

people constructively across the boundaries of public agencies, levels of government, and/or public, private, and civic spheres to carry out a public purpose that could not otherwise be accomplished." This opens up the field of play to a wide variety of actors, which Agranoff and McGuire (2003) consider necessary to solve problems and create public value that cannot be facilitated by a single organization or approach. From the standpoint of local provision of human relations services, the NPG/M paradigm has clear functional importance in that, despite the lip service that elected officials usually pay to promoting healthy intergroup relations and growing community capacity, there is often little in the way of monetary and personnel resources attached to photo ops and other public relations opportunities.

Hence, government–business collaboration can have a key impact on the co-production of public services and capacity-building processes within disadvantaged communities (see Brudney, 1983; Ostrom, 1996) leading to improvement in services and increased engagement in citizenship functions and social capital (Bovaird, 2007; Levine, 1984; Marschall, 2004). But successful coproduction—despite the growing interest in recent decades—depends in large measure on buy-in from citizen groups in areas such as education, sustainability, and public safety, especially among minority groups (Davis & Ostrom, 1991; Folz, 1991; Marschall, 2006; Percy, 1987; Pestoff, Brandsen, & Verschuere, 2012; Rousseau, 1995; Schneider, 1987). This suggests that programs designed to bring group members into a structured learning and experiential environment have a critical role to play in fostering coproduction activities for community members, including young people.

We see coproduction as part and parcel of the YA program in that it ensconces youth in the actual learning process of generating the basic ingredients of coproduction: education, engagement, and analytical skills. Established in 2012, the City HRC YA program provides high school youth ages 14–17 years from all socio-economic backgrounds with the opportunity to generate productive relationships with various youth groups through peer-to-peer interaction and activities. Additionally, YAs participate in civic-engagement activities designed to increase their knowledge and expertise in the areas of policy, legislation, civic-process, and functions of local, state and federal government.

Through curriculum-based workshops, volunteer events, field trips, travel, and activities designed to increase participation in the civic process, YAs broaden their minds and their experience caches in the areas of leadership, innovation, and advocacy.

CORE GOALS OF THE HRC YA INITIATIVE

1. Utilize the history and resources inside Los Angeles City Hall as a tool to affect youth populations
2. Provide youth with leadership tools, skill sets, and advanced knowledge of how to engage local government
3. Encourage civic leaders and government agencies to work collaboratively in providing youth with quality civic and educational experiences
4. Inspire youth populations to be leaders by using California and the U.S. as laboratories for learning through multiple travel opportunities both in and out of state
5. Create a fun environment for learning where youth are comfortable offering their perspectives and opinions on issues and policies that affect their communities

THE YA CURRICULUM MODEL

1. *Introduction to Government*: provides youth with an overview of government and its structure at the local, state, and federal levels
2. *Los Angeles History*: provides an historical overview of the City of Los Angeles and its evolution and transformation over the years
3. *Civic Engagement*: uses civic participation templates to engage youth interest and expand on their knowledge base of facilitation and policy subject matter
4. *Social Justice and Organizing*: provides youth with a safe space to define areas of need in their respective communities and to develop the skill set needed to be civically engaged
5. *Human Relations*: offers a basic understanding of human relations concepts, intergroup dynamics, and conflict management techniques
6. *Professional and Personal Development*: equips youth with basic interpersonal skills and appropriate professional conduct reflective of day-to-day interactions in the workplace

Each of the above subjects represents a path to building community capacity indirectly through enabling city youth to effectively engage in co-production. City HRC works diligently to ensure that the YA program is successful in providing these services to youth participants. But, as stated, programmatic success in the wake of lean funding for government human relations programs requires cross-sector partnerships to make the initiative more than just a program on paper. Just as capacity building is an indirect factor in improving community status, delivering on the articulated YA program core goals and curriculum requires collaboration with partners from a variety of sectors, including

Figure 2.3 **The Building Blocks of Youth Capacity in Los Angeles**

and especially business. The partnership between business and government represents an opportunity for YA participants to see both government and private-sector entities in action. As a result, participants are afforded a more holistic look at the institutions and market sectors that will drive public policy making and economic growth during their adult lives.

Considering how personal, professional, and communal development is spurred by well-paying vocational opportunities, youth may grow in their relative capacities by seeing firsthand how an industry operates through examples of leading firms in a specific sector. Here, the input of the business partner is clearly indirect in facilitating YA program deliverables, but this input is critical nonetheless. In pursuing developmental value creation, City HRC and business partners produce a joint outcome of benefit to the constituencies and missions of both entities. But both also remain free to pursue a variety of opportunities outside of the specific government–business collaboration. It is in this value creation context that we consider the work of City HRC and Google LA with the YA program participants.

GOOGLE LA

Google LA gives a high priority to outreach and partnerships with public and private organizations. As part of its annual efforts, the company sponsors events and provides grants in various academic development areas (with a concentration in science, technology, engineering, and math [STEM]–related fields). Company outreach, how-ever, is not limited to tech-based organizations. The Boys and Girls Club, for example, has long been featured as a partner in the greater Los Angeles area. As Google LA team member Julie Wiskirchen noted in an interview for this chapter, "If an organization approaches us, we will try to help them."

STEM education efforts are also supported through the Google RISE Award, which places a particular emphasis on computer science training among underrepresented groups. At the same time, the company provides free Google Apps for accredited non-profit K–12 schools, colleges, and universities, as well as the Google Teacher Academy, to empower teacher technology use in the classroom. Finally, Google LA sponsors the Community Affairs grant, which ranges from $5,000 to $25,000 and focuses on propos-als in STEM, carbon reduction, the technology ecosystem, technology infrastructure for non-profits, and efforts to bridge the digital divide (see London, Pastor, & Rosner, 2008 for a review of this issue). From these examples, it is clear that Google LA sees itself playing a supportive role in providing the scaffolding necessary to encourage capacity building in various communities. The effect, however, is intentionally indirect and com-munally based.

According to Wiskirchen, Google LA has "no interns formally." The popular 2013 Vince Vaughn movie *The Internship* appears to show a one-off internship opportunity at Google's Mountain View headquarters. However, the LA office is a member of the Los Angeles Chamber of Commerce, the Venice Chamber of Commerce (which is the city section closest to the company headquarters), and the LAX Coastal Area Chamber of Commerce. As such, informal networking opportunities will crop up, which may lead to employment possibilities down the road.

Despite the lack of direct, company-wide initiatives, Google LA encourages "employees in Los Angeles to come up with innovative and meaningful ways to support our community." Wiskirchen cites the GoogleServe initiative, which occurs in June, as a key example of the outreach the company provides. At the same time, the com-pany supports its employees ("Googlers") by making corporate donations to approved nonprofit organizations (up to $12,000 annually). Googlers also offer their time and support outside of the corporate structure, including serving as volunteers to work with local homeless populations and as advisors for a robotics program at a high school near Google LA's office.

The lack of formal internship opportunities helps to illustrate why we consider the Google LA and City HRC partnership as a developmental partnership form, rather than an example of the reciprocal or symbiotic varieties. Although the YA program receives the benefit to its curriculum and goals in the opportunity for student ambassadors to visit and learn from Google personnel, Google does not receive a direct supply of intern tal-ent from the YA program in return. Almost as if it were intentionally positioning itself as an indirect support broker, Google LA encourages partnerships with community and government organizations, while stopping short of inducting community members into direct, formal relationships with the company. While one might view this policy as a cynical business ploy out of a corporate public relations textbook, when viewed from the standpoint of government–business partnerships in the NPG/M paradigm, Google LA's approach is well-suited for the kind of connection that City HRC and the YA program prefer. After all, the YA program is not a temp agency or a vocational school. It, instead, functions as a capacity builder for youth from underserved communities. As such, the taste of Google LA facilitated in the partnership is precisely the type of opportunity from which the youth ambassadors can learn as they chart their own courses of community engagement and capacity building.

The most tangible manifestation of the City HRC/Google LA relationship is the youth ambassadors' visits to the Google office. One example is an in-person YA visit to the Google LA office on November 15, 2013. To a large extent, the experience bore a substantial resemblance to *The Internship* film. The vibe and practices at the Google LA office—including the cafes with free food—were on clear display for the YAs. More importantly, YAs were able to sit in on presentations about Google+, Google Glass, and other related company platforms. They were also able to gain advice and perspective from several Google LA event hosts.

Generally, the Google LA hosts made a point of encouraging the youth ambassadors to pursue opportunities that allow them to "do cool things that matter." The YAs were encouraged to keep in touch with the Google LA office as they continue their education and consider college options. The importance of the experience was in the YA program's facilitation of ambassador access to Google as an example of where the YAs' developing interests and skill sets might take them professionally. This is the kind of "rubbing elbows" event that is often limited to expensive prep schools and private liberal arts colleges (where the benefit of attendance is normally measured in the connections made across business and government). From a co-production standpoint, this kind of "face time" opportunity demonstrated to the YAs that—despite their less affluent socio-economic backgrounds—they too can fit well in the world's primary economic and political environs. In terms of building capacity and increasing efficacy, the YA/Google LA partnership is an exemplar cross-sectional undertaking.

The youth ambassadors' reaction to the 2013 visit was as one might expect. All 16 attendees were effusive in their praise for Google and expressed a sense of awe for what they had just experienced collectively and individually. It was also clear from the comments and facial expressions of all the attendees that they had received a very rare glimpse into the inner workings of one of the world's most important and valuable companies. This level of access—something that would not be possible for these youth ambassadors without the unique developmental partnership between City HRC and Google LA—fostered a level of individual confidence and perspective-broadening that may lead the ambassadors to both grow in their personal capacity and use this growth to increase civic and political engagement.

To be sure, effects stemming from the City HRC/Google LA partnership are indirect, but such is the reality with many initiatives undertaken within the human relations framework. Perhaps ironically, the indirect nature of the government–business partnership we have examined in this chapter also describes the process by which this arrangement developed in the first place. After all, although Google LA represents a

Figure 2.4 **Tips for Developing Cross-Sector Partnerships**

willing business-sector partner whose organizational ethic fits well with the YA program's focus, the future success of human relations efforts across governments will be determined by the ability of public-sector practitioners to create and sustain similar developmental partnerships. There is, of course, no set path to accomplishing this task. Based on our experience with the City HRC/Google LA collaboration, however, we offer the following points for consideration (see Figure 2.4). These cover aspects related to ensuring participant growth and developing the cross-sector relationships themselves.

KEY POINTS FOR PARTNERSHIP DEVELOPMENT

- **Promote principal/participant empowerment.** The cross-sector model between City HRC and Google LA was successful, in part, because the YA program was designed to focus on making individual youth ambassadors part of the decision-making process in designing the year-long curriculum, events, and task responsibilities. While the ambassadors' experience and ability varied in this regard, even those least acclimated to these tasks were brought into the decision-making process. What is more, each YA was empowered to provide real-time feedback on the program's activities, which fed directly into task and curricular redesigns for future YA cohorts. From our perspective, developing communities through youth capacity building begins with the very programs that are intended to encourage individual and collective voice. This design aspect should be built into programs from the beginning to ensure participants see their capacity and related skills grow throughout their program participation.
- **Don't be afraid to ask, again.** Developing cross-sector relationships often requires organizers to hone personal levels of persistence and creativity. Although the realization of government and business collaboration can be exhilarating, these

opportunities are not readily apparent or easy to take advantage of (at least in many cases). Hence, government practitioners should think about the types of partnerships they wish to develop, with attendant goals in mind. They should also approach the partnership process with the expectation that relationships will need cultivation in advance of realizing specific programmatic outcomes. Such developmental partnerships require a willingness to ask for opportunities to explore collaborative options with the business sector, even if one is turned down several times in doing so. As with many other aspects of professional life, rejection is part of a larger process whereby one works toward goal realization with those who will become willing and worthwhile partners. Getting to this point, however, requires the persistence of those who are not afraid to ask to develop cross-sector relationships and be rejected at points along the way. Certainly, one must have a thick skin in these circumstances and recognize that the willingness of potential organization partners to develop cross-sector collaborations may change over time (which is why asking again is a good idea).

- **Avoid the quid pro quo.** Given the way Google LA approaches its community action policies, one of the most advantageous decisions by the YA program administrators was not to enter into discussions that would make Google responsible for providing a pre-determined and conventional series of outputs. This understanding formed the basis of the developmental partnership between the YA program and Google LA. However, the arrangement was as beneficial for City HRC as it was for Google. We suggest that even in cases where a different partnership form is the goal, practitioners should avoid discussion of quid pro quo–like arrangements, at least initially. Though transactional aspects of a partnership may develop over time, our view is that government offices in the human relations sector should avoid situations in which municipalities are expected to provide tangible and reliable outputs to external partners over the long term. Until and unless government funding priorities change, human relations shops will be best served not to promise more than they can realistically deliver. Avoiding quid pro quo relationships with the business sector will help.

- **Go outside established lanes.** Creating the kind of cross-sector relationships described in this chapter necessitates government personnel looking for ways that they may assume responsibility for establishing and/or encouraging public–business partnerships, even if this work is outside of the established responsibilities of their position. This may require a degree of finesse in garnering support among coworkers and supervisors in taking on additional responsibilities. Admittedly, this kind of action may not always be feasible for both political and administrative reasons. However, where it is possible to forge coalitions within government departments in developing a game plan for approaching businesses in creating cross-sector partnerships, taking steps outside established lanes may have substantial payoffs both personally and professionally.

- **Grow and adjust organically.** There is a natural tendency within organizations to build on successful initiatives by making them permanent programs complete with recurring budget lines, staff assignments, and event periodicity. Although these developments may prove useful in some cases, they may actually make the continued success of cross-sector relationships less likely. Just as we cautioned against quid pro quo arrangements, we advise practitioners to approach government and business partnerships with a healthy dose of flexibility. Generally speaking, those working in human relations departments are already accustomed to a high level of fluidity in their work, so applying this last recommendation should be considered a natural outgrowth of the important work they already do in promoting capacity building among youth and other constituencies.

REFERENCES

Agranoff, R., and McGuire, M. (2003). *Collaborative public management: New strategies for local governments.* Washington, DC: Georgetown University Press.

Alford, J., and Hughes, O. (2008). Public value pragmatism as the next phase of public management. *American Review of Public Administration, 38,* 130–148.

Bowen, S. (2001). *Language barriers in access to health care.* Ottawa: Health Canada.

Bovaird, T. (2007). Beyond engagement and participation: User and community coproduction of public services. *Public Administration Review, 67,* 846–860.

Brudney, J. L. (1983). The evaluation of coproduction programs. *Policy Studies Journal, 12,* 376–385.

Burke, E. M. (1999). *Corporate community relations: The principle of the neighbor of choice.* Westport, CT: Praeger.

Chaskin, R.J. (2001). Building community capacity: A definitional framework and case studies from a comprehensive community initiative. *Urban Affairs Review, 36,* 291–323.

Davis, G., & Ostrom, E. (1991). A public economy approach to education: Choice and coproduction. *International Political Science Review, 12,* 313–335.

Emerson, K., Natbatchi, T., and Balogh, S. (2012). An integrative framework for collaborative governance. *Journal of Public Administration Research and Theory, 22,* 1–29.

Fogelson, R. M. (1967). White on black: A critique of the McCone Commission on the Los Angeles riots. *Political Science Quarterly, 82,* 337–367.

Folz, D. H. (1991). Recycling solid waste: Citizen participation in the design of a coproduced program. *State and Local Government Review, 23,* 98–102.

Freudenberg, N., Pastor, M., and Israel, B. (2011). Strengthening community capacity to participate in making decisions to reduce disproportionate environmental exposures. *American Journal of Public Health, 101*(S1), S123-30. doi: 10.2105/AJPH.2011.300265.

Googins, B. K., & Rochlin, S. A. (2000). Creating the partnership society: Understanding the rhetoric and reality of cross-sectional. . . . *Business and Society Review, 105,* 127–145.

Levine, C. H. (1984). Citizenship and service delivery: The promise of coproduction. *Public Administration Review, 44,* 178–187.

Logsdon, J. (1991). Interests and interdependence in the formation of social problem-solving collaborations. *Journal of Applied Behavioral Science, 27*(1), 23–37.

London, R. A., Pastor, Jr., M., & Rosner, R. (2008). When the divide isn't just digital: How technology enriched afterschool programs help immigrant youth find a voice, a place, and a future. *Afterschool Matters, 7,* 1–11.

Marschall, M. J. (2004). Citizen participation and the neighborhood context: A new look at the coproduction of local public goods. *Political Research Quarterly, 57,* 231–244.

Marschall, M. J. (2006). Parent involvement and educational outcomes for Latino students. *Review of Policy Research, 23,* 1053–1076.

Moore, C., & Pierre, J. (1988). Partnership or privatization? The political economy of local economic restructuring. *Policy and Politics, 16*, 169–178.

Norton, B.L., McLeroy, K.R., Burdine, J.N., Felix, M.R.J., and Dorsey, A.M. (2002). Community capacity: Concept, theory, and methods. In Ralph J. DiClemente, Richard A. Crosby, and Michelle C. Kegler (Eds.), *Emerging theories in health promotion practice and research: Strategies for improving public health*. New York: Wiley.

Osborne, S. (2006). Editorial: The new public governance? *Public Management Review, 8*, 377–387.

_____. (2010). *The new public governance? Emerging perspectives on the theory and practice of public governance*. New York: Routledge.

Ostrom, E. (1996). Crossing the great divide: Coproduction, synergy, and development. *World Development, 24*, 1073–1087.

Percy, S. L. (1987). Citizen involvement in coproducing safety and security in the community. *Public Productivity Review, 10*, 83–93.

Perkins, D.D., Hughey, J., and Speer, P.W. (2002). Community psychology perspectives on social capital theory and community development practice. *Journal of Community Development Society, 33*, 33–52.

Pestoff, V., Brandsen, T., and Verschuere, B. (Eds.). (2012). *New public governance, the third sector, and co-production*. New York: Routledge.

Putnam, R.D. (2001). *Bowling alone: The collapse and revival of American community*. New York: Simon and Schuster.

Raeburn, J., Akerman, M., Chuengsatiansup, K., Mehia, F., and Oladepo, O. (2006). Community capacity building and health promotion in a globalized world. *Health Promotion International, 21*(S1), 84–90.

Rousseau, D. (1995). *Psychological contracts in organizations: Understanding written and unwritten agreements*. Thousand Oaks, CA: Sage Publications.

Ryan, N. (2001). Reconstructing citizens as consumers: Implications for new modes of governance. *Australian Journal of Public Administration, 60*, 104–109.

Saegert, S. (1993). Survey of residents of currently and previously city-owned buildings in the Bronx. In M. Cotton (Ed.), *Housing in the balance: Seeking a comprehensive policy for city-owned housing*. New York: Task Force on City Owned Property.

Sampson, R. J., Raudenbush, S. W., & Earls, F. (1997). Neighborhoods and violent crime: A multilevel study of collective efficacy. *Science, 277*(5328), 918–924.

Schneider, A. L. (1987). Coproduction of public and private safety: An analysis of bystander intervention, 'protective neighboring', and personal protection. *Western Political Quarterly, 40*, 611–630.

Smith, M., Mathur, N., & Skelcher, C. (2006). Corporate governance in a collaborative environment: What happens when government, business, and civil society work together? *Corporate Governance, 14*, 159–171.

Sullivan, H., & Skelcher, C. (2002). *Working across boundaries: Collaboration in public services*. Basingstoke: Palgrave Macmillan.

Taylor, R.B. (1996). Neighborhood responses to disorder and local attachments: The systemic model of attachment, social disorganization, and neighborhood use value. *Sociological Forum, 11*, 41–74.

Waddell, S. (1999). New institutions for the practice of corporate citizenship: Historical, intersectional, and developmental perspectives. *Business and Society Review, 105*, 107–126.

Wettenhall, R. (2003). The rhetoric and reality of public-private partnerships. *Public Organization Review: A Global Journal, 3*, 77–107.

Wright, B.H., Bryant, P., and Bullard, R.D. (1994). Coping with poisons in Cancer Alley. In Robert D. Bullard (Ed.), *Unequal protection: Environmental justice and communities of color*. San Francisco: Sierra Club.

Part II

Regulation

3

Business–Government Collaboration in Rulemaking

Regulating Carbon Emissions from Motor Vehicles

Ian C. Graig

On August 9, 2011, President Barack Obama announced that the U.S. was for the first time setting fuel consumption and greenhouse gas (GHG) emissions standards for heavy-duty (HD) commercial trucks and buses. The announcement, which closely followed an agreement with the auto industry to set stringent new fuel economy and GHG emissions rules for passenger cars and light trucks, was part of a broader administration effort to address climate change—an initiative that would become known as the "Climate Action Plan" during President Obama's second term in office.

Few areas of policymaking in the U.S. have been more contentious in recent years than environmental policy, particularly as it relates to clean air standards and efforts to address climate change. In the years since Barack Obama became president, proposals from the Environmental Protection Agency (EPA) to use its authority under the Clean Air Act to control greenhouse gas and other emissions have been subject to lengthy legal challenges and often-intense opposition from industry groups and members of Congress. The process of writing rules that would regulate GHG emissions from power plants, industrial facilities, and other "stationary sources" has proven to be particularly contentious.

In contrast, the process for writing rules to regulate GHG emissions from motor vehicles (or "mobile sources") has proven to be a generally collaborative or cooperative one. In the case of those regulations, the EPA and the Department of Transportation's National Highway Traffic Safety Administration (NHTSA) have worked closely with motor vehicle and engine producers—and with state regulators and environmental groups—in formulating proposed standards, test procedures, etc. As a result, although conservative legal activists, climate "skeptics," and general business organizations have criticized the proposed standards, the proposals have met with surprisingly little opposition from most segments of the automotive industry.

The heavy-duty truck and bus standards announced by President Obama in August 2011 (the "HD truck rule") were clearly written through a collaborative process. Federal and state regulators worked together with industry on a potentially contentious issue over several years to develop proposals that met the regulatory agencies' goal of reducing GHG emissions and fuel consumption—but did so in a manner that was acceptable to most motor vehicle and engine producers and in fact met certain key industry goals. As a result, the announcement of those standards generally received a positive reaction not only from environmental groups, which were also involved in the rulemaking process, but also from automotive component suppliers and the truck, bus, and engine producers that would have to comply with the new standards. Those who participated in the process commented publicly and privately about its collaborative or cooperative nature (Kahl, 2011).[1]

The collaborative nature of this regulatory process can in part be attributed to factors unique to the heavy-duty vehicle emissions standards and the industries affected by those regulations, but it can also be attributed to several factors with implications for business and government collaboration in general and for the rule-making process in particular. This case study will explore in some detail the process through which the HD truck rule was written in an effort to highlight those factors that helped foster a cooperative process. The case study is based on an extensive review of the formal rulemaking documents, the comments filed by companies and other interest groups and the agency responses to those comments, the publicly available records of meetings between interest groups and agency officials, and the public announcements of government, industry, and interest group representatives involved in that process, as well as press coverage and analysis of the HD truck rule. It is also based on an extensive review of government–industry cooperation before the formal rulemaking began, as well as the statutory bases for the rule making and the record of the earlier related rulemakings (such as the writing of the light-vehicle GHG emissions and fuel economy rules). Finally, the case study draws on formal and informal exchanges between the author and representatives of industry, environmental groups, and regulatory agencies who were directly involved in the process.

Before turning to the HD truck rule itself, however, it is important to review briefly first the rulemaking process and then the literature on how business and other interest groups can influence that process.

THE RULEMAKING PROCESS

The Administrative Procedure Act of 1946 (APA), which established the fundamental principles of the federal rulemaking process, defines a *rule* as "an agency statement of general or particular applicability and future effect designed to implement, interpret, or prescribe law or policy." As Cornelius Kerwin and Scott Furlong wrote in their widely used study of rulemaking, the key features of rules are that they "originate in agencies, articulate law and policy limited only by authorizing legislation, and have either a broad or narrow scope but are always concerned with shaping future conditions" (Kerwin & Furlong, 2011, p. 7). Federal agencies issue thousands of final rules each year based on laws passed by Congress that either require or authorize them to do so (Copeland, 2009).[2] Some of these rules are extremely brief and have a direct impact on a small number of individuals, groups, or companies; others run for hundreds of pages in the *Federal Register* and have a broad nationwide impact. In almost all circumstances, legislation passed by Congress contains comparatively broad and general language, and lawmakers rely, to quote Kerwin and Furlong again, "on rulemaking to supplement legislation rather than attempt to enact laws that answer all questions and anticipate all circumstances" (Kerwin & Furlong, 2011, p. 29).

What prompts an agency to propose a new rule? In some cases, Congress passes a law that includes a clear mandate to write a new rule, setting a deadline for the agency to publish its final rule and for that rule to take effect. In many other cases, however, an agency undertakes to write a new rule based on more broadly defined authority—for example, to address an emerging problem or issue that the agency concludes is within its statutory authority under laws already passed by Congress.[3] As will be discussed below, the latter situation better describes the writing of the HD truck rule, though aspects of that rulemaking process (such as the development of fuel consumption standards) were based on more clearly defined Congressional requirements.

The rulemaking process currently followed by most federal agencies is based on the nearly 70-year-old APA and several other key laws and executive orders. These include the National Environmental Policy Act (NEPA), which requires federal agencies to prepare an Environmental Impact Statement (EIS) for any rule that will potentially have a

Figure 3.1 **The Rulemaking Process**

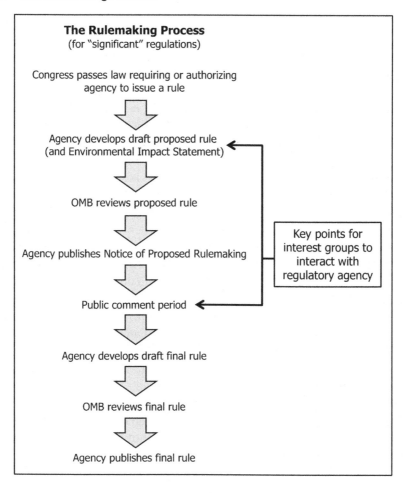

significant impact on the environment, and executive orders requiring additional impact analyses and reviews of "significant" regulations. The HD truck rule, which had the potential for significant economic and environmental impact, was subject to those additional requirements.

The process is most notably characterized by "notice and comment" procedures designed to ensure that federal agencies solicit and consider public comments when writing regulations. Under those procedures, federal agencies publish a Notice of Proposed Rulemaking (NPRM) that explains the proposed rule in detail, solicit and respond to public comments about the proposal, and then develop and publish a final rule. This "notice and comment" process is used in most cases by most federal agencies, including the EPA and NHTSA. Kerwin and Furlong argue that rulemaking provides "opportunities for and dimensions to public participation" that are rarely available during Congressional consideration of legislation (Kerwin & Furlong, 2011, p. 31). Others are less convinced, arguing that rulemaking procedures have a largely symbolic impact.[4]

THE ROLE OF BUSINESS AND OTHER INTEREST GROUPS

A key issue in the literature on rulemaking, and one of great importance in this review of the HD truck rule, is the role played by interest groups, including companies and business associations, in the rulemaking process. Interest groups clearly seek to influence regulators indirectly by lobbying the White House or Congress, but the "notice and comment" nature of federal rulemaking offers interest groups (companies, trade associations, environmental and other issues advocacy groups, etc.), state and local government agencies, and individuals an opportunity at several points to provide comments directly to regulators. Interest groups often say participation in rulemaking is as important or more important than other forms of influencing government policy, including lobbying Congress or the White House, mobilizing "grassroots" activity, making political contributions, and conducting litigation (Furlong & Kerwin, 2005, pp. 353–370).

Organized interests, including business groups, are among the most active participants in the rulemaking process. Marissa M. Golden found that business interests (corporations, utilities, and trade associations) submitted between 66.7% and 100% of the comments received by the EPA and NHTSA in the formal public comment periods of eight rulemakings, for example, though "business did not present a united front" in its comments (Golden, 1998, pp. 245–270). The active participation of business interests is hardly surprising since, as Cary Coglianese has noted, "it takes a high level of technical sophistication to understand and comment on regulatory proceedings" (Coglianese, 2006, p. 943). Rulemaking in fact requires considerable substantive and technical expertise, playing to the strengths of interest groups like trade associations and businesses (Furlong & Kerwin, 2005, p. 361; Kerwin & Furlong, 2011, pp. 34–35). Susan and Jason Webb Yackee argue that agencies may be particularly responsive, at least in the case of relatively noncontroversial rulemakings, to comments from business groups that understand the complex data and studies essential to writing complicated and technical rules (Yackee & Yackee, 2006).

Business groups filed the most formal comments with the EPA and NHTSA during the writing of the HD truck rule, as will be noted below, though environmental and other interest groups also filed a significant number of comments. Individuals filed far fewer comments through Regulations.gov and other methods, with the exception of certain interest group–generated electronic mass-comment filings.[5]

The clearest opportunity to offer comments occurs during the formal public comment period that follows publication of a NPRM, but opportunities may be available well before the publication of a NPRM. Some of the most important work on a proposed rule can be done *before* the publication of the NPRM, a period that can last for a number of years (Testimony of William F. West, 2006). In a study of 42 rulemaking procedures, William West found that 36 involved interactions before the NPRM between the regulatory agency and nongovernmental actors, especially groups with which regulators were familiar (West, 2004).

During this "initiation" phase, agencies gather extensive information that is used in developing a proposed rule (Government Accountability Office, 2009). "Some observers have concluded that the most critical part of the process occurs before a proposed rule is published in the *Federal Register*," Curtis Copeland of the Congressional Research Service (CRS) has noted, "and (for significant rules) possibly even earlier."[6] These more informal interactions offer interest groups an opportunity to influence the formulation of a rule at its very early stages.

In fact, interest groups rate informal contact with an agency prior to publication of the NPRM, along with coalition formation, to be the most effective methods for influencing the regulatory process (Kerwin & Furlong, 2011). As will be seen, these early interactions were vitally important in setting the collaborative tone in the writing of the HD truck rule. Interest groups that have early interactions with regulatory agencies also tend to file formal written comments during the "notice and comment" period.[7] Most of the groups that interacted with the EPA and NHTSA early in the writing of the HD truck rule also filed formal comments after the NPRM was published.

On a most basic level, federal agencies seek input from the public when writing a rule because they are required by law to do so. The idea that business groups can offer technically sophisticated comments points to other potential motivations, however.[8] Business and other interest groups can provide regulatory agencies with new information and expertise during the rulemaking process, while also protecting the agency and its rules from future court challenges (Yackee, 2006). The judicially enforced "procedural accountability" of the rulemaking process, in William West's words, forces agencies to clarify the technical and legal justifications for their actions (West, 2004).

The rulemaking process allows agencies to discern the policy concerns of those affected by a proposed rule. As Laura Langbein and Cornelius Kerwin (2000) note, "Just as Congress writes vague legislation when the likely consequences are unclear because of political uncertainty or technical complexity—shifting responsibility onto the relevant agency—so also is the implementing agency responding to congressional preferences when it does the same thing by shifting responsibility for the specifics to the affected parties" (p. 611).[9] Golden notes that the rulemaking process can resemble an "issue network" based on the exchange of information, in which federal agencies often served as arbiters among other participants and not merely as co-equals in the network (Golden, 1998).

A cooperative or collaborative approach does raise a concern that has long been part of the debate on rulemaking and interest group influence: the idea of regulatory "capture," or the theory that the regulatory process is often captured by the regulated industry and operated primarily for its benefit. According to capture theory, regulators develop a close relationship with and an orientation toward the regulated industry, resulting in a process that is essentially controlled by that industry. This process leads to regulations written to serve the interests of the regulated industry rather than the public. Daniel Carpenter and David Moss define capture as the "result or process by which regulation, in law or application, is consistently and repeatedly directed away from the public interest and toward the interests of the regulated industry, by the intent and action of the industry itself" (Carpenter & Moss, 2014, p. 13; Novak, 2014). Capture theory is embraced both by liberals concerned about economic concentration and the influence of business on public policy and by conservatives concerned about the expansion of government and the inefficiency of regulation—though Carpenter and Moss argue that capture is often "misdiagnosed" to explain any regulatory problem (Carpenter & Moss, 2014).

It does not appear that regulatory capture applies in the writing of the HD truck rule, as will be argued below. Of course, cooperation and collaboration in the regulatory process can raise the question of capture: as Ian Ayers and John Braithwaite (1991) have noted, "The very conditions that foster the evolution of cooperation are also the conditions that promote the evolution of capture." But "negotiation and compromise—explicit and implicit—are ubiquitous elements" of any rulemaking process, as Kerwin and Furlong note (Kerwin & Furlong, 2011, p. 289). This was clearly the case in the writing of the HD truck rule.

The discussion above hints at the rationale behind a cooperative and collaborative approach like that seen in the writing of the HD truck rule: once it becomes clear that a rule will be written, all of the parties involved in a rulemaking have a stake in writing an effective rule that offers something to regulators, the regulated industry, and other interested parties. Government and nongovernmental "stakeholders," including both business and non-business groups, realize that more can be gained through collaboration and cooperation, dialogue, and utilizing multiple sources of scientific, technical, and economic knowledge, than through an adversarial process.[10]

SETTING THE STAGE: LIMITING GHG EMISSIONS FROM LIGHT VEHICLES

To understand why the HD truck rule was written through a collaborative rather than adversarial process, it will be important to put the effort to reduce GHG emissions from heavy-duty vehicles within the broader context of regulating vehicle emissions in general and addressing climate change in particular.

The U.S. first set standards to control emissions of traditional "criteria" pollutants (such as hydrocarbons [HC] and carbon monoxide [CO]) from motor vehicles in the early 1970s, and first set Corporate Average Fuel Economy (CAFE) standards for passenger cars and light trucks a few years later.[11] These standards provided the foundation for a new undertaking launched by the Obama administration: the effort to control GHG emissions from motor vehicles, which account for 23% of total U.S. GHG emissions.

During his successful presidential campaign, Barack Obama vowed that, if elected, he would implement policies designed to address climate change by reducing GHG emissions. He called on Congress to pass cap-and-trade legislation or enact a carbon tax. In the absence of Congressional action, however, he vowed to take steps to reduce GHG emissions using existing law.

A 2007 decision by the U.S. Supreme Court in *Massachusetts v. Environmental Protection Agency* provided the legal basis for the Obama administration to do so. In that groundbreaking decision, the Court found that greenhouse gases could be considered pollutants under the Clean Air Act (CAA). If the EPA determined that GHG emissions endangered public health and welfare, the agency could then use its authority under the CAA to regulate those emissions.[12]

The George W. Bush administration opposed using the CAA to regulate GHG emissions, however, and the EPA had not completed work on such an "endangerment finding" when Obama became president. Obama's choice to head the EPA, Lisa Jackson, vowed that she would move quickly on the issue (Samuelsohn, 2009). Within three months of Jackson's confirmation by the Senate, the EPA had issued a preliminary finding that carbon dioxide and five other greenhouse gases contribute to air pollution that endangers public health and welfare.[13]

Acting on the basis of that endangerment finding,[14] President Obama announced on May 19, 2009, that the EPA would begin writing rules under the CAA to limit greenhouse gas emissions from passenger cars and light trucks. The EPA would act jointly with NTHSA, which would raise federal fuel economy standards for those vehicles. The two issues were clearly related: the best way to reduce GHG emissions by gasoline- or diesel-fueled motor vehicles is to improve their fuel efficiency.[15] The announcement meant that, for the first time ever, automakers would be required to cut vehicle GHG emissions on a national basis. Such a new and potentially far-reaching regulatory initiative is often met with resistance by the industry that will be most directly affected—but that was not the case in this instance.

A NATIONAL STANDARD

Representatives of the United Auto Workers union and several leading automotive companies joined President Obama when he announced that the EPA and NHTSA would propose GHG emissions and fuel economy standards for passenger cars and light trucks. They were there because the Obama administration's "national program" to reduce GHG emissions would offer the auto industry two things that it desired: certainty about future regulations and consistency of regulations on a national basis. The latter point was particularly important because, although the federal government has clear jurisdiction over fuel economy rules, each state has two options in terms of regulating vehicle emissions: federal or California regulations.

The Clean Air Act preempts state vehicle emissions standards with one exception: the state of California, whose emissions rules predate those of the federal government, is allowed to enact its own vehicle emissions standards, provided they are as stringent as federal standards and the EPA first grants a waiver from federal preemption. The Clean Air Act Amendments of 1977 allowed other states ("Section 177 states") to adopt motor vehicle emission standards that are identical to California standards, provided California has received a waiver from federal preemption.[16]

In 2002, California had passed a law requiring automakers to make significant cuts in GHG emissions from light vehicles sold in the state. In 2005, the California Air Resources Board (CARB) issued regulations requiring a 30% cut in such emissions by 2016. At least 12 other states indicated they would adopt the California emissions standards. In 2007, however, the EPA rejected California's request for a waiver from federal preemption. In doing so, the Bush administration prevented California and the other states from regulating GHG emissions from motor vehicles.[17]

Lisa Jackson vowed during her confirmation hearings before the Senate in early January 2009 that she would review that decision if confirmed as EPA administrator (Davies, 2009). Later in January, President Obama directed the EPA to revisit the Bush administration's decision to block California from implementing its rules limiting GHG emissions from vehicles (The White House, 2009). On July 8, 2009, the EPA granted California a waiver of federal preemption, allowing the state to implement its GHG emissions rules ("California State Motor Vehicle Pollution Control Standards; Notice of Decision Granting a Waiver of Clean Air Act Preemption for California's 2009 and Subsequent Model Year Greenhouse Gas Emission Standards for New Motor Vehicles," 2009).

President Obama's earlier announcement of the national program to reduce vehicle emissions overshadowed the waiver decision, however, because California agreed as part of the national program to defer to federal GHG emissions standards through model year (MY) 2016 rather than implement its own rules. California retained the right to request a waiver from federal preemption after MY 2016, however.

The automakers who joined President Obama in announcing his national policy had signaled their willingness to support the administration initiative largely because, since tougher regulations seemed a given with a new president committed to implementing them, the national policy offered automakers the clarity of one nationwide standard for GHG emissions.[18] A single nationwide standard would fulfill a key goal of the auto industry, because it would greatly simplify the process of certifying new vehicles as being in compliance with emissions standards.[19] In exchange for California agreeing to the national policy, the automakers agreed to stop legal efforts to block California from setting GHG emissions standards for vehicles.[20]

On May 22, 2009, the EPA and NHTSA announced their joint rulemaking, and they published a proposed rule on September 28 (Environmental Protection Agency and Department of Transportation, 2009). The agencies finalized the light-vehicle rule on

April 1, 2010, and published it on May 7.[21] The auto industry offered generally positive comments about the rule, in large part because it avoided a system of piecemeal regulation by federal and state agencies (Broder, 2010).

THE HD TRUCK RULE: EARLY ORIGINS

The writing of the GHG emissions and fuel-efficiency standards for passenger cars and light trucks set the stage for the writing of similar rules for HD trucks, buses, and engines, since the EPA's endangerment finding had also cited HD vehicles as a source of GHG emissions that endanger public health and welfare. On May 21, 2010, President Obama called on the EPA and NHTSA "to establish fuel efficiency and greenhouse gas emissions standards for commercial medium- and heavy-duty vehicles beginning with model year 2014, with the aim of issuing a final rule by July 30, 2011" (Office of the Press Secretary, the White House, 2010).[22]

The process of writing those rules began years earlier, however. In the aftermath of the *Massachusetts v. EPA* decision, for example, the EPA started considering how to respond to the Court's decision and how potentially to regulate GHG emissions from a variety of sources. The EPA released an Advance Notice of Proposed Rulemaking (ANPR) on July 11, 2008, summarizing the agency's work on the issue. The EPA had considered several potential approaches to reducing GHG emissions from HD vehicles and engines. Those approaches focused on improving engine technology, reducing aerodynamic drag or tire rolling resistance to improve fuel efficiency, introducing hybrid and other advanced technologies, and changing the operation of heavy vehicles (e.g., reduced idling).[23]

In doing so, the EPA drew on the experience of the 21st Century Truck Partnership, a collaborative R&D program between the Department of Energy and several leading HD vehicle and engine producers and component firms that was established in 2000. This public–private partnership, which built on earlier pre-competitive collaborative programs such as the Combustion Research Facility (CRF) at Sandia National Laboratories and on the cooperative R&D programs of the Energy Department's Office of Vehicle Technologies, had produced a technology roadmap for reducing HD vehicle emissions (Board on Energy and Environmental Systems, Division on Engineering and Physical Sciences, National Research Council, 2012; 21st Century Truck Partnership, 2000).

NHTSA also started to study this issue well before the launch of formal rulemaking. The Energy Independence and Security Act of 2007 (EISA) gave NHTSA the authority for the first time to implement a commercial HD vehicle "fuel-efficiency improvement program." EISA also directed NHTSA to adopt and implement "test methods, measurement metrics, fuel economy standards, and compliance and enforcement protocols that are appropriate, cost-effective, and technologically feasible" for commercial HD vehicles. EISA gave NHTSA authority to establish separate standards for different classes of HD vehicles. NHTSA was required to provide not less than four full years of lead time before companies had to comply with the regulations and three full model years of "regulatory stability."[24]

Congressional efforts to set fuel-efficiency standards for HD trucks and buses were also shaped by the experience of the EPA's SmartWay program. SmartWay is a voluntary program, established in 2004, that certifies trucks and trailers as meeting fuel-efficiency criteria based on certain design characteristics. SmartWay members include the EPA as well as trucking companies, rail carriers, logistics firms, manufacturers, retailers, and other federal and state agencies. Certification by SmartWay allows shippers, manufacturers, and carriers to use the SmartWay logo in marketing, which is important because some firms prefer to ship with carriers that use SmartWay-certified equipment. In addition, the state of California in 2008 adopted rules that would require tractor trailers operating within the state to utilize SmartWay technologies.

As part of its effort, SmartWay, in collaboration with industry and academia, studied methods for measuring the fuel efficiency of long-haul, delivery, and other HD vehicles. The EPA worked under SmartWay to find better methods for measuring aerodynamic drag, tire-rolling resistance, and other criteria to determine fuel efficiency. Most notably, SmartWay focused on finding testing methods to overcome a key stumbling block in setting HD fuel-efficiency standards: the need to use an approach other than the miles-per-gallon standard used to measure light-vehicle fuel economy. Commercial HD vehicles carry a wide variety of loads, perform a wide variety of tasks, and come in a wide range of configurations. As a result, the consensus was that a "performance-based" measure of fuel efficiency needed to be developed for HD vehicles—a consensus built through years of cooperation between the EPA and its partners in the SmartWay program.[25]

EISA also mandated NHTSA to contract with the National Academy of Sciences (NAS) for a report on the viability of HD vehicle fuel-efficiency regulations. The Transportation Research Board (TRB) of the NAS formed a committee composed primarily of research scientists and engineers at national laboratories, universities, and automotive firms to prepare the Congressionally mandated study. Their report called for the development of a performance-based method to measure vehicle fuel efficiency that took into account fuel consumption per unit of payload carried (i.e., load-specific fuel consumption, or LSFC), setting different LSFC standards based on vehicles' functions. NHTSA used the report, which assessed the technologies and approaches that could be used to improve the fuel efficiency of medium- and heavy-duty vehicles, in shaping its proposed regulations.[26]

On June 14, 2010, NHTSA published a notice of intent to prepare a draft Environmental Impact Statement to analyze the potential environmental impact of new HD truck fuel-efficiency regulations, as required by the National Environmental Policy Act. The notice offered four alternative approaches that NHTSA could adopt to regulate medium- and heavy-duty vehicle fuel efficiency, ranging from a rule that merely set engine performance standards to rules that combined an engine standard with vehicle performance standards for Class 8 tractors only; all Class 2b to Class 8 vehicles; or trailers and all Class 2b to Class 8 vehicles.[27] (Vehicle classes are determined by weight, with Class 8 vehicles being the heaviest.)

NHTSA's proposed alternatives highlight the fact that the rule would be the first of its kind for HD vehicles and thus required an entirely new regulatory design. As a result, NHTSA needed input from stakeholders (industry, trade associations, environmental groups, etc.) to help with the design of the standard. This was particularly true because of the complex and unique structure of the HD-vehicle industry, with its wide array of vehicle types, weights, and uses, as well as the diverse nature of the firms active in that industry.[28]

In response to its request for comments, NHTSA received public submissions from more than 40 individuals, companies, trade associations, and other groups. The comments were largely focused on questions related to the possible scope of the regulations, that is, whether the regulatory process should focus on engines only, Class 8 tractors only, or the entire class of medium- and heavy-duty vehicles; whether it should include trailers; etc.[29]

THE PROPOSED RULE

Based on the foundation built through SmartWay, the 21st Century Truck Partnership, the TRB study, and NHTSA's work on the draft EIS, NHTSA and the EPA drafted a proposed rule to set fuel consumption and GHG emissions standards for HD trucks. The agencies sent the proposed rule to the White House Office of Management and Budget (OMB), which must review all "significant" regulatory proposals, on August 13, 2010. OMB concluded its review on October 22.[30]

The NPRM was published in the *Federal Register* on November 30. The agencies proposed establishing GHG emissions and fuel consumption standards for HD engines and "heavy-duty (HD) trucks," which were defined as all highway vehicles that were *not* covered by the light-vehicle CAFE and GHG emissions rules—in other words, all Class 2b through Class 8 medium- and heavy-duty commercial vehicles.[31]

The agencies stated their intent to take an approach that would make maximum use of existing technologies to achieve substantial annual reductions in GHG emissions and fuel consumption—an approach that eased industry concerns. In doing so, the agencies were able to cite the work of SmartWay and the 21st Century Truck Partnership, which indicated the potential for up to a 40% reduction in GHG emissions from a typical HD truck in the near term and the possibility of greater reductions in the long term through improvements in truck and engine technologies.[32]

Publication of the proposed rule started a 60-day clock ticking for public comments, which were due on or before January 31, 2011. Since this was a joint rulemaking, any comments submitted to the EPA docket were considered to have been submitted to the NHTSA docket, and vice versa. The agencies also held two public hearings on the proposed rule, on November 15, 2010, in Chicago, and on November 18, 2010, in Cambridge, Massachusetts.

The proposed rule, which covered 304 pages in the *Federal Register*, contained the agencies' proposed GHG emissions and fuel-consumption standards and requests for

Table 3.1

Regulatory Timeline: The Heavy-Duty Truck Rule

Early industry–government collaboration and regulatory actions on heavy-duty truck fuel efficiency	1980s	Beginnings of cooperative R&D between DOE and heavy-duty truck and engine firms
	2000	21st Century Truck Partnership established
	2004	SmartWay program established
	2007	EISA gives NHTSA authority to implement fuel efficiency standards for heavy-duty vehicles and mandates NAS study on such standards
Key developments in the regulation of greenhouse gas emissions	2007	*Massachusetts v. EPA* decision
	July 30, 2008	Environmental Protection Agency (EPA) publishes ANPR on regulating greenhouse gas (GHG) emissions in response to *Massachusetts v. EPA*
	November 4, 2008	Barack Obama elected president
	April 24, 2009	EPA endangerment finding
	May 19, 2009	President Obama announces intention of EPA and NHTSA to propose rules setting fuel economy and GHG emissions standards for light-duty vehicles
	May 7, 2010	EPA and NHTSA publish final rule setting fuel economy and GHG emissions standards for light-duty vehicles
Key steps in writing the heavy-duty truck rule	May 21, 2010	President Obama releases memorandum calling on EPA and NHTSA to propose rules setting heavy-duty vehicle fuel consumption and GHG emissions standards
	June 14, 2010	NHTSA publishes a Notice of Intent to prepare an EIS on potential heavy-duty vehicle fuel consumption and GHG emissions standards
	August 13, 2010	NPRM submitted to OMB for review
	October 2010	EPA and NHTSA complete Draft Regulatory Impact Analysis
	October 22, 2010	OMB completes review of NPRM
	October 25, 2010	EPA and NHTSA sign NPRM (published in *Federal Register* on November 30, 2010)
	November 2010	EPA and NHTSA hold public hearings on proposed rule
	January 31, 2011	60-day public comment period closes
	June 6, 2011	EPA and NHTSA submit final rule to OMB for review
	June 13, 2011	NHTSA completes Financial Environmental Impact Statement
	August 2011	EPA and NHTSA complete Regulatory Impact Analysis
	August 8, 2011	OMB completes review
	August 9, 2011	President Obama announces final rule (published in *Federal Register* on September 15, 2011)

public comments on several specific aspects of the proposal. It also summarized feasibility assessments used by the agencies in preparing the proposals, including assessments of engine, tractor, aerodynamic, tire, weight reduction, idle reduction, transmission, hybrid, and other technologies. The proposed rule included averaging, banking, and trading (ABT) provisions to help firms meet the standards,[33] and the agencies' proposals for compliance, certification, and enforcement. Finally, the proposed rule contained the agencies' estimates of its impact on climate change and non-GHG emissions and of the cost of compliance.

The agencies broke HD vehicles into three categories for regulatory purposes: *Class 7 and Class 8 combination tractors*, i.e., the heavy trucks ("tractors") that haul trailers; *Class 2b through Class 8 vocational vehicles*, such as emergency vehicles, motor homes, shuttle buses, transit buses, school buses, and delivery, utility, dump, refuse, cement, or tow trucks; and *Class 2b and Class 3 heavy-duty pickup trucks and vans.* The agencies also proposed GHG emissions and fuel-consumption regulations for the engines used in those vehicles.

In breaking the HD truck market into these three segments, the agencies drew on their experience with the trucking sector through SmartWay and other programs, as well as comments offered by HD vehicle and engine producers and trucking and transit companies during the rulemaking process. Such segmentation reflects the diverse nature of the HD truck market and the fact that those trucks are used for such a wide range of purposes. The proposal did not cover trailers—much to the disappointment of environmental groups and of regulators in California and other states—though the agencies considered doing so and requested comments on whether they should propose rules on trailers in the future.

As in the MY 2012–16 light-vehicle CAFE and GHG emissions standards, the agencies harmonized the proposed HD fuel-consumption and GHG emissions standards and coordinated implementation timelines: the GHG emission standards proposed by the EPA would take effect starting in MY 2014, while the vehicle fuel-consumption standards proposed by NHTSA would be voluntary in MY 2014–15 and become mandatory in MY 2016. Early compliance would be allowed in MY 2013. The NHTSA standards became mandatory later than the EPA standards because of lead-time requirements under the EISA, the law that authorized NHTSA to propose fuel consumption standards for heavy vehicles.

The agencies received 2,981 public submissions during the 60-day comment period that followed publication of the proposed rule. Comments were filed by heavy-vehicle producers, components firms, trucking fleet operators, trade associations representing several industry groups, general business associations, environmental groups, state agencies, libertarian and anti-regulation groups, and individuals.[34]

The sources of the most extensive comments received and directly addressed by the agencies can be assessed through the EPA's formal response to public comments. In that response, the EPA addressed in some detail the comments submitted by over 110 commentators. Companies or business groups, including industry or sectoral trade associations, filed the largest number (66) of comments to which the EPA responded, though the EPA also responded to comments from 15 environmental groups and 11 state government agencies or related associations, as well as a smaller number of general interest groups and individuals. The EPA's responses focused on such relatively narrow issues as test procedures, the GHG emissions model, and certification, but also on general support for or opposition to the HD truck rule (Assessment and Standards Division, Office of Transportation and Air Quality, Environmental Protection Agency, 2011).[35]

The comments from truck manufacturers, components firms, and trucking industry groups were generally positive. Although often raising concerns about specific provisions within the proposals, these groups offered largely positive comments about the overall rule, the proposed regulatory approach, and the process through which the rule was written. For example, the Green Truck Association, an affiliate of the National Truck Equipment Association, stated its support for the EPA's and NHTSA's "regulatory approach to this complex issue" (Green Truck Association, 2011).

The lengthy comments from the Engine Manufacturers Association (EMA) and Truck Manufacturers Association (TMA) cited the fact that the agencies had worked closely with EMA, TMA, and their members in crafting the proposed rules, going on to note "the vast amount of common ground that the Agencies and the regulated industries, including the members of EMA and TMA, have been able to develop." EMA and TMA called that common ground "the linchpin" to the implementation of the rules (Engine Manufacturers Association and the Truck Manufacturers Association, 2011).

The heavy truck and engine industry, including EMA, made several suggestions for specific changes to be made before the rule was finalized, including suggested changes in early compliance credits or rules to encourage wider use of natural gas or hybrid vehicles. The Volvo Group, a major heavy truck manufacturer, argued that the start date should be delayed. Daimler Trucks North America expressed appreciation "for the opportunity over the past many months to have worked with the Agencies in the development of the proposed rule" and added that "the Agencies have listened to Daimler's concerns and suggestions"—though Daimler went on to offer 100 pages of very specific comments on virtually all aspects of the proposed rule (Wallace King Domike & Reiskin, 2011).[36]

Energy industry and umbrella business associations, as well as libertarian and anti-regulation groups, filed generally negative comments. These groups raised doubts about the agencies' assessments on technical feasibility, cost, and implementation timelines, but often focused less on the HD truck proposal itself than on the fact that it was based on the EPA's endangerment finding.

The U.S. Chamber of Commerce, for example, stated in its comments that "The Chamber believes that the Clean Air Act is not the appropriate tool to address greenhouse gas emissions" (Chamber of Commerce of the United States of America, 2011). The Coalition for Responsible Regulation, a group of companies and associations in the energy and other industries, argued that the proposed rule "relies upon a faulty finding that GHGs, including CO^2, endanger public health or welfare" (Holland & Hart and Vernon & Elkins, 2011).

Environmental groups such as the Natural Resources Defense Council, praised the proposed rule, though they also generally argued for even tougher regulations. Many environmental groups and state clean-air regulators, drawing on the experience of the SmartWay program, called for the addition of a standard for trailers. The National Association of Clean Air Agencies, an association of state, territorial, and regional clean-air regulators, stated that it "respectfully disagrees" with the failure to include a standard for trailers, while calling on the EPA and NHTSA to make the standards for all three vehicle categories more stringent (National Association of Clean Air Agencies, 2011; Natural Resources Defense Council, 2011; State of California, Air Resources Board, 2011). Yet these critiques were contained within generally positive comments about the proposed rule.

THE FINAL RULE

The EPA and NHTSA reviewed the thousands of comments filed in response to the proposed rule, including the comments filed in response to the agencies' specific requests. On August 9, 2011, a bit more than seven months after the close of the comment period, President Obama announced that the EPA and NHTSA had finalized a regulation (a "final rule") to set the first-ever standards for fuel consumption and GHG emissions for gasoline and diesel heavy-duty engines and HD trucks and buses. In making the announcement, Obama was joined at the White House by representatives of the HD trucking industry.

The standards affect virtually every highway vehicle *not* covered by the light-vehicle GHG emissions and CAFE rules. The "structure of the program and the stringency of the standards" in the final rule were essentially the same as in the proposed rule. The final rule broke HD vehicles into three categories for regulatory purposes: Class 7 and Class 8 combination tractors, which are required to reduce fuel consumption and GHG emissions by roughly 20% by MY 2018; Class 2b through Class 8 vocational vehicles, which are required to make a 10% cut; and Class 2b and Class 3 heavy-duty pickup trucks and vans, which are required to make a 15% cut in fuel consumption and emissions. The rule also sets standards for engines used in those vehicles. The agencies responded to public comments by making changes in the testing and reporting requirements and in the emissions compliance model; making the averaging, banking, and trading program more flexible; and taking steps to further encourage the development of innovative technologies (Environmental Protection Agency and Department of Transportation, 2011).[37]

The reaction to the announcement was generally positive, reflecting the fact that the EPA and NHTSA had consulted closely with truck and engine manufacturers, fleet operators, and environmental groups in writing the new standards. EMA and TMA stated their strong support for "a uniform national program" and praised the EPA and NHTSA for "their willingness to listen to manufacturers' concerns." The American Trucking Association (ATA), which like EMA sent a representative to the White House announcement of the final rule, said the standards were "welcome news," as ATA members would benefit from more fuel-efficient trucks. Smaller trucking firms were more negative, with the Owner-Operator Independent Drivers Association stating that the "flawed, one-size-fits-all rule" would hurt small trucking firms. The Diesel Technology Forum said improvements in diesel-engine efficiency would offer opportunities for early gains in fuel efficiency and that many of the proposed technology solutions are "off the shelf" and would be embraced more readily in the marketplace due to the regulations (Obama Administration Announces First Fuel Economy Standards for Medium and Heavy Trucks, 2011). In fact, the rules have been characterized by some active in the rulemaking process as targeting "low-hanging fruit" that allowed GHG emissions and fuel consumption to be reduced without requiring any major technological breakthroughs.[38]

Reaction by environmental groups was generally positive, with the Sierra Club praising the rules as an important first step and the Environmental Defense Fund stating that "thanks to these new standards, everybody wins: truck drivers save money at the pump, America imports less foreign oil, and we all get to breathe cleaner air" ("Obama Unveils . . . ," 2011). The Union of Concerned Scientists stated that "the new standards will shift clean truck technology into gear," enabling truck manufactures to quickly adopt clean, fuel-efficient technology that in turn will reduce shipping costs and boost jobs and wages (Union of Concerned Scientists, 2011).

COLLABORATION WITHOUT CAPTURE

The detailed review above indicates clearly that the HD truck rule was written through a process marked by a high level of collaboration or cooperation between business and government. That cooperation took place within a traditional rulemaking process, though it started well before the formal publication of a proposed rule. It built on years of interaction between industry and the regulatory agencies through government–industry research programs, certification of compliance with "criteria" emissions rules, the writing of earlier emissions regulations, etc.

As noted above, such long-term relationships between regulatory agencies and regulated industries always raise a concern about regulatory capture. Capture does not seem to apply in the case of the HD truck rule, however, in part because of the complexity of the process through which this rule was written: the rulemaking involved two separate regulatory agencies that rely on different authorizing laws, have different though overlapping areas of regulatory jurisdiction, and have differing records of cooperation with the industries they regulate. Nongovernmental participants found differences in terms of which agency was more willing to engage in detailed discussions, though representatives of industry and environmental groups alike found regulators to be responsive on the whole.[39]

The regulated industry in this case is also a highly complex one, especially when one considers not only those firms that must directly comply with the HD truck rule—vehicle and engine manufacturers—but also their suppliers and customers. As a result, industry "stakeholders" were not unanimous in their views on the specifics of the rulemaking. These circumstances do not point toward capture.

It is also important to note that industry representatives were not the only nongov-ernmental stakeholders involved in this process from its earliest stages. Most notably, environmental groups played an active role in the process starting soon after the Supreme Court ruling in *Massachusetts v. EPA*, participating in the EPA's earliest consideration of whether and how to regulate GHG emissions. As a result, their views influenced the agency's earliest decisions on reducing GHG emissions from mobile sources, which had a direct impact on the HD truck rule. In addition, the political leadership of the Obama administration, with its commitment to addressing climate change, also influenced the early stages of the rulemaking process. That process also received a great deal of media attention due to its broad potential economic and environmental impact. In light of all this, although the regulated industry could and did influence the HD truck rule, it cannot be said that it "captured" either of the regulatory agencies. Rather, as described in this case study, the HD truck rule offers an excellent example of a collaborative approach to regulation, one that led to an outcome clearly acceptable to most of the key participants in the rulemaking process.

Looking forward, it is difficult to say whether the collaborative experience of writing the first HD truck rule will carry forward as regulators and industry begin to shape the "Phase II" heavy-duty rule that will take effect starting in MY 2018. The EPA, NHTSA, and the political leadership of the Obama administration made it clear throughout the process described above that they planned to write a second and more stringent HD truck rule, and work on that Phase II rule began almost immediately after the first rule was finalized. Depending on the size of emissions cuts required, the Phase II rule could pose a greater challenge for industry than the first HD truck rule. The "payback" period for trucking companies is certain to be longer with the Phase II rule. There may be greater disagreement within industry than there was during the writing of the first rule.[40] But the collaborative process through which the first rule was written certainly raises hope that industry and regulators can continue to collaborate in shaping regulations that reduce GHG emissions in a manner that is acceptable to vehicle and engine manufactur-ers, motor carriers, trucking companies, and other stakeholders.

CONCLUSION

The GHG emissions and fuel-consumption rules for HD vehicles were written through a generally collaborative process, one in which regulatory agencies, industry, trade asso-ciations, and environmental groups worked together to shape rules that achieved much of the desired environmental outcome in a manner acceptable to most of the parties. The vast majority of those involved in the rulemaking process had clearly determined that they had more to gain more from a cooperative than from an adversarial approach. Why was that the case?

One important factor is that the rules *offered something for most of the groups partici-pating in the process*, including the HD vehicle and engine industries, the environmental groups, and the federal agencies that collaborated with them. The industry got a degree of certainty about regulatory standards over several years and, more importantly, a national program applying the same standards in all 50 states. The federal regulatory agencies, in return, were able to set the first-ever GHG emissions and fuel-consumption rules for an important segment of vehicles, one responsible for significant emissions of CO_2 and other greenhouse gases and significant annual consumption of diesel fuel in particular (most of the vehicles affected by the rule run on diesel rather than gasoline). California regulators may have favored more stringent standards but, by agreeing to participate in the national program, they were able to lessen the risk of legal challenges and take important steps to start reducing GHG emissions by HD vehicles operating in their state. Environmental groups also may have favored more stringent standards, but they clearly viewed these rules as an important first step in reducing HD vehicles' GHG emissions—particularly since the EPA and NHTSA indicated that a second phase of HD vehicle rules was already envisioned.

A second key factor is the vehicle and engine industries were willing to collaborate with regulators in promulgating the rules in part because *it was clear that the Obama administration intended to move forward with standards to reduce GHG emissions, with or without industry cooperation.* During the presidency of George W. Bush, the vehicle and engine industry believed that the White House was unlikely to support an effort to use the Clean Air Act to regulate GHG emissions, even after the Supreme Court ruling in *Massachusetts v. EPA*. Before the 2008 elections, it also seemed unlikely that Congress would pass and the president sign legislation requiring the motor vehicle industry to reduce GHG emissions. Once Obama took the oath of office, however, it quickly became clear that his administration intended to move forward to address climate change and reduce GHG emissions from mobile and stationary sources alike. It also seemed possible that Congress, with Democratic majorities in both houses after the 2008 elections, would pass climate-change legislation that could affect motor vehicles and transportation fuels. The vehicle and engine industries decided that it was better to have a seat at the table and work with federal regulators to shape the new regulations.

The vehicle and engine industries also understood that *GHG emissions regulations were not just likely in the United States but also in key overseas markets.* The European Union and Japan in particular were exploring ways to reduce GHG emissions from vehicles. Most of the companies active in the motor vehicle and engine industries sell products in Europe and Asia as well as in North America and needed to develop ways to reduce GHG emissions from the vehicles and engines sold in those markets as well. Those companies had an interest in regulations that would allow them to develop products that could be sold in several national markets, not just one. Whereas emissions of traditional "criteria" pollutants are regulated differently in each global market, GHG emissions lend themselves to a more global regulatory approach because reducing fuel consumption is clearly the best way to reduce GHG emissions. Such global regulatory concerns were of little interest to smaller firms active in just the U.S. market or to motor carriers or fleets that buy HD vehicles for use only in North America—groups that were less supportive of the HD truck rule.

A fourth key factor—and one that is not unique to the writing of the HD rules—is competitive advantage: while individual companies are often hesitant to say so publicly, some of the HD vehicle, engine, and component firms participating in the rulemaking process believed that *they could gain a competitive advantage from the GHG emissions and fuel-consumption standards.* This has often been the case with the writing of new automotive regulations, though it is more obvious in the case of certain motor vehicle safety rules than with emissions rules. The potential for competitive advantage resulting from the HD rules became particularly clear in the debate about technology credits, as companies sought to ensure that such credits would be available for technologies that they produce.[41]

It is also important to remember that, when President Obama first proposed regulating GHG emissions from HD vehicles, the path forward had already been paved by a more politically active industry: the light-duty vehicle industry. There is some overlap between the light- and heavy-duty vehicle industries—vehicle companies like General Motors and Ford are involved in both, as are many important component suppliers—but many of the leading companies in the very diverse HD vehicle industry do not produce passenger cars or other light vehicles. They had watched closely as the light-duty industry collaborated with regulators during the writing of the GHG emissions and fuel-efficiency standards for passenger cars and light trucks, however. The light-duty industry has a great deal of political clout—automakers such as General Motors, Ford, Chrysler, Toyota, and Honda have long had a major presence in Washington—and the major automakers helped shape the contours of the complicated process of writing the GHG emissions rules. *The precedent of a successful effort to write light-duty GHG emissions and fuel economy rules was thus very important in setting the stage for a collaborative effort to write the HD rules.*

The HD industry's extensive experience working with the EPA on the regulation of traditional "criteria" emissions was also vitally important when the EPA started discussions with the industry about regulating GHG emissions. In its July 2008 ANPR, for example, the EPA stated that the agency "would rely on our past experience addressing the multifaceted characteristics of this sector," noting that the industry was familiar with the equipment and test procedures that could be used to regulate GHG emissions. The EPA also noted in its July 2008 ANPR that the agency was aware HD engine manufacturers "have already achieved GHG emissions reductions through the introduction of more efficient engine technologies,"[42] based in part on cooperative programs like SmartWay. *The importance of SmartWay and other business-government collaborations cannot be overstated*: the SmartWay program not only provided data upon which the GHG emissions rules could be based, it also gave the industry confidence that the EPA understood the HD market and the concerns of engine and vehicle manufacturers and of carriers.[43] That was particularly important in light of the complex nature of the commercial HD vehicle market and of regulating HD vehicle emissions, which increased the importance of the HD industry's technical expertise during the rulemaking process.

The years of collaboration through SmartWay and other programs also make it clear that, whereas the formal rulemaking process went quickly, this was possible only because federal regulators had been working closely with industry for several years to address some of the most difficult challenges in reducing GHG emissions and fuel consumption by HD vehicles. This points to the most important conclusion that can be drawn from the experience of writing the GHG emissions rules for HD vehicles: *A collaborative regulatory process is far more likely when regulators and industry can build on years of experience working together before the formal rulemaking process begins.* Such long-running collaboration ensures that regulators are familiar with the industry, its key players, and their most important concerns and issues—and that industry has a similar familiarity with the key regulators. This by no means can or should ensure that either regulators or industry will be completely satisfied by the results of the regulatory process, but it makes it far more likely that the process will be a collaborative one whose end result avoids the fierce political and legal challenges that have been typical of environmental regulation in recent years. In fact, the collaborative nature of the process through which the GHG emissions rules for motor vehicles were written is particularly striking because it occurred during a period in which the Obama administration's environmental policies were the subject of intense criticism (Lee, 2014).[44]

Such early collaboration is often found in the writing of complex rules. As Kerwin and Furlong note, "communication between interest groups and agencies prior to the proposed rulemaking is quite common" (Kerwin & Furlong, 2011), and, as noted above, critical decisions are often made prior to the publication of a proposed rule—a period that can last for several years. This was clearly the case in the writing of the HD rules, where the issues surrounding efforts to make HD vehicles and engines more fuel-efficient were explored for years by federal agencies, vehicle and engine manufacturers, and trucking companies through SmartWay and other programs.

As the above discussion makes clear, the collaborative nature of this regulatory process can in part be attributed to factors unique to the HD vehicle emissions standards and the industries affected by those regulations. It can also be attributed to factors, summarized below, with implications for business–government collaboration in general and for the rulemaking process in particular. The lesson of this case study is that business, government, and other stakeholders can, under the right conditions, collaborate on writing a rule even if it concerns a highly contentious and adversarial issue like climate change.

KEY POINTS

- Business–government collaboration in the rulemaking process can result in regulations that achieve societal goals, such as reducing emissions that endanger public health and safety, at a cost acceptable to regulated businesses and their customers.
- Such collaboration is possible within the structures of the traditional rulemaking process when a majority of those involved determine that they have more to gain more from a cooperative approach than from an adversarial one.
- Such collaboration is most easily achieved in cases where the regulations offer something to all of the parties involved, including business and government.
- The risk that such collaboration will lead to regulatory "capture" is greatly reduced by the early involvement of public interest groups and other non-business

stakeholders and when companies involved in the regulated business are not unanimous in their views on the rulemaking.

- Individual businesses can be more interested in collaboration with regulators in cases where they see competitive advantage potentially resulting from the rulemaking process.
- A collaborative rulemaking process is most likely when business and government can build on a long history of working together on similar issues before the formal rulemaking process begins.

ACKNOWLEDGMENT

I would like to thank the officials at trade and industry associations, environmental groups, companies, and regulatory agencies who offered their comments, on condition of anonymity, about the process through which the light- and heavy-duty vehicle greenhouse gas emissions and fuel efficiency rules were written. I would also like to thank my colleagues at Global Policy Group for our many discussions over the years about environmental policy and its impact on the automotive industry. Finally, I would like to thank my wife Laurie for her editorial suggestions and support.

NOTES

1. In terms of the collaborative nature of the rulemaking, Margo T. Oge, the director of the Office of Transportation and Air Quality within EPA's Office of Air and Radiation, stated afterward that the HD truck rule "shows what can be done when people with faith are willing to work hard, use common sense to achieve a common cause." See: Martin Kahl, "Margo Oge provides the EPA's take on the US MD/HD final rule," *Automotive World*, October 6, 2011 (based on the public comments of Oge at a conference at which the author also spoke). See also: Written statement of Margo T. Oge, Subcommittee on Energy and Power, Committee on Energy and Commerce, U.S. House of Representatives, July 17, 2012. Similar comments about the collaborative nature of the process were made by representatives of industry and environmental groups and regulatory agencies in email exchanges with the author after the HD truck rule was finalized.

2. Copeland notes that federal agencies issue 3,000 to 4,000 final rules each year. During the eight years of the Clinton administration, an average of 4,740 final rules and 3,253 proposed rules were published each year (Kerwin and Furlong [2011], p. 19).

3. Such a decision to write a new rule can be driven by the leadership of a regulatory agency, outside pressure from the White House or other political actors, or a petition for rulemaking filed by an outside party.

4. See, for example, William West's review of scholarly assessments of the effects of rulemaking in (West, 2004, pp. 66–80).

5. Cary Coglianese concluded in a 2006 article that, even with the development of "e-rulemaking" in which public comments can be filed electronically via the Regulations.gov website and rulemaking documents and comments can be read through on-line dockets, "regulatory agencies continue to garner only the most modest, if not trivial, level of involvement by ordinary citizens" (Coglianese, 2006).

6. (Copeland, 2009), p. i. The importance of the pre-NPRM period has led some agencies in certain major rulemakings to issue an Advance Notice of Proposed Rulemaking to solicit comments even before the launch of the regulatory process.

7. Opinions vary on the impact of formal filings but, in a study of 40 rules promulgated by four federal agencies, Susan Webb Yackee found that interest group comments submitted during the formal comment period can, and often do, affect the final rule (Yackee, 2006).

8. Jason Webb Yackee and Susan Webb Yackee note that business groups often file "higher quality" comments than other groups (Yackee and Yackee, 2006).

9. Langbein and Kerwin make the comment in a discussion comparing negotiated rulemaking and conventional rulemaking, but it clearly applies to both approaches (2000). Negotiated regulation (also known as "reg neg," or regulatory negotiation) is an alternative approach to rulemaking in which representatives of federal agencies and affected interest groups formally negotiate a proposed rule. The approach, which first emerged in the 1980s and was subsequently authorized through the *Negotiated Rulemaking Act of 1990*, was used most notably by EPA and the Transportation Department. Its use has declined significantly in recent years. The HD truck rule was written using a conventional rulemaking process.

10. This description of collaboration draws on Neil Gunningham's description of the collaborative approach to regulation found in the Environment Improvement Plans of the Victorian Environmental Protection Authority in Australia (Gunningham, 2009). Much of the literature on cooperative or collaborative approaches to regulation focuses on enforcement (Scholz, 1984). Many of the underlying concepts about cooperation apply to rulemaking as well, however.

11. The *Clean Air Act* requires EPA to set ambient air quality standards for six commonly found air pollutants, which are also known as "criteria" pollutants. The first federal standards limiting motor vehicles' emissions of "criteria" pollutants—HC and CO tailpipe emissions and HC crankcase emissions—were enacted through the *Motor Vehicle Pollution Control Act of 1965* and took effect in MY (model year) 1968. (The state of California had adopted similar standards that took effect earlier, in MY 1966.) EPA has since enacted a series of more stringent federal standards (Tier 0, Tier 1, Tier 2, Tier 3) affecting passenger car and light truck tailpipe and evaporative emissions of "criteria" pollutants. The first emissions standards for heavy-duty vehicles and engines took effect in MY 1988. EPA has since set more stringent standards for "criteria" pollutant emissions that were phased in over MY 2004–07, with a second set of standards phased in over MY 2007–10. NHTSA has regulated light-vehicle fuel efficiency by setting CAFE standards for passenger cars since MY 1978 and for light trucks since MY 1979. Those rules require an automaker to meet a standard for sales-weighted fuel economy (in miles per gallon) for its fleet of vehicles sold in the U.S. in a model year. In 2007, Congress required NHTSA to increase light vehicle fuel efficiency to at least 35 mpg by MY 2020.

12. A good discussion of the legal issues raised in *Massachusetts v. EPA* and other legal cases can be found in (O'Leary, 2013).

13. (Environmental Protection Agency, "Proposed Endangerment and Cause or Contribute Findings for Greenhouse Gases under Section 202(a) of the *Clean Air Act*," 2009) The primary greenhouse gas emitted from vehicles is carbon dioxide, or CO2, but vehicles also emit methane (CH4), nitrous oxide (N2O), and hydrofluorocarbons (HFCs).

14. The endangerment finding was finalized in December 2009. See: Environmental Protection Agency, "Endangerment and Cause or Contribute Findings for Greenhouse Gases Under Section 202(a) of the *Clean Air Act*", 2009.

15. Office of the Press Secretary, The White House, "President Obama Announces National Fuel Efficiency Policy," 2009. In terms of CAFE, NHTSA would rely on an "attribute-based" approach that required vehicles with a smaller "footprint" to meet more stringent standards than larger vehicles—an approach that the agency had first used in writing "reformed" CAFE rules for MY 2008–11 light trucks.

16. The rules related to California emissions regulations and waivers from federal pre-emption may be found in Section 209 —State Standards of the *Clean Air Act*. According to Section 209(e)(2), EPA should grant such a waiver unless the agency finds that California: was "arbitrary and capricious" in finding that its standards were at least as protective of public health and welfare as applicable federal standards; does not need such standards to meet "compelling and extraordinary conditions"; or California's standards and enforcement procedures are not consistent with Section 209.

17. California's GHG emissions rules, which were enacted as part of its second generation low-emission vehicle program (LEV II), were implemented through CARB Resolution 04–28, September 24, 2004, which was approved by California's Office of Administrative Law on September 15, 2005. The rules included test procedures to control GHG emissions from passenger cars, light trucks, and medium-duty passenger vehicles. EPA's denial of California's request for a waiver from federal pre-emption can be found at: Environmental Protection Agency, "California State Motor Vehicle Pollution Control Standards; Notice of Decision Denying a Waiver of *Clean Air Act* Preemption for California's 2009 and Subsequent Model Year Greenhouse Gas Emission Standards for New Motor Vehicles" 2008.

18. Some questioned whether two of those automakers, GM and Chrysler, were in a position to fight the Obama administration at a time when the federal government was helping them as they faced bankruptcy (Broder, 2009).

19. Under section 203 of the *Clean Air Act*, an automaker must obtain a certificate of conformity indicating compliance with federal emissions standards prior to selling a new vehicle in the U.S. The automaker does so by submitting test data and other information to EPA to demonstrate that a vehicle or engine family conforms to those standards. An automaker must go through the certification process with California to sell new vehicles in California and states that have adopted California emissions regulations.

20. The commitment letters from the automakers and their trade associations, and from the state of California, can be found at: www.epa.gov/otaq/climate/letters.htm#2009al

21. The rules, which apply to MY 2012-MY 2016 passenger cars, light trucks, and medium-duty passenger vehicles (MDPVs), require a 30% cut in GHG emissions to an average of 250 grams/mile of CO_2 and a average fuel economy of 34.1 mpg by MY 2016. Automakers are expected to meet the GHG standards largely by improving fuel economy, though they can also get credit for reducing hydrofluorocarbon and CO_2 emissions through improvements in air-conditioning systems. (Environmental Protection Agency and Department of Transportation, 2010).

22. The president also called on the two agencies by September 30, 2010, to publish a letter of intent to write new GHG emissions and fuel economy rules for MY 2017-MY 2025 light vehicles. (Office of the Press Secretary, the White House, 2010) Vehicles with a GVWR between 8,500 lbs and 26,000 lbs are at times called medium-duty vehicles, though such vehicles can also be called heavy-duty vehicles.

23. The ANPR was formally published in the *Federal Register* on July 30. (Environmental Protection Agency, 2008) EPA received 18,055 comments that were posted to its docket, though Regulations. gov indicates that the total number of comments could exceed 280,000 when bulk submissions are included.

24. The final version of the EISA (P.L. 110–140) gave NHTSA flexibility in setting fuel economy standards for medium- and heavy-duty vehicles. The original Senate version of the EISA would have mandated such standards and defined a specific annual percentage increase in fuel efficiency.

25. See Transportation and Regional Programs Division, Office of Transportation and Air Quality, Environmental Protection Agency, 2007. The development of test protocols was also related to efforts to establish a method for determining whether vehicles met fuel-efficiency requirements for hybrid heavy-vehicle tax credits.

26. Committee to Assess Fuel Economy Technologies for Medium- and Heavy-Duty Vehicles, Board on Energy and Environmental Systems, Transportation Research Board, *Technologies and Approaches to Reducing the Fuel Consumption of Medium- and Heavy-Duty Vehicles* (Washington: The National Academies Press, 2010).

27. The *National Environmental Policy Act* requires federal agencies both to consider the potential direct and indirect environmental impact of proposed rules and reasonable alternatives, including "no action." In its June 2010 notice, NHTSA invited public comments on the scope of the EIS analysis, describing alternative approaches that it was considering in this "scoping process." In addition to the four alternatives, NHTSA also requested comment on a "no action" alternative that assumed NHTSA

would not issue a rule, which was included to serve as an analytical baseline. See Department of Transportation, "Notice of Intent To Prepare an Environmental Impact Statement for New Medium- and Heavy-Duty Fuel Efficiency Improvement Program" [Docket No. NHTSA–2010–0079], *Federal Register,* June 10, 2010 (75 FR 33565).

28. This point was highlighted in an April 10, 2014, email exchange between the author and a top official at a trade association who was actively involved in the formulation of the regulations. In its July 2008 ANPR (73 FR 44354), EPA had also considered different options for regulating GHG emissions from heavy-duty trucks, including: a regulatory program based on an engine CO_2 standard or a weighted GHG emissions standard; a heavy-duty truck GHG emissions rule modeled on light-duty vehicle emissions test procedures, using a weighted measure that would account for payload or work performed by the truck; or, as a complement to those approaches, allowing trucking fleets to generate GHG emissions credits through the use of advanced technologies.

29. The comments filed with NHTSA can be found in Docket ID No. NHTSA-2010–0079. Comments were filed by several heavy-duty vehicle, engine, and component producers, including Cummins, Daimler Trucks North America, Navistar, Volvo, Allison Transmission, and Eaton; trade associations, including the National Truck Equipment Association, American Bus Association, Truck Trailer Manufacturers Association, National Automobile Dealers Association, and American Trucking Association; the U.S. Chamber of Commerce; environmental and energy efficiency groups, including the American Council for an Energy Efficient Economy, Environmental Defense Fund, and the Sierra Club; and several state government environmental agencies or departments.

30. Executive Order 12866, which was signed in 1993, requires that the OMB's Office of Information and Regulatory Affairs (OIRA) review all "significant" regulatory actions, which is defined as those actions likely to have an annual economic impact of $100 million or more, create a serious inconsistency with an action taken by another agency, materially affect mandatory spending programs, or raise novel legal or policy issues. See: Executive Order 12866, "Regulatory Planning and Review," *Federal Register*, October 4, 1993 (58 FR 51735). That executive order replaced Executive Order 12291, signed by President Reagan, which had first required OMB reviews of significant rulemakings.

31. Environmental Protection Agency and Department of Transportation (2010). The two agencies had signed the NPRM on October 25. A good summary of the proposed rule can be found in: Office of Transportation and Air Quality, Environmental Protection Agency, "EPA and NHTSA Propose First-Ever Program to Reduce Greenhouse Gas Emissions and Improve Fuel Efficiency of Medium- and Heavy-Duty Vehicles: Regulatory Announcement" (EPA-420-F-10–901), October 2010. The term "HD Trucks" as used in the proposed rule incorporates work trucks and commercial medium- and heavy-duty on-highway vehicles under the definition used in the EISA, which gave NHTSA authority to regulate fuel consumption by such vehicles. The definition of "HD Trucks" is similar to the definition of heavy-duty vehicles used by EPA in regulating criteria emissions, which includes several classes of heavy-duty vehicles (HDVs) ranging from HDV-2b (gross vehicle weight rating [GVWR] of 8,500 lbs-10,000 lbs) to HDV-8 (GVWR of 33,000 lbs and above). NHTSA and other Transportation Department agencies use a slightly different definition of vehicle classes for the purposes of federal safety regulations that groups commercial trucks and buses in both medium- and heavy-duty classifications.

32. See EPA's July 2008 ANPR (73 FR 44354) for a detailed review of the basis for those assertions. See also Cullen and Bynum (2008).

33. Averaging, banking, and trading, which was first used by EPA for heavy-duty truck emissions in the 1990s, refers to the "averaging" of emissions over engine families produced by the manufacturer, the "banking" of credits to offset emissions from the same or other engine families produced by the manufacturer in future model years, and the "trading" of credits by sale to another manufacturer to offset emissions from that firm's engine families. ABT programs are designed to increase flexibility in complying with emissions standards. A good brief description of ABT programs can be found in: Ellerman, Joskow, and Harrison, Jr., "Emissions Trading in the U.S.: Experience, Lessons, and Considerations for Greenhouse Gases," prepared for the Pew Center on Global Climate Change, May 2003, pp. 27–29.

34. Based on data found on Regulations.gov.

35. The 65 commentators in "general support" of the rule included a broad mix of companies, business associations, environmental groups, and state agencies. The 11 commentators included in "opposition" to the rule included a small number of companies, several business associations, and several conservative interest groups.

36. DTNA stated that it had suggested "a rule that considers the GHG reduction potential of the entire vehicle and its integrated components, including its engine, and is neutral as to the technologies that manufacturers may use to meet the specified standards." See: Daimler Trucks North America, Detroit Diesel Corporation, Mercedes Benz USA, and Daimler Buses North America, undated.

37. President Obama had announced the standards in August. See: The White House, Office of the Press Secretary, "White House Announces First Ever Oil Savings Standards for Heavy Duty Trucks, Buses," August 9, 2011. NHTSA had earlier released its Final Environmental Impact Statement (FEIS), which was prepared in cooperation with EPA and the Transportation Department's Federal Motor Carrier Safety Administration. See: National Highway Traffic Safety Administration, "Medium- and Heavy-Duty Fuel Efficiency Improvement Program: Final Environmental Impact Statement," June 13, 2011. EPA also published detailed responses to many of the public comments filed in response to the NPRM (see citation in footnote 62).

38. This description was used in an April 10, 2014, email exchange between the author and a regulatory specialist at a trade association who was involved in the rulemaking.

39. Based on email exchanges between the author and participants in the process. Industry and interest group participants were unanimous in their comments that cooperation with EPA was easier during the rulemaking.

40. The payback period is the time required for the buyer of a heavy truck, for example, to "pay-back" the higher cost of a vehicle meeting new standards with the cost savings resulting from lower fuel consumption. These concerns about collaboration in writing the Phase II rules were raised by several trade and industry association officials in email exchanges with the author, though the officials were also all hopeful that the Phrase II process will be a collaborative one.

41. In terms of the HD industry, emissions rules not only have an impact on the relative competitiveness of each manufacturer's product; they also can prompt an industry-wide "pre-buy" that greatly affects the pattern of HD truck sales. In the case of EPA's MY 2007 heavy-duty emissions rules, for example, a combination of high prices and technology uncertainty led to a substantial increase in purchases of Class 8 trucks during the two years (2005–06) before the new rules took effect. A study by NERA Economic Consulting, for example, estimates that the "pre-buy" totaled 120,000 additional units beyond a baseline projection. In the two years after the rules took effect, however, there was a "low buy" in which carriers bought 180,000 units less than baseline. (See: David Harrison and Mark LeBel, "Customer Behavior in Response to the 2007 Heavy-Duty Engine Emission Standards: Implications for the NOx Standard," NERA Economic Consulting, November 14, 2008.) The first phase of the GHG emissions and fuel consumption rules did not have such a large impact, though the second (post-2018) phase could have a larger impact on the HD truck market if they require more significant (and expensive) technological changes.

42. 73 FR 44354 (section quoted appears on page 44456). It should be noted that, while heavy-duty vehicle and engine firms had long dealt with EPA on emissions regulations, they had little experience in dealing with NHTSA on the issue of fuel efficiency (as opposed to safety).

43. This point was emphasized in an April 8, 2014, email exchange between the author and an official at an industry group who was an active participant in the rulemaking process.

44. See, for example, Carol E. Lee, "Rare Detente: New EPA Chief and Industry," *The Wall Street Journal*, March 7, 2014, which highlights difficult relations between EPA and industry during the time Lisa Jackson served as EPA administrator.

REFERENCES

21st Century Truck Partnership. (2000, December). *Technology roadmap for the 21st century truck program*, 21CT-001.

Assessment and Standards Division, Office of Transportation and Air Quality, Environmental Protection Agency. (2011, August). *Greenhouse gas emissions standards and fuel efficiency standards for medium- and heavy-duty engines and vehicles: EPA response to comments document for joint rulemaking* (EPA-420-R-11-004).

Ayers, I., & Braithwaite, J. (1991, Summer). Tripartism: Regulatory capture and empowerment. *Law and Social Inquiry*, *16*(3), 435–496.

Board on Energy and Environmental Systems, Division on Engineering and Physical Sciences, National Research Council. (2012). *Review of the 21st century truck partnership, second report*. Washington, DC: National Academies Press.

Broder, J. M. (2009, May 18). Obama to toughen rules on emissions and mileage, *The New York Times*.

Broder, J. M. (2010, April 1). U.S. issues limits on greenhouse gas emissions from cars, *The New York Times*.

Carpenter, D., & Moss, D. (2014). Introduction. In D. Carpenter & D. Moss (Eds.), *Preventing regulatory capture: Special interest influence and how to limit it* (p. 13). New York: Cambridge University Press.

Chamber of Commerce of the United States of America. (2011, January 31). *Comments Re: Greenhouse gas emissions standards and fuel efficiency standards for medium- and heavy-duty engines and vehicles*, Docket ID No. EPA-HQ-OAR-2010-0162 and NHTSA-2010-0079.

Coglianese, C. (2004, Spring). E-Rulemaking: Information technology and the regulatory process. *Administrative Law Review*, *56*(2), 353–402.

Coglianese, C. (2006, March). Citizen participation in rulemaking: Past, present, and future. *Duke Law Journal*, *55*(5), 943.

Copeland, C. W. (2009, July 20). *The unified agenda: Implications for rulemaking transparency and participation*, R40713. Congressional Research Service.

Cullen, A., & Bynum, C. (2008, June 12). Environmental Protection Agency, Memorandum to Docket ID No. EPA-HG-OAR-2008-0318, Subject: *Summary of greenhouse gas emission control technologies for heavy-duty trucks*.

Daimler Trucks North America, Detroit Diesel Corporation, Mercedes Benz USA, and Daimler Buses North America. (undated). *Comments Re: Greenhouse gas emissions standards and fuel efficiency standards for medium- and heavy-duty engines and vehicles*, Docket ID No. EPA-HQ-OAR-2010-0162 and NHTSA-2010-0079.

Davies, F. (2009, January 14). EPA nominee pledges to quickly review California's emissions standard. *San Jose Mercury News*.

Department of Transportation. (2010, June 10). *Notice of Intent to prepare an environmental impact statement for new medium- and heavy-duty fuel efficiency improvement program*, Docket No. NHTSA-2010-0079, *Federal Register*, (75 FR 33565).

Ellerman, A. D., Joskow, P. L., & Harrison, Jr., D. (2003, May). *Emissions trading in the U.S.: Experience, lessons, and considerations for greenhouse gases* (pp. 27–29). Prepared for the Pew Center on Global Climate Change.

Engine Manufacturers Association and the Truck Manufacturers Association. (2011, January 31). *Comments Re: Greenhouse gas emissions standards and fuel efficiency standards for medium- and heavy-duty engines and vehicles*, Docket ID No. EPA-HQ-OAR-2010-0162 and NHTSA-2010-0079.

Environmental Protection Agency. (2008, July 30). *Regulating greenhouse gas emissions under the Clean Air Act: Advanced notice of proposed rulemaking*, EPA-HQ-OAR-2008–0318; FRL-8694-2, RIN 2060-AP12, *Federal Register*, (73 FR 44354).

Environmental Protection Agency. (2009, April 24). *Proposed endangerment and cause or contribute findings for greenhouse gases under Section 202(a) of the Clean Air Act*, EPA-HQ-OAR-2009–0171; FRL-8895-5, RIN 2060-ZA14, *Federal Register*, (74 FR 18886).

Environmental Protection Agency. (2009, July 8). *California State Motor Vehicle Pollution Control Standards; Notice of decision granting a waiver of Clean Air Act preemption for California's 2009 and subsequent model year greenhouse gas emission standards for new motor vehicles*, FRL–8927–2, *Federal Register*, (74 FR 32744).

Environmental Protection Agency. (2009, December 15). *Endangerment and cause or contribute findings for greenhouse gases under Section 202(a) of the Clean Air Act*, EPA-HQ-OAR-2009-0171; FRL-9091-8, RIN 2060-ZA14, *Federal Register*, (74 FR 66496).

Environmental Protection Agency and Department of Transportation. (2009, May 22). *Notice of upcoming joint rulemaking to establish vehicle GHG emissions and CAFE standards*, FRL-8909-3, RIN 2060-ZA15, *Federal Register*, (74 FR 24007).

Environmental Protection Agency and Department of Transportation. (2009, September 28) *Proposed rulemaking to establish light-duty vehicle greenhouse gas emission standards and corporate average fuel economy standards; Proposed rule*, EPA-HQ-OAR-2009-0472; FRL-8959-4; NHTSA-2009-0059, RIN 2060-AP58; RIN 2127-AK90, *Federal Register*, (74 FR 49454).

Environmental Protection Agency and Department of Transportation. (2010, May 7). *Light-duty vehicle greenhouse gas emission standards and corporate average fuel economy standards; Final rule*, EPA-HQ-OAR-2009-0472; FRL-9134-6; NHTSA-2009-0059, RIN 2060-AP58; RIN 2127-AK50, *Federal Register*, (75 FR 25325).

Environmental Protection Agency and Department of Transportation. (2011, September 15). *Greenhouse gas emission standards and fuel efficiency standards for medium- and heavy-duty engines and vehicles: Final rule*, EPA-HQ-OAR-2010–0162; NHTSA-2010-079, *Federal Register*, (76 FR 57106).

Executive Order 12866. (1993, October 4). *Regulatory planning and review, Federal Register*, (58 FR 51735).

Furlong, S. R., & Kerwin, C. M. (2005, July). Interest group participation in rule making: A decade of change. *Journal of Public Administration Research and Theory*, 15(3), 353–370.

Green Truck Association. (2011, January 28). *Comments Re: Greenhouse gas emissions standards and fuel efficiency standards for medium- and heavy-duty engines and vehicles*, Docket ID No. EPA-HQ-OAR-2010-0162 and NHTSA-2010-0079.

Golden, M. M. (1998, April). Interest groups in the rule-making process: Who participates? Whose voices get heard? *Journal of Administrative Research and Theory*, 8(2) 245–270.

Government Accountability Office. (2009, April 20). *Federal Rulemaking: Improvements needed to monitoring and evaluation of rules development as well as transparency of OMB regulatory reviews* (GAO-09-205).

Gunningham, N. (2009, March). The new collaborative environmental governance: The localization of regulation. *Journal of Law and Society*, 36(1), 145–166.

Harrison, D., & LeBel, M. (2008, November 14). *Customer behavior in response to the 2007 heavy-duty engine emission standards: Implications for the NOx Standard*. NERA Economic Consulting.

Holland & Hart and Vernon & Elkins on behalf of the Coalition for Responsible Regulation. (2011, January 27). *Comments Re: Greenhouse gas emissions standards and fuel efficiency standards for medium- and heavy-duty engines and vehicles*, Docket ID No. EPA-HQ-OAR-2010-0162 and NHTSA-2010-0079.

Kahl, M. (2011, October 6). Margo Oge provides the EPA's take on the US MD/HD final rule. *Automotive World*.

Kerwin, C. M., & Furlong, S. R. (2011). *Rulemaking: How government agencies write law and make policy* (4th ed.). Washington, DC: CQ Press.

Langbein, L. I., & Kerwin, C. M. (2000, July). Regulatory negotiation versus conventional rule making: Claims, counterclaims, and empirical evidence. *Journal of Public Administration Research and Theory*, 10(3), 611.

Lee, C. E. (2014, March 7). Rare detente: New EPA chief and industry. *The Wall Street Journal*.

National Association of Clean Air Agencies, NCAA Mobile Sources and Fuels Committee. (2011, January 31). *Comments Re: Greenhouse gas emissions standards and fuel efficiency standards for medium- and heavy-duty engines and vehicles*, Docket ID No. EPA-HQ-OAR-2010-0162 and NHTSA-2010-0079.

Natural Resources Defense Council. (2011, January 31). *Comments Re: Greenhouse gas emissions standards and fuel efficiency standards for medium- and heavy-duty engines and vehicles*, Docket ID No. EPA-HQ-OAR-2010-0162 and NHTSA-2010-0079.

Novak, W. J. (2014). A revisionist history of regulatory capture. In D. Carpenter & D. Moss (Eds.), *Preventing regulatory capture: Special interest influence and how to limit it* (pp. 25–48). New York: Cambridge University Press.

Obama Administration Announces First Fuel Economy Standards for Medium and Heavy Trucks. (2011, August). *TruckingInfo.com*.

Obama Unveils First Fuel Efficiency Rule for Heavy Duty Trucks. (2011, August 10). *Environmental News Service*.

Office of the Press Secretary, The White House. (2009, May 19). *President Obama announces national fuel efficiency policy*.

Office of the Press Secretary, The White House. (2010, May 21). *Presidential memorandum regarding fuel efficiency standards*.

O'Leary, R. (2013). Environmental Policy in the Courts. In N. J. Vig & M. E. Kraft (Eds.), *Environmental policy: New directions for the 21st century* (8th ed., pp. 135–156). Los Angeles: CQ Press.

Samuelsohn, D. (2009, March 10). Leaked EPA document shows greenhouse gas endangerment finding on fast track. *The New York Times*.

Scholz, J. T. (1984). Cooperation, deterrence, and the ecology of regulatory enforcement. *Law and Society Review, 18*(2), 179–224.

State of California, Air Resources Board. (2011, January 31). *Comments Re: Greenhouse gas emissions standards and fuel efficiency standards for medium- and heavy-duty engines and vehicles*, Docket ID No. EPA-HQ-OAR-2010-0162 and NHTSA-2010-0079.

Testimony of William F. West, Subcommittee on Commercial and Administrative Law, House Committee on the Judiciary. (2006, December). *Interim report on the administrative law, process and procedure project for the 21st century,* Committee Print No. 10, 109th Congress, 2nd Session.

Transportation and Regional Programs Division, Office of Transportation and Air Quality, Environmental Protection Agency. (2007, November). *SmartWay fuel efficiency test protocol for medium and heavy duty vehicles* (Working Draft), EPA420-P-07-003.

Union of Concerned Scientists. (2011, August 9). *New truck standards will lower emissions, create jobs and reduce oil consumption*.

Wallace King Domike, & Reiskin on behalf of the Volvo Group. (2011, January 31). *Comments Re: Greenhouse gas emissions standards and fuel efficiency standards for medium- and heavy-duty engines and vehicles*, Docket ID No. EPA-HQ-OAR-2010-0162 and NHTSA-2010-0079.

West, W. (2004, January/February). Formal procedures, informal processes, accountability, and responsiveness in bureaucratic policy making: An institutional policy analysis. *Public Administration Review, 64*(1), 66–80.

The White House, Presidential Memorandum for the Administrator of the Environmental Protection Agency. (2009, January 26). Subject: *State of California request for waiver under 42 U.S.C. 7543(b), the Clean Air Act*.

Yackee, J. W., & Yackee, S. W. (2006, February). A bias towards business? Assessing interest group influence on the U.S. bureaucracy. *The Journal of Politics, 68*(1), 128–139.

Yackee, S. W. (2006, January). Sweet-talking the fourth branch: The influence of interest group comments on federal agency rulemaking. *Journal of Public Administration Research and Theory, 16*(1), 103–124.

4

Smart Community Engagement

Challenges and Opportunities in Transforming and Emerging Industries

Jian Cui

INTRODUCTION

In response to widespread public concerns over oil and gas development, especially the new shale energy development enabled by directional drilling and hydraulic fracturing (a.k.a "fracking"), the American Petroleum Institute (API) released its first official *Community Engagement Guidelines* (the API Guidelines) in July 2014. These guidelines help oil and gas companies with stakeholder management and community engagement (API, 2014). A stakeholder is defined as "any person, group or entity that has interest or concern in an organization and its activities. . . [who] can affect or be affected by the organization's actions, objectives and policies" (API, 2014, p. vi). Bearing this in mind, the guidelines provide a lifecycle framework for effective community engagement through five key steps: entry, exploration, development, operation/production, and exit. This active framework addresses the complexities of a U.S. oil and gas industry in transformation, including risk, mistrust, and the common engagement strategies that have failed.

To a large extent, the API Guidelines imply a global trend of environmental politics and an intense stalemate in public relations facing not only the oil and gas industry (or specifically the unconventional oil and gas industry), but also areas of renewable energy. What remains to be answered is how to construct win-win relations between public and private leaders in addressing the risks associated with technological diffusion. These industries face three main challenges when engaging the community in such a changing environment.

First and foremost, modern community engagement in an emerging or transforming industry no longer deals with the simple ideology of "Not In My Back Yard" (or "NIMBY-ism"): reasonable compensation, "effective" communication, or relocation of operations. Take the process of unconventional gas development as an example. Fracking widely affects the environment and socio-economics. Its wide impacts rewrite the calculation formula for benefits and costs for countless individuals and groups. Straightforward expediencies fail to fit this new game, in which the stakes are defined and paid differently.

Adding complexity is an environmental movement escalated to regional and even global levels. This threatens the ability of a single company in meeting various expectations across communities. The scope of stakeholders and their intellectual and financial capacities might far exceed what a corporation can handle on its own. This new generation environmental movement has dramatically complicated the external environment of business.

Last, new technologies reframe the risk perceptions of the public, which might prevent effective communication even if the industry works to build better transparency. Because the public decides the social legitimacy of any new or classic industry, a flawed or inaccurate collective perception will negatively affect public relations and impose additional costs into the market. Such inaccuracies may stem from radical denouncement of an entire industry by environmental lobbyists or the belief that corporate leaders are either ignorant or behind the times. The conventional approach to community engagement emphasizes multiple measures without indicating the conditions under which one measure would be better used than another. A consensus between the industry and the community may be hardly approachable without in-depth analysis of what the characteristics of such perceptions are, how these perceptions are constructed, and how they interact with other factors in affecting the ultimate efficiency of engagement.

In sum, several missing elements in current engagement strategies might prevent efficient construction of healthy public relations at the local and global levels. These missing elements involve understanding various types of stakeholders, including their stakes in the development process, roles in the general anti-industry movement, and perceptions of the driving technologies. Whereas the first two elements apparently fit into conventional community engagement language, the third element does not occupy a conceptual niche in conventional guidelines. In our context of transforming and emerging industries, however, risk perception acts as a leveraging factor between the first two elements, thereby shaping the constitution of the stakeholder environment where the industry is embedded.

This chapter intends to introduce an alternative framework of smart community engagement by focusing on various types of stakeholders and how they interplay with others in determining the outcome of corporate engagement in challenging communities. We will first contextualize our analysis in the area of unconventional gas development driven by the common application of hydraulic fracturing (a.k.a., fracking). Then after reviewing the global anti-fracking movement, we will identify the promises and perils for sustainable development in a given context. Next, we will construct an action framework for smart engagement by integrating the given industrial context with the relevant building blocks of social license, bounded rationality, and common-pool resource. By developing the API Guidelines in an innovative way, our framework offers a dynamic and contingent way to address the specific questions we are centering on. Finally, we will discuss the implications of this framework under several conditions.

CONTEXT: HYDRAULIC FRACTURING AND THE
ANTI-FRACKING MOVEMENT

In the past decade, shale gas development, as an emerging fossil fuel industry, has burgeoned globally and especially in the U.S., where energy security has been prioritized at the federal level. The advanced well-stimulation technique (technically known as high-volume hydraulic fracturing or informally referred to as "fracking") produces one third of total natural gas today (USEIA, 2014) and is projected to reach 49% by 2035. Growing domestic production is also expected to continue to make the U.S. less dependent on natural gas imports from Canada while triggering exports to Mexico and more distant foreign markets (Brent, Countries, Arabia, & Hub, 2014). However, from the U.S., where the industry has been pioneered in scale, to countries such as France, Bulgaria, and Czech Republic, where the sentiment regarding the industry has gone beyond general concerns over environmental and health risks into patriotism against foreign involvement (Wood, 2013), global debates on risks associated with the industry have never waned.

Among all concerns, wide attention is paid to the environmental and health risks associated with the activities of operating hydraulic fracturing, as well as other stages of production of unconventional extraction (Krupnick, Gordon, & Olmstead, 2013). However, there are two main areas of concern regarding fracking. First, the risks associated with the industry and its stimulation techniques are more complex than the traditional approach to resource extraction. Besides the common risks of mining and extraction processes, shale gas development also carries the risks of habitat disruption from construction; methane and volatile organic compounds (VOC) air pollution; freshwater depletion; surface water contamination from fracturing fluid spills, wastewater discharges, and wastewater impoundment; and groundwater contamination from poorly constructed or maintained wells (Konschnik & Boling, 2014).

Second, the scale of the industry and its intensity in interfering with private lives has catalyzed public debate and the anti-fracking movement within the U.S. and across the continents (Strategic Center for Natural Gas and Oil, 2013). Local communities hosting fracking companies can be both rural and populated urbanized regions. Stakeholders include both local residents, who are more diverse, empowered, and engaged than before, and concerned citizens, experts, and elites who actively join the anti-fracking movement via online forums, direct donations, or professional debates. Stakeholders access information that is no longer solely provided by the industry or specific companies, but by a global community, where information is available in various flavors.

In addition to such intertwined features, it is critical to understand what stakeholders are expecting, as expressed in the anti-fracking movement, and how they get engaged in the movement, which implies appropriate responses by companies. According to the latest report released by Control Risks, a London-based global risk and strategic consulting firm, four demands have been expressed throughout the global anti-fracking movement: (1) greater compensation for environmental and ecological losses; (2) further studies on the risks associated with hydraulic fracturing, particularly regarding water contamination; (3) moratoriums and bans on fracking (as a means to buy time to build stronger political will against the industry); and (4) tighter regulation in jurisdictions where governments are widely criticized for their susceptibility to coercion and weak enforcement of environmental regulations (Wood, 2013). Additionally, the anti-fracking movement, spread globally via grass-roots activities, online and social media, and global networking, mirrors a more diverse and empowered environmental side, with which shale gas companies have to engage when engaging the community.

CONCEPT AND FRAMEWORK

Social License Theory

The first relevant body of literature centers on corporate overcompliance behaviors that broadly interest scholars in corporate social responsibility, regulation, and environmental policy analysis. Numerous studies address the linkages among multiple forms of enforcement and compliance at various levels (Delmas & Toffel, 2004). In addition to formal structures for enforcement, communities and other stakeholders affect corporate policy individually through citizen lawsuits and collectively through making official complaints; voting for local moratoriums, or boycotting certain companies or goods. Although the literature focusing on informal structures for enforcement has been criticized for not including the role of intermediate agencies, such as industrial associations or quasi-governmental agencies (e.g., the International Standard Organization), in making the linkage between informal enforcement and corporate compliance truly functional (Darnall & Carmin, 2005), the literature increasingly provides evidence of social pressure in influencing the decision making of firms through market competition or community entry (Gunningham, 1995; Hoffman, 1999; Jennings & Zandbergen, 1995; Nash & Ehrenfeld, 1997; O'Hare, 1982; Powell & Dimaggio, 1991; Scott, 2013).

Gunningham, Kagan, and Thornton provided a theoretical framework for explaining the relationship between industry and society, regardless of the presence of formal enforcement of environmental compliance (Gunningham, Thornton, & Kagan, 2005). In their theory, *social license* is defined as the demands on and expectations for a business enterprise that emerge from neighborhoods, environmental groups, community members, and other elements of the surrounding civil society. When formal regulation is weak or underfunctioning, these social parties evaluate corporate performance and decide whether to grant the social license to the company to operate in a specific community. The social license can take the form of one-time acceptance given by main stakeholders of a community, an ongoing reputation of one firm, or acceptance of a whole industry that grows across regions over time.

Theory of Legitimacy Construction

Though providing us tools to understand the interaction between business and society at the macro level without the constraining presence of formal authority, the social license theory is less helpful in explaining how social expectations have been constructed, especially when the development project is as controversial and uncertain as those undertaken by industries in unconventional gas development. In response, we introduce the theory of legitimacy construction as another building block of our action framework.

Black explains the mechanism of legitimacy construction from the perspective of governance while assuming bounded rationality underlying human decision making (Black, 2008). Originally coined by Herbert Simons and others, individual rationality is limited by the information individuals have, the cognitive limitations of their minds, and the finite amount of time they have to make a decision. Rather than going through a full rational process of finding optimal choices with given information, decision makers often apply heuristics to simplify the problem at hand. In addition, people tend to ignore important issues they are less capable of comprehending, while miscalculating the real benefits and costs of the decision in a certain intellectual and informational context (Elster, 1985; Kahneman, 2003; March, 2009; Simon, 1991, 1997). Such "cognitive limitations" of actual humans lead to categorizing stakeholders into three types, differentiating the process of legitimacy construction, and determining the main goals of each stakeholder in interacting with the business.

The first mechanism is morally based, which is consistent with the goals or the procedure to achieve corporate legitimacy. For example, when an industry is based on a human-induced process that alters the environment, promoting that industry will always negatively affect human welfare, according to environmentalists and other individuals with specific ideologies. The second mechanism is pragmatically based, which is directly or indirectly driven by personal interest. In such a situation, stakeholders mainly seek to maximize their own gains, either politically or economically, without caring much for social externalities, ethics, or key uncertainties underlying the industry. Lastly, society constructs legitimacy through a cognitive process as members come to accept the facts regarding the development process or techniques adopted by the business, given the available information and individuals' cognitive capacity. This mechanism is constrained by both the quality and the sequence of information, but it is also relatively neutral compared with the other two mechanisms in evaluative legitimacy.

Accordingly, there are three types of stakeholders interplaying with business, which then have to develop appropriate strategies for community engagement. In response to the morally or ideologically driven stakeholders, compensation may be impractical or impossible. When negotiating with pragmatic stakeholders, public relations budgets will determine efficient communication and the ability to reach an agreement. For cognitive stakeholders, who would neither ignore new findings to update their viewpoint nor change their minds for money, simply lobbying or providing information only from industrially funded research may not work. Such categories shed light on community

engagement in general while specifically fitting into the context of emerging and transforming industries, where perceptions of the industry and the needs of many involved
stakeholders are often more complex and unaligned.

Collective Action and the Problem of Common-pool Resource

Finally, we introduce the problem of collective action as another building block of our
action framework. What makes community engagement unique and more challenging
in unconventional shale gas development as well as in other emerging and transforming
industries is that companies are not only competitors with each other, but also potential
partners in acquiring the social license for the whole industry from ideological, rent-
seeking, and skeptic stakeholders. On the one hand, for stakeholders with access to
information on industrial performance in different regions from various sources, their
decision on the social license or "legitimacy" would depend more on the general performance of several companies than on just the entering company trying to engage with the
community while running business there. On the other hand, laggard companies that do
not have the budget for abating pollution nor for investing in public relations would not
be willing to contribute to the social license application. According to Olson (1971), the
efficiency of such effort would be largely affected by the size of the industry as well as
the cost to do so.

Meanwhile, a common-pool resource is a type of good for which the production and
maintenance is costly but excluding free-riding consumption would also be pricey if
not impossible (Ostrom, Walker, & Gardner, 1992). In this theory, players would only
decide to limit their consumption of the resource or contribute to its preservation at a
sufficient level when the degradation of the resource substantially affects their own welfare in both the short and long runs. If, in framing the legitimacy (or the social license
granted by specific communities) of developing shale gas as a kind of common-pool
resource, late-entering companies use the social license during their development for
free while decreasing the total reputation of the industry through violations or widely
acknowledged misdeeds, they are likely to mobilize a new round of anti-fracking movements at local levels or to compel more stringent intervention by formal institutions.

Summary

In sum, we find three bodies of literature especially helpful for us to construct the action
framework of smart community engagement. While the first two theories provide useful intellectual tools to better understand stakeholders and their roles in determining
the social and political environment where unconventional gas development occurs, at
the macro and micro levels respectively, the third theory offers us a useful lens to peer-
analyze the industry. In other words, we suggest that managing stakeholders via multiple
strategies is as pivotal as planning interactions with other companies in a collective way
in modern community engagement.

Table 4.1

Summary of Theoretical Building Blocks

		Peer-company Evaluation (Common-pool Resource)	
		Collaborative	Free-riding
Stakeholder Evaluation (Social License and Legitimacy Construction)	Ideologically driven		
	Cognitively driven		
	Pragmatically driven		

Thus, we provide a 3×2 matrix to simplify our three theoretical building blocks (see Table 4.1). As Table 4.1 shows, the ultimate goal in analyzing stakeholders is to identify key stakeholder types and their rationality regarding the industry or its operating process. Based on this, a company can predict the level of social expectation such stakeholders would establish for the whole industry or the targeting company. Meanwhile, the main goal in evaluating peer companies is to assess to what extent they would be willing to collaborate to acquire the social license.

ACTION FRAMEWORK OF SMART COMMUNITY ENGAGEMENT AND STAKEHOLDER MANAGEMENT

Categorized Matrix with Integrated Dimensions

Our action framework includes a multiple-stage engagement built on the latest API Guidelines and the three theoretical building blocks discussed above. The purpose of this framework is not to provide an alternative model of community engagement, but rather to provide a toolkit for stakeholder assessments and an action framework for efficient community engagement. In this framework, community is defined as both external and internal. External community means stakeholders from the hosting community: regulators or local leaders from environmental and citizen groups, churches, or educational institutions. Internal community means companies running their business in or close to the hosting community, including competitors, suppliers, and contracted service companies. The framework provides an integrated and dynamic tool that extends the usefulness of the API Guidelines by providing more nuances in how to evaluate the external community environment and how to identify the conditions under which specific engagement strategies are more likely to succeed. Thus, the theoretical summary (see Table 4.1) can also serve as an Analytic Matrix of External and Internal Communities (see Table 4.2).

Table 4.2

Analytic Matrix of External and Internal Communities

		Internal Community Evaluation	
		Collaborative	Free-riding
External Community Evaluation	Ideologically driven		
	Cognitively driven		
	Pragmatically driven		

When analyzing the external community, we ask two questions before implementing any community engagement regarding social license and legitimacy construction: (1) How much does the stakeholder expect from the company or the industry, and (2) how costly it is to meet such an expectation in order to gain the social license to operate? With these questions in mind, managers know how to design communications between them and the key stakeholders, as suggested by the API Guidelines. At the same time, such questions can also guide managers to better allocate their budget for public relations when they are dealing with diverse stakeholders in one community or a number of different communities. Meanwhile, the matrix highlights the main goal of internal community evaluation: to assess competitors from an alternative perspective. As discussed earlier, the social license to operate, especially for a transforming or emerging industry, would benefit companies seeking permits and local support with no cost. In other words, if it is publicly believed that the industry will benefit society without endangering ecology and public health, companies can more easily gain policy support, local job applicants, and general legitimacy. Such social support might result from long-term lobbying efforts or pollution mitigation by leading companies, for instance. In such a context, it is always crucial to evaluate the industrial community alongside the given stakeholders' types to determine the different costs of collaboration.

We thus suggest that the internal-community evaluation needs to assess how collaborative other companies can be, in terms of their willingness and ability to invest in either abating certain pollutions or communicating with the stakeholders in an informative, transparent, and mutually respectful way. Given that these efforts won't be free and the time available for managers to build up an ally can be extremely limited, the proportion of late-entry companies that would freeride the painstaking process can be predicted at a high level.

Continuum Model of Smart Community Engagement

However, this matrix may not be helpful in practice, given that the boundaries between different types may be blurred. Furthermore, measures to label the stakeholders and other companies with the right type may not be appropriate or available in various contexts. We can modify the matrix by changing the categorized dimensions into quantifiable

Figure 4.1   **Continuum Model of Smart Community Engagement**

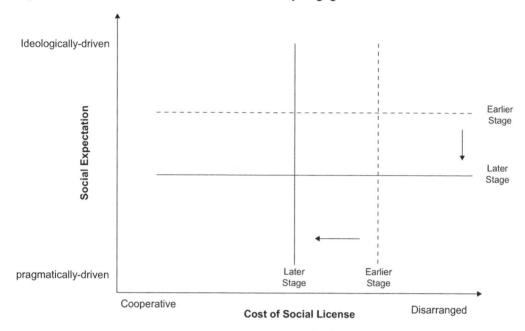

continuums, along which both the external and internal communities could be better measured.

Figure 4.1 illustrates how evaluations of external and internal communities can be integrated in a more flexible and realistic way. The *x*-axis measures the cost of applying for the social license to operate: the higher the cost, the less likely a company would be to construct a collaborative relationship with stakeholders and potential partners from the industrial community. The *y*-axis measures the type of stakeholders in terms of the level of social expectation of preferred corporate behaviors: the higher the level of expectation, the harder it will be for corporations to meet the standard and thus gain the social license.

As previously discussed, morally driven stakeholders set the highest expectations, in which the ecological environment should be preserved as untouched and errors will not be tolerated. Pragmatically driven stakeholders, who make decisions based on net benefit, will grant the license to the industry if they expect that doing so will result in improvements over the status quo. For these stakeholders, companies do not need to invest additional resources to improve corporate behaviors or contribute to collective action. Between the two extremes lay cognitively driven stakeholders, who may make painstaking efforts to evaluate the performance of the targeted companies with available information and may be partly driven by ethical or economic motivations at the same time. Though this type of stakeholder may increase the cost of community engagement and require extra effort in investigation, self-regulation, or both, this group of stakeholders can help committed corporations gain legitimacy when external and internal communities are both challenging. This group of stakeholders also represents the new generation of citizens, who are intellectually empowered in public deliberation, active in requesting new information, able to process raw and complex information, and ready to make independent decisions.

For internal communities, the modified framework Moreno longer assumes a dichotomy between collaborative and non-collaborative. Relaxing this assumption helps the modified framework to better capture the dynamics and complexity of the industrial community. In the case of unconventional gas development, the industry is more diverse and decentralized than the traditional oil and gas industry (Konschnik & Boling, 2014). Small companies have disappeared rapidly during the last decade, whereas big companies have increased in size and integrity by mergers and acquisition. Such phenomena make it impossible to stabilize the type of companies in the previous matrix and call for a more flexible perspective to assess the companies' potential roles in the transforming industry.

Evaluation of the internal community might be more challenging than evaluation of the external community. The difficulties may come from firms' competing interests in both the short and long runs, as well as different visions for the future. Furthermore, companies may be concerned with the problem of free-riders if they decide to participate in a collective effort to build a better public image, an improved industrial reputation, or a new quasi-authority agency. In the normal case, the larger the number of participants, the harder it will be for such collaboration to be formed and sustained.

However, the external community may pressure companies to join forces when facing equal levels of public distrust or skepticism. Although it is practical for individual companies to appropriately deal with pragmatically driven stakeholders by making them better off after the development, it is hard for individual companies to meet without collaborative efforts an extremely high social expectation that has been established by morally driven stakeholders. Such challenges from the external community might to some extent help establish industrial-level or regional-level cooperation among companies in order to meet the high social expectations or establish an entity from which late-coming, free-riding companies are excluded. Through this latter strategy, a company does not simply apply for a social license that could be used by other companies, but rather constructs another level of legitimacy only granted to contributing firms. This labeled legitimacy can be a high-end license only available to advanced corporations, such as that described by the Center for Sustainable Shale Development (CSSD) in their mission statement.[1]

Parallel Diagnosis of External and Internal Communities

In order to appropriately assess the external and internal communities, several questions need to be asked in a sequential way. As shown in Figure 4.2, we suggest a parallel approach to assessing both external and internal communities. The approach provides a common structure to frame questions applicable to analyzing stakeholders

Figure 4.2   **Parallel Approach to External and Internal Communities**

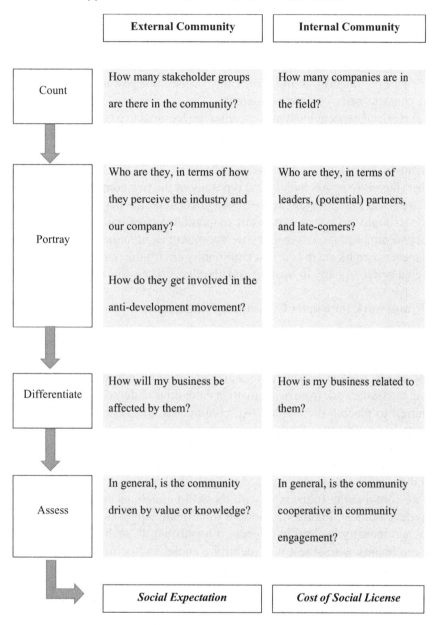

	External Community	**Internal Community**
Count	How many stakeholder groups are there in the community?	How many companies are in the field?
Portray	Who are they, in terms of how they perceive the industry and our company? How do they get involved in the anti-development movement?	Who are they, in terms of leaders, (potential) partners, and late-comers?
Differentiate	How will my business be affected by them?	How is my business related to them?
Assess	In general, is the community driven by value or knowledge?	In general, is the community cooperative in community engagement?
	Social Expectation	*Cost of Social License*

and companies. In the first step, we suggest companies quantify the size of the community. In the next step, we recommend companies collect qualitative data to describe the community in detail. This step portrays the community more in-depth and thus helps managers intuitively engage with the other players in the arena; it also provides critical information to weigh the importance of each category.

In the next step, managers should differentiate the general community by evaluating the stake their company has with each category. The patterns discovered through this analysis can determine the scope of the "core community" with which companies can strategically engage. By "core community," we mean the collection of players—stakeholders who represent the external community and companies who represent the internal community—who make up either the majority of the community or the most powerful force in influencing the main characteristics of each community. The core external community determines what level of social expectation that companies are required to meet and how the company can create social consensus around industrial performance and the risks associated with the industry. The core internal community determines the likelihood a company can build a partnership to achieve or maintain its legitimacy.

The last stage is to assess the general typology of the two communities. Although the earlier categorical matrix offers heuristics to understand the players' categories, it fails to provide a simple and cohesive measure to qualitatively examine the two communities as interactive dimensions. Given the core communities identified in the differentiation stage, managers can locate the current community environment in the continuum matrix and design a better strategy to manage stakeholders and engage communities.

Action Framework for Smart Community Engagement

This section provides several conceptual and analytic tools for conducting community analysis in order to smartly engage with changing and challenging communities, especially in the context of emerging and transforming industries, such as shale. By modifying the framework from using distinct categories to describe external and internal communities, to placing them along two continuums, the Continuum Model of Smart Community Engagement expands our understanding of the complexity of communities in a more realistic way. Although this description can be conducted through parallel diagnosis, both quantitative and intuitive, that process is still static in the sense that it does not distinguish the conditions used to apply the tools.

Now we combine the framework with the API Guidelines in the specific context of shale gas development. Figure 4.3 shows a situation in which anti-fracking sentiment is prevalent and industry leadership is weak, if not absent. In such a context, external and internal community assessment will identify a social and political environment with a very high social expectation and few companies that could be potential partners. If managers decide to invest in community engagement, the rate of free-riding could be high, suggesting the outcome of engagement is likely to be inefficient. Meanwhile, though several engagement strategies are available, the engagement may not be successful, given that both the level of social expectation and the cost of social license exceed the boundary of smart engagement.

At the mature stage, where the risks associated with the industry become less salient to the public or more knowledge has been created to solve some of the earlier concerns, the social and political environment is located within the boundary where a bundle of smart engagement measures can be feasible (Figure 4.4). For example, when an industry

Figure 4.3 **Smart Community Engagement at Early Stage of Development**

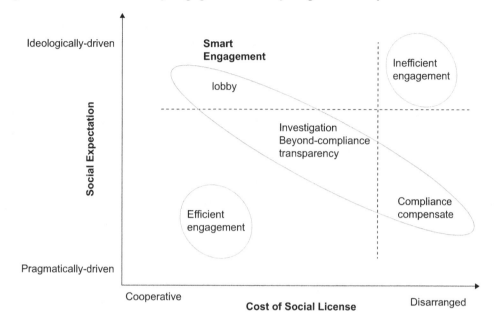

Figure 4.4 **Smart Community Engagement at Later Stage of Development**

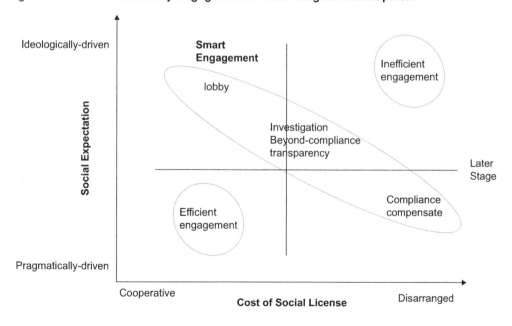

faces a high level of social expectation but has strong cooperation among companies and leaders, lobbying can be a feasible tool to engage with communities, along with other means suggested by the API Guidelines. When stakeholders care more about the facts regarding the risks and benefits of the development, it is appropriate to collaborate with other companies to invest in investigation, to self-regulate beyond the official standards, and to provide information to build industrial-wide transparency. Finally, if the majority or the most powerful stakeholders are pragmatically driven, managers can choose basic compliance with formal regulations and compensate citizens only when hazards cause real losses. In these cases, managers ignore free-riders or rather free ride themselves, given the scattered internal community.

In sum, the assessment of external and internal communities informs managers in locating their social and political environment within a broad conceptual map (Figures 4.3 and 4.4), where various stages of development fit. Built on the five-stage Community Engagement Life Cycle Model developed by the API Guidelines, we can assume that the later the stage of development, the more mature both external and internal communities will be. By "mature" we mean an increase in the cognitive ability of stakeholders who establish the social expectation for the industry, as well as greater capacity for corporate collaboration across the industry to achieve the social license to operate. Once the assessment falls into the lower left region of the model (Figure 4.4), smart engagement is unnecessary. Any straightforward engagement measures will be as efficient as they are in conventional industries.

CONCLUSION

In this chapter, we have presented a framework for smart community engagement that addresses the challenges of stakeholder management. The framework is built on the multiple-stage engagement model developed by the latest API Guidelines and three relevant theoretical building blocks regarding external and internal communities. The purpose of the framework is not to prescribe a magic must-do list to managers troubled by challenging communities, skeptical residents, or radical environmental advocates. Instead, the framework is intended to be a broad and flexible guide to reflect many new challenges in the industrial field. The framework identifies several factors affecting the effectiveness of engagement efforts, while also suggesting a number of opportunities to overcome those restrictions, if not individually.

Importantly, it is necessary to understand several extensions in applying the framework. First, though it does not explicitly define companies as "stakeholders," the framework integrates the industry into the framework as the internal community by emphasizing its key role in interacting with other non-corporate stakeholders. In the dynamic approach suggested by the model, corporate stakeholders may vary in importance during different stages of the development. Without comprehending such potential roles in non-market settings, a company cannot succeed long in the market.

Next, the framework has a potential implication beyond the context we have focused on this chapter. We foresee two merging trends in energy and the environment, represented in this chapter by shale gas development and the global anti-fracking movement.

The first is that technological development and diffusion introduces a bundle of associated risks that often appear faster than new regulations. Oftentimes, companies have to engage with hosting communities before all the rules are clear and appropriate, which results in the companies being less capable of addressing various concerns from environmental groups and the general public. Second, the scope of industry's involvement in citizens' daily lives has triggered the evolution of a global network seeking to oppose or redirect this involvement. Such initiatives can be well-funded, intellectually capable, and politically empowered. They are not only changing the macro-level environment for lobbying, but also setting up the local conditions in which community engagement occurs. The framework provides managers in these industries a tool to analyze local opposition through answerable questions from which they can develop engagement strategies that are more appropriate in a given context.

The framework may be more useful when additional information is available, such as the budget for public relations, the market price of the product, operational costs, long-term market projections, and the presence of a credible trade association or an independent audit agency. This information determines the opportunity costs used by managers to decide whether to invest in the social license project either individually or collectively. Otherwise, managers will be narrowly focused and ignore the negative externalities they have put into the environment or the community. This perspective offers an alternative application of our framework: for regulators and other players in governance to be able to predict the response of companies to external pressures and direct those responses favorably.

Finally, the framework may be used as a strategic planning tool, especially for leading companies in the field. The original framework assumed the company is an average company in the field. In accordance, the company needs to locate the leaders in the field to work together if its managers decide to respond to the stakeholders more responsibly. In such a case, the extent to which a controversial industry can be improved is set as given. The real options available for managers were simply "follow" or "free-ride." But at a leading firm, managers can look for the optimal solution with given information, such as the general status of the industry, the major type of stakeholders, and the potential partners who can be united to form the core internal community, so that late-comers can either be excluded or labeled. In this case, our framework is not a modified model of community engagement, but rather a strategic tool for building leadership in a challenging sociopolitical context.

KEY POINTS

- Driven by technology diffusion and its various risks, as well as the concerns of evermore empowered citizens, smart engagement determines the success of local engagement by individual companies and global development of the whole industry.
- Smart engagement provides a strategic tool that helps analyze the internal and external environments, replaces the customer-based calculation with a stakeholder-based rationale, and provides a more nuanced guide to appropriate corporate responses to various social pressure.

- Smart engagement identifies the role of leadership in constructing and maintaining the public image of emerging and transforming industries in the dynamic and complex environment.
- Smart engagement enables community leaders and citizens to better predict the behaviors of entering companies in unfamiliar industries, resulting in more effective communication in maintaining their own rights and interests.

Figure 4.5   Oil and Gas Project Life Cycle, Five Phase Model

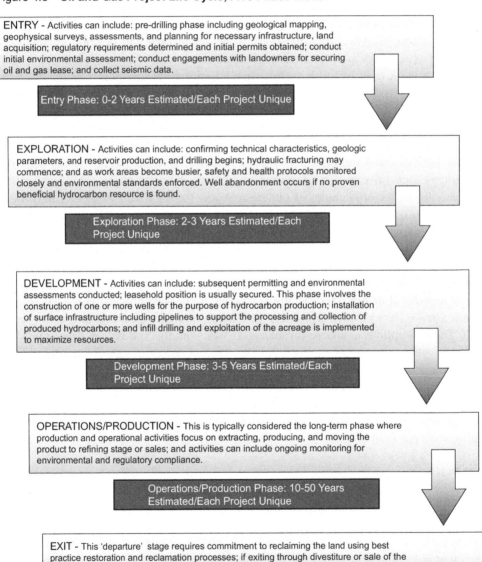

ENTRY - Activities can include: pre-drilling phase including geological mapping, geophysical surveys, assessments, and planning for necessary infrastructure, land acquisition; regulatory requirements determined and initial permits obtained; conduct initial environmental assessment; conduct engagements with landowners for securing oil and gas lease; and collect seismic data.

Entry Phase: 0-2 Years Estimated/Each Project Unique

EXPLORATION - Activities can include: confirming technical characteristics, geologic parameters, and reservoir production, and drilling begins; hydraulic fracturing may commence; and as work areas become busier, safety and health protocols monitored closely and environmental standards enforced. Well abandonment occurs if no proven beneficial hydrocarbon resource is found.

Exploration Phase: 2-3 Years Estimated/Each Project Unique

DEVELOPMENT - Activities can include: subsequent permitting and environmental assessments conducted; leasehold position is usually secured. This phase involves the construction of one or more wells for the purpose of hydrocarbon production; installation of surface infrastructure including pipelines to support the processing and collection of produced hydrocarbons; and infill drilling and exploitation of the acreage is implemented to maximize resources.

Development Phase: 3-5 Years Estimated/Each Project Unique

OPERATIONS/PRODUCTION - This is typically considered the long-term phase where production and operational activities focus on extracting, producing, and moving the product to refining stage or sales; and activities can include ongoing monitoring for environmental and regulatory compliance.

Operations/Production Phase: 10-50 Years Estimated/Each Project Unique

EXIT - This 'departure' stage requires commitment to reclaiming the land using best practice restoration and reclamation processes; if exiting through divestiture or sale of the asset, then reclamation becomes the responsibility of purchaser.

Exit Phase: 0-2 Years Estimated/Each Project Unique

Source: From API Guidelines, P4

NOTE

1. The CSSD is a Pittsburgh-based independent 501(c)(3) nonprofit organization whose mission is to support continuous improvement and innovative practices through performance standards and third-party certification, as a center of excellence for shale gas development. Funded by philanthropic foundations and participating energy companies, CSSD is intended to promote collaborative efforts by industry and its stakeholders called for by the Shale Gas Production Subcommittee of the U.S. Secretary of Energy's Advisory Board. www.sustainableshale.org/about/

REFERENCES

American Petroleum Institute. (2014). *Community engagement guidelines*. Washington, DC: API Publishing Services. Retrieved from www.api.org/globalitems/~/media/Files/Policy/Exploration/100-3_e1.pdf

Black, J. (2008). Constructing and contesting legitimacy and accountability in polycentric regulatory regimes. *Regulation & Governance, 2*(2), 137–164. doi:10.1111/j.1748-5991.2008.00034.x

Darnall, N., & Carmin, J. (2005). Greener and cleaner? The signaling accuracy of U.S. voluntary environmental programs. *Policy Sciences, 38*(2–3), 71–90. doi:10.1007/s11077-005-6591-9

Delmas, M., & Toffel, M. W. (2004). Stakeholders and environmental management practices: An institutional framework. *Business Strategy and the Environment, 13*(4), 209–222. doi:10.1002/bse.409

Elster, J. (1985). *Sour grapes: Studies in the subversion of rationality* (1st ed., p. 177). Cambridge: Cambridge University Press. Retrieved from www.amazon.com/Sour-Grapes-Studies-Subversion-Rationality/dp/0521313686

Gunningham, N. (1995). Environment, self-regulation, and the chemical industry: Assessing responsible care. *Law & Policy, 17*(1), 57–109. doi:10.1111/j.1467-9930.1995.tb00139.x

Gunningham, N., Thornton, D., & Kagan, R. (2005). Motivating Management: Corporate Compliance in Environmental Protection, *Law & Policy, 27*(2), 289–316. Retrieved from http://scholarship.law.berkeley.edu/facpubs/628

Hoffman, A. J. (1999). Institutional evolution and change: Environmentalism and the U.S. chemical industry. *Academy of Management Journal, 42*(4), 351–371. doi:10.2307/257008

Jennings, P. D., & Zandbergen, P. A. (1995). Ecologically sustainable organizations: An institutional approach. *Academy of Management Review, 20*(4), 1015–1052. Retrieved from http://professor.business.ualberta.ca/pjennings/~/media/business/FacultyAndStaff/SMO/PJennings/Documents/JenningsandZandbergen1995EcologicallySustainableOrganizationsAMR.pdf

Kahneman, D. (2003). A perspective on judgment and choice: Mapping bounded rationality. *American Psychologist, 58*(9). Retrieved from www2.econ.iastate.edu/tesfatsi/JudgementAndChoice.MappingBoundedRationality.DKahneman2003.pdf

Konschnik, K. E., & Boling, M. K. (2014). Shale Gas development: A smart regulation framework. *Envionrmental Science & Technology, 48*(15), 8404–8416. doi:10.1021/es405377u

Krupnick, A., Gordon, H., & Olmstead, S. (2013). *Pathways to dialogue: What the experts say about the environmental risks of shale gas development* (p. 81). Washington, DC. Retrieved from www.rff.org/centers/energy_and_climate_economics/Pages/Shale-Gas-Expert-Survey.aspx

March, J. G. (2009). *Primer on decision making: How decisions happen* (p. 308). New York: Free Press. Retrieved from www.amazon.com/Primer-Decision-Making-Decisions-Happen/dp/1439157332

Nash, J., & Ehrenfeld, J. (1997). Codes of environmental management practice: Assessing their potential as a tool for change. *Annual Review of Energy and the Environment, 22*(1), 487–535. doi:10.1146/annurev.energy.22.1.487

O'Hare, M. (1982). Information strategies as regulatory surrogates. In E. Bardach et al. (Eds.), *Social regulation: Strategies for reform* (pp. 221–236). San Francisco, CA: Institute for Contemporary Studies.

Olson, M. (1971). *The logic of collective action*. Cambridge, MA: Harvard University Press. Retrieved from www.hup.harvard.edu/catalog.php?isbn=9780674537514

Ostrom, E. Walker, J., & Gardner, R. (1992). Covenants with and without a sword: Self-governance is possible. *The American Political Science Review, 86*(2), 404. doi:10.2307/1964229

Powell, W. W., & Dimaggio, P. J. (1991). *The new institutionalism in organizational analysis.* Chicago, IL: University of Chicago Press. Retrieved from www.press.uchicago.edu/ucp/books/book/chicago/N/bo3684488.html

Scott, W. R. (2013). *Institutions and organizations: Ideas, interests, and identities* (4th ed., p. 360). Los Angeles, CA: Sage Publications, Inc. Retrieved from www.amazon.com/Institutions-Organizations-Ideas-Interests-Identities/dp/1452242224

Simon, H. A. (1991). Bounded rationality and organizational learning. *Organization Science, 2*(1), 125–134. Retrieved from www.jstor.org/discover/10.2307/2634943?uid=3739864&uid=2&uid=4&uid=3739256&sid=21105251816013

Simon, H. A. (1997). *Models of bounded rationality, Vol. 3: Emperically grounded economic reason* (p. 479). Cambridge, MA: The MIT Press. Retrieved from www.amazon.com/Models-Bounded-Rationality-Vol-Emperically/dp/0262193728

Strategic Center for Natural Gas and Oil. (2013). *Modern Shale gas development in the United States: An update* (pp. 1–79).

USEIA. (2014). *U.S. crude oil and natural gas proved reserves, 2012* (p. 48). Retrieved from www.eia.gov/naturalgas/crudeoilreserves/pdf/uscrudeoil.pdf

U.S. Energy Information Administration (2014). *Short-term Energy Outlook (STEO).* Retrieved from www.eia.gov/forecasts/steo/archives/dec14.pdf

Wood, J. (2013). *The global anti-fracking movement: What it wants, how it operates and what's next* (p. 24). London: Control Risks Group Limited. Retrieved from www.epl.org.ua/images/pdf/what_is_antishale_movement.pdf

5

Balancing Environment and Business through Governance

Nature Protection Policies in De Alde Feanen National Park, The Netherlands

Katharine A. Owens

INTRODUCTION

De Alde Feanen,[1] (see Figures 5.1 and 5.2) a 2,500-hectare wetland in the center of the Province of Friesland, is the final area in the Netherlands under discussion to potentially gain national park status. To achieve national park status, stakeholders must develop a management plan outlining how the area will meet the requirements of a national park. This entails forming a deliberative body of stakeholders, the *overlegorgaan*. This governing group does not make new policy but rather works to agree on a plan within existing regulations. Over 20 environmental policies apply to the area at various levels of government, including municipal, provincial, national, European, and international. The *overlegorgaan* includes an independent chairman and 17 individuals representing government, environmental organizations, recreation organizations, and water management organizations. This complex process includes many stakeholders with a range of goals.

Within this group, two players hold opposing views about limiting park access by recreational boaters. The nature organization It Fryske Gea supports access restrictions as a way to halt what they describe as ecological degradation within De Alde Feanen. The primary group opposing these measures is the recreation organization De Marrekrite, which maintains that the proposed decrease in boating access will negatively affect recreation rights in the park and, therefore, affect many businesses associated with recreational boating.

This case study details how the *overlegorgaan* makes decisions about the nature area, taking into consideration government regulation as well as environmental and business interests. The analysis describes the motivation, information levels, and power balance between stakeholders, revealing how these characteristics influence their behavior. It also shows how trust, lobbying and the importance of goals influence decision making. This assessment highlights the ways actors shape policy decision making and gives insight into how stakeholders might find balance in management.

Figure 5.1 **De Alde Feanen, a Fen Complex, Shown in Medium Gray with Waterways in Dark Gray[2]**

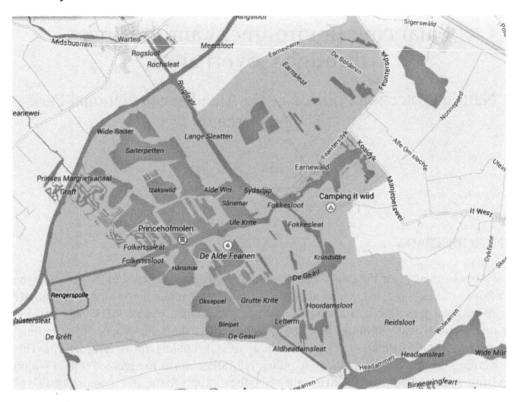

Figure 5.2 **Location of De Alde Feanen (Indicated by the White Star) Relative to the Northern Coast of the Netherlands[3]**

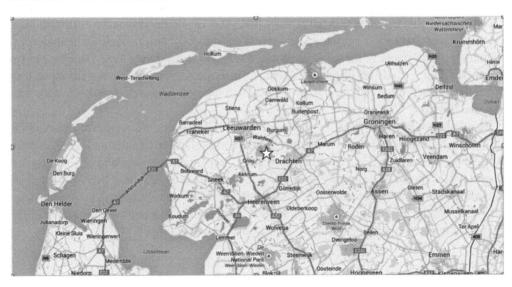

LITERATURE REVIEW

Dutch Wetlands

Throughout history, the Dutch have manipulated wetlands for agriculture and human habitation, as well as in support of flood control and navigation. Once a vast marshland, the west of the Netherlands would be regularly flooded without the support of dikes and other water management structures (Bijker, 2002; Dicke, 2001; Kaijser, 2002; Reuss, 2002). This emphasis on physically manipulating and managing water led to a sophisticated social water management system. Dutch water boards (*waterschappen*) developed in the 12th century, though these groups appeared later in the northern part of the country (Kaijser, 2002). Water boards historically included a disproportionate number of farmers and landowners (Kuks, 2002). In this way, not surprisingly, water board policy emphasized safety and agriculture at the expense of environmental concerns until the 1970s, when the environment gained more general prominence (Dicke, 2001; Kuks, 2002). Water boards continue to be used in the Netherlands for water management.

Water boards are a form of democratic governance featuring voting privilege based on a "profit-payment-participation principle (those having an interest in water management may participate and have to pay for water services in proportion to their interest)" (Bijker, 2002; Kuks, 2002, p. 2). Water boards are one tool used in Dutch society to manage a complex resource like a wetland complex. Economically, Dutch wetlands are a tourist destination and provide public goods, such as controlling flooding, improving water quality, and providing wildlife habitat (*MLNV*, 2008). Wetland preservation, conservation, and restoration can cause friction among stakeholders in a densely populated country like the Netherlands (Owens, 2008). This analysis seeks to better understand how stakeholders in this case make decisions about the Dutch wetland De Alde Feanen.

Governance Strategies for the Intersection of Business and Environment

Researchers offer varying recommendations to policy actors seeking to integrate environment and business goals in complex decision-making processes. In particular, researchers highlight water management as requiring attention (Huntjens et al., 2011; Sivapalan, Savenije, & Blöschl, 2011), as it is considered to be more often about problems of governance than problems of technical management (Özerol, de Boer, & Vinke-de Kruijf, 2013). Water management projects are understood to be complex decision-making arenas, with a range of actors, scales, goals, and policies (Owens & Bressers, 2013; Özerol et al., 2013). Medd and Marvin (2007) write that "strategic intermediaries play a critical role in reconnecting the multiple spatialities of water" (p. 16). Huntjens et al. (2011) describe the interwoven nature of water management systems, finding "information management and social (cooperation) structures are interlinked," which they term the "socio-cognitive dimension of water management regimes" (p. 160). Sivapalan et al. (2011) recommend conceptualizing this work as socio-hydrology, "the science of people and water . . . aimed at understanding the dynamics and co-evolution of coupled human-water systems" (p. 2). Researchers concur that water management can be a complex arena for decision making and, as such, may benefit from various instruments of governance.

Governance or management strategies may include green alliances, the co-production of knowledge, boundary-spanning mechanisms, and negotiated agreements. Arts (2002) defines green alliances as "collaborative partnerships between environmental NGOs and business that pursue mutually beneficial ecological goals" and that, in a way, circumvent government (p. 27–28). Arts (2002) examines the strengths and weaknesses of so-called green alliances of business and nongovernmental organizations (NGOs), finding they "are flexible, non-bureaucratic coalitions that bring together additional resources for private environmental policy making," but concurrently "are not . . . embedded in the 'core business' of companies and in formal public policy making on the environment" (p. 35). He also warns that due to the "opposite 'nature' of [these partners] . . . in terms of power and worldview," these are "highly unstable" coalitions (Arts, 2002, p. 35). In this way, green alliances offer both advantages and disadvantages.

Edelenbos, van Buuren, and van Schie (2011) discuss problems in agreeing on information when stakeholders have a range of views on a given issue. They find that "experts, bureaucrats and stakeholders use different norms and criteria for knowledge production, ranging from scientific validity (experts), policy usefulness (bureaucrats) and social validity (stakeholders)" (p. 683). In essence, this range of perspectives yields different understanding of the information (Edelenbos et al., 2011). To overcome this problem of differently valuing information, they suggest co-producing knowledge, which the group will then recognize as convincing enough for decision making (Edelenbos et al., 2011). As a strategy this may combat issues of distrust among stakeholders.

Cash and Moser (2000) define boundary organizations as "institutions which serve to mediate between scientists and decision-makers, and between these actors at different scales" (p. 109). Boundary-spanning strategies are used to facilitate interaction among stakeholders. Cash and Moser (2000) see boundary organizations as interceding where science meets policy decision making. It is also possible to envision boundary work occurring across scales and interests (Kearney, Berkes, Charles, Pinkerton, & Wiber, 2007; Owens, 2010). Boundary organizations are not by definition cooperative, but instead interactive: they enable both "connection and separation across boundaries" (Cash & Moser, 2000, p. 115). Boundary spanning is deemed especially applicable to decision making in the environmental realm, which is often by definition crossing "scales . . . [and] different sets of social, environmental and economic interests" (Cash & Moser, 2000; Medd & Marvin, 2007, p. 10). Star and Griesemer (1989) portray boundary objects as "both plastic enough to adapt to local needs and the constraints of the several parties employing them, yet robust enough to maintain a common identity across sites" (p. 393). Boundary-spanning approaches may cross scales to improve decision making and or cooperation.

De Clercq (2002) defines negotiated agreements as those "between public (national, federal or regional) authorities and industry, wherein both parties commit themselves to reali[z]e the environmental goals stated in the negotiated agreement " (p. 3). Bressers, de Bruijn, and Lulofs (2009) describe the power of negotiated agreements in Dutch policy implementation as a tool that works well with "internal stresses" and has legitimacy within the business community, yet lacks "clear orientation towards radical innovations" (p. 74). They note that allowing an "avoidance of trench warfare between government and business" and "the attainment of 'feasible' objectives" are important advantages of negotiated agreements (p. 74). It should be noted that Bressers and de Bruijn (2005) write that the success of tools like negotiated agreements are influenced by national culture and may depend on the national context.

Balancing environmental and business goals through governance strategies is complex work but not an impossible goal. Green alliances may allow for flexible, informal solutions. Co-producing knowledge may build trust (in information) among stakeholders. Boundary-spanning approaches may have the capacity to cross scales to improve decision making and or cooperation. Particularly Dutch strategies such as negotiated agreements have a reputation for success. This chapter presents an analysis of how stakeholders interact in a decision-making context about one Dutch wetland, with special attention to each of these strategies in the process.

Contextual Interaction Theory

Analysis of past projects allows one to better understand how government, business, and environmental stakeholders work together (or fail to). The contextual interaction theory (CIT) examines the motivation, information, and power balance among key stakeholders, evaluating these characteristics to better understand *how* actors make decisions about a resource (Bressers, 2004; Owens, Hughes, & Skoczenski, 2013). Using motivation, information, and power, the theory creates a hypothesis of what will happen among process participants (e.g., cooperation, forced cooperation, opposition, obstruction, learning toward cooperation, or no interaction). It is important to note that motivation, information, and power are not capriciously chosen as important among a host of equally important variables, but as having descriptive power above that of other variables (Bressers, 2004; Owens, 2008; Owens & Bressers, 2013). Use of the theory enables consistent and replicable decision-making analysis.

BACKGROUND INFORMATION

Stakeholders

To help understand the stakeholders involved in decision making for De Alde Feanen and their roles, I use Dente, Fareri, and Ligteringen's (1998) system of categorizing actors by the type of objective they have in the process. Actors with a *process objective* are concerned with their "role in the decision making process and not so much on the actual solution to the problem that will emerge" (Dente et al., 1998, p. 203). In contrast, an actor with a *content objective* "perceives that the debated option confers predominantly either costs or benefits" (Dente et al., 1998, p. 203). In other words, some stakeholders have more at "stake" than others.

The *overlegorgaan* is made up of 19 individuals: a secretary and independent chairman as well as 18 people representing 17 groups (It Fryske Gea merited two representatives) (Hemmen, 2005). Table 5.1 describes each member and their objectives. Objectives are translations from Dutch, taken from a report for *overlegorgaan* members about the project (Hemmen, 2005). Within the *overlegorgaan* there are two advisory committees and a research committee:

- *The Advisory Group for Management, Design, and Monitoring* includes representatives from the municipalities of Smallingerland, Tytsjerksteradiel, and Boarnsterhim; the Province of Friesland; De Marrekriet; and It Fryske Gea. It is overseen by the *overlegorgaan* secretary.
- *The Advisory Group for Information, Education, and Recreation* includes representatives from IVN Consultancy Friesland; National Park De Alde Feanen Secretary, Coordinator for Information and Education, and Administrator for Information and Education; It Fryske Gea; Province of Friesland; the municipalities of Smallingerland, Boarnsterhim, and Tytsjerksteradiel; Dienst Landelijk Gebied; village representatives of Earnewald, Oudega en De Veenhoop, Warten, Grou, and Wergea; Algemene Nederlandse Wielrijdersbond (ANWB); Watersportverbond Noord; Recreatieschap De Marrekrite; TROEF; and De Verenigingen voor Vreemdelingen Verkeer.
- The *Research Platform Alde Feanen* includes the Van Hall Institute,[4] Wetterskip Fryslân (the Frisian Water Authority), It Fryske Gea, and Dienst Landelijk Gebied (DLG)[5]. This is an ongoing committee set with the task to scientifically monitor the ecology of the national park.

This case revolves around accepting a management plan that increases the scope of protection within the park by reducing boating access. It Fryske Gea supports these

Table 5.1

Members of the *Overlegorgaan*, Their Objectives, and Actor Type

Organization	Objectives	Actor Type
Overlegorgaan secretary and independent chairman	Coordinates all actors to agree on a management plan for the park.	Process
Province of Friesland (Provincial-level government)	Administrates and coordinates the Province of Friesland and attends to the residents' interests.	Process
Smallingerland, Boarnsterhim, and Tytsjerksteradiel (Municipal-level government)	Administrates and coordinates the municipality and attends to the residents' interests.	Content

Organization	Objectives	Actor Type
Frisian Water Authority (Provincial-level water governance agency)	Water, sea defense, and dike management in the province.	Process
Waterboard Lauwerswalden[6] (Water governance agency)	Water management in the area, including, among other things, De Alde Feanen.	Process
De Friese Millieu Federatie (Provincial-level environmental group)	Strengthens nature and the landscape in the Province of Friesland.	Content
It Fryske Gea (Provincial-level environmental group)	Conserves, preserves, and develops nature and the landscape in Friesland.	Content
De vereniging voor Dorpsbelang van Earnewald, Oudega en De Veenhoop (An interest association representing the citizens of three villages)	Attends to the interests of their members (the whole village, not individual interests), as well as to the municipalities and other authorities.	Content
De vereniging voor Dorpsbelang van Warten, Grou and Wergea (Interest association for three villages)	Attends to the interests of their members (the whole village, not individual interests), as well as to the municipalities and other authorities.	Content
De Verenigingen voor Vreemdelingen Verkeer (National tourism association)	Attends to tourism interests, for tourists and for local recreationalists.	Content
De Noordelijk Land- en Tuinbouworganisatie (Regional farmers' association)	Stands for a healthy agricultural sector with good future perspectives.	Content
De Noord Nederlandse Watersportbond (Regional recreational organization)	Represents the interests of water-sport participants in the northern region of the Netherlands.	Content
Het Recreatieschap De Marrekrite (Provincial recreational organization)	Balances and coordinates development of water sports, particularly promoting suitable infrastructure.	Content
De Vereniging van Friese Rondvaartondernemers (Regional business organization)	Stands for the interests of Frisian boating manufacturers.	Content
De HISWA (Handel Industrie En Scheepvaart in de Waterrecreatie) vereniging en de RECRON (Industry trade organizations for boating and recreation, respectively)	Represents the interests of recreation entrepreneurs and water-sport participants.	Content
De Vereniging De Princehof en Eigenaren Recreatievestiging Friesland (Provincial recreation organization)	Attends to the interests of owners of vacation and recreation homes and houseboats.	Content
Ministerie van Landbouw, Natuur en Voedselkwaliteit regio noord (Ministry of Agriculture, Nature, and Food–Northern region)	In relation to De Alde Feanen, protects an important ecosystem and establishes a national park with accompanying objectives.	Process

Note: Translated from Dutch from Hemmen, 2005 (p. 22).

measures as a way to halt what they see as the degradation of De Alde Feanen. It believes changing access will fulfill policies already applied to the area, such as the Birds and Habitat Directives and the National Ecological Network. The primary group opposing these measures is the recreation group De Marrekrite. De Marrekrite finds the proposed changes limit recreation rights in the park. Success for either It Fryske Gea or De Marrekrite represents a loss for the other.

It Fryske Gea[7] is a provincial nonprofit nature protection organization that manages more than 50 nature reserves with a total surface area of over 19,000 hectares and has more than 25,000 members (It Fryske Gea, 2014). It Fryske Gea advocates incorporating strict guidelines about accessibility into the framework of the national park management plan. The specification will include reducing motor boat access to core areas of the park, which it believes will help maintain the area's ecological integrity. Het recreatieschap De Marrekrite, founded in 1957, promotes the creation and maintenance of infrastructure facilities for recreational boaters (De Marrekrite, 2014).

Policies

Several levels of policy apply to the fen complex known as De Alde Feanen. Internationally, it is a Ramsar Convention Wetland of International Importance (Ramsar, 2014). At the European level, policies include the 1979 Bird Directive–Special Protection Zone (*De Vogelrichtlijn—Speciale Beschermingszone*), the 1992 Habitat Directive (*Habitatrichtlijn*), and the 2000 Water Framework Directive (*Europese Kaderrichtlijn Water*).

Nationally, the area falls under the 1990 Nature Policy Plan–National Ecological Network (*Natuurbeleidsplan, Ecologische Hoofdstructuur*), the 1995 Greenspace Structural Frameworks I and II (*Structuurschema's Groene Ruimte I en II*), the 1998 Memorandum: Nature Management (*Nota Natuurbeheer*), the 1998 and 2004 Nature Protection Laws (*Natuurbeschermingswet*), the 2000 Memorandum: Nature, Woods and Landscape 21st Century (*Nota Natuur, Bos en Landschap 21e eeuw*), the 2000 Water Policy for the 21st Century (*Waterbeleid voor de 21e eeuw*), the 2000 Second Water Household Plan Friesland (*Dreaun troch it wetter*), the 2002 Flora and Fauna Laws (*Flora en Faunawet*), and the 2002 Memorandum: Choose Recreation (*Nota Kiezen voor Recreatie*).

Provincial policies affecting De Alde Feanen include the 1994 Regional Plans (*Streekplannen*), the 1995 Regional Plan Concerning the Blue Zone (*Streekplan uitwerking De Blauwe Zone*), the 1998 Memorandum: Nature Management (*Nota Natuurbeheer*), the 2000 design project Swette-De Burd (*Herinrichtingsprojecten Swette-De Burd*), the 2000 Friesland lakes project (*Friese Meren Project*), the 2002 Policy Memorandum: Recreation and Tourism (*Beleidsnota Recreatie en Toerisme*), and the 2005 design project De Alde Feanen (*Herinrichtingsproject De Alde Feanen*). Municipal-level policies also apply to the park, including Zoning Plans for Rural Areas (*Bestemmingsplan Buitengebied*) for the municipalities of Tytsjerksteradiel and Boarnsterhim.

In general, one can say that in the Netherlands, European law manifests itself through more specific policies at lower levels of government (Owens, 2008). Although all of these policies apply to the area, none of them specifically address the issue of boating access. The stakeholders developing this national park management plan must gain the approval of the national government, and yet the exact details of the plan may take many forms.

METHODOLOGY

I used a semi-structured interview instrument to learn the history of these policy interactions and to measure motivation, information, and power of stakeholders. Analysis of interviews produced motivation, information, and power scores for each interviewee. These scores, analyzed with Contextual Interaction Theory, produced a hypothesis about the ensuing interaction. In other words, given the motivation, information, and power scores, the theory produces a hypothesis of the kind of interaction that will occur (e.g., cooperation, opposition, obstruction, etc.).

Using case-study methodology (Yin, 2003), I assessed relevant documents and conducted interviews with key actors. Interviewing is one way to understand more about participant motivations, information level, and perceptions regarding power balance. Interviewing gives insight into how participants connect meaning with events (Berg, 2001). The semi-structured instrument included asking predetermined questions systematically, with the expectation of probing at times beyond given answers (Berg, 2001).

To understand local history and the development of the management plan for the national park De Alde Feanen, I interviewed members of the *overlegorgaan*. The Advisory Group for Management, Design, and Monitoring proved to be particularly critical to the decision-making process. In an early interview, the *overlegorgaan* secretary described them as the stakeholders with "the ability to change things" within the process. Analysis stemmed from interviews with five members of this committee,[8] the *overlegorgaan* secretary, and a representative from the Frisian Water Authority. Of the seven interviews for this case, five were conducted in-person and recorded. One interview took place over the telephone and was not recorded. In one in-person interview, there were tape recording difficulties. Notes were taken during each interview to ensure documentation. I transcribe and then assessed each interview to determine motivation, information, and power scores.

Motivation

The motivation score includes the stakeholder's own motivation and potential sources of external pressure. Their own motivation encompasses their compatibility with implementation goals, as well as normative, economic, social, and political influences. In addition, stakeholder motivation incorporates work-related goals, as well as attitudes toward the program objective and the other stakeholders' goals. Finally, a measure of self-effectiveness contributes to the motivation score. When interviewing about motivation, there was an awareness to follow up with probing questions if there was an indication that higher authorities or external pressure affected the stakeholders. This allowed recognizing situations in which outside influence thwarts or galvanizes a

Table 5.2

Underlying Concepts for Motivation, Example Questions, and Subsequent Interview Questions

Type of Motivation	Example Questions	Interview Questions
Compatibility with implementation goals	What were the goals of this project?	8, 9
Normative	Do you feel it is your civic duty to participate in this project?	13c, 19
Economic	Was this project important to your community?	19
Social	Was the community at large involved in this decision? How important is it to you that community members are satisfied with the results?	14, 20, 22, 23
Political	Did politicians support this project?	15a
Work-related motivation	Does your organization have goals for wetlands in the area?	10a, 10b, 11, 12, 27, 29
Attitude toward the program objective	Do you find wetland restoration is an important part of wetland policy in general?	13a, 13b, 16a, 17a, 18a, 18b, 21
Attitude toward other stakeholders	Would you describe any of the stakeholders as being targeted by this project (positively or negatively)? For example, if the project is implemented, who has the most to gain, and who has the most to lose?	8
Self-effectiveness	During this process, if something is important to your group and others disagree, what do you think are your chances of attaining goals important to you?	33, 40

stakeholder's own motivation. See Table 5.2 for example interview questions and how they link to each element of the motivation score.

Information

Information includes accessibility to information and the transparency of the process for stakeholders. Information and communication that reduce uncertainties promote ease in implementation (Rothstein, 1998). Winter and May (2001) note that awareness of a given regulation *and its specifics* are preconditions for compliance (my emphasis). Stakeholders may lack awareness of regulations for many reasons, including newness or lack of publicity (Winter & May, 2001). They may also lack understanding about requirements or the means for compliance (Winter & May, 2001). Here, measuring information includes policy awareness and understanding policy requirements and benefits. Additionally, it involves knowledge of other stakeholders and the level of documentation available. It also includes accessibility to information, the simplicity or complexity of

Table 5.3

Underlying Concepts for Information, Example Questions, and Subsequent Interview Questions

Type of Information	Example Questions	Interview Questions
Policy awareness	What is the policy or program supporting this wetland project?	24
Policy requirements	Are the requirements of this policy clear to you?	25, 26
Policy benefits	Does implementing this policy bring benefits to your organization?	27
Knowledge of stakeholders and qualifications	Can you name other actors or stakeholders involved?	4, 29
Documentation, including lack of	How would you describe the information your organization receives about this policy program?What are your impressions of this information in terms of quantity?	28, 30a, 30b, 30c, 31a, 32
Accessibility, including lack of	During the decision-making process, did you find yourself dependent on others for information?During the project, did you find a lack of information existed between yourself and other actors?	28, 30a, 31a, 32
Process complexity, uncertainties	Are there things you are uncertain about that hamper your activities regarding this project?	33

information, and understanding of the process as a whole. Table 5.3 identifies the underlying concepts that compose the information score, as well as examples of interview questions that correspond with the concepts.

Power

Power is not solely about decision making; it also includes non-decision making (Lukes, 2005). Here, power includes resources dedicated to supporting or fighting the given implementation, the reputation of the actor's power, and the ability to control a situation. Resources include the ability to strengthen or weaken a given individual, organization or agency, such as finances, personnel, and time. The reputation of power is an important facet, centering on how stakeholders perceive each other in the process. The reputation of power is true until it is challenged and fails. Power, in terms of controlling a situation, divides into formal and informal facets. Formal power is that given to a group, agency, or individual according to the law (e.g., a regulator). Informal power derives from other channels (e.g., coalition building, using the press, raising awareness, lobbying, etc.). It is important to understand who has formal power, while also taking into account who

Table 5.4

Underlying Concepts for Power, Example Questions, and Subsequent Interview Questions

Type of Power	Example Questions	Interview Questions
Resources	Did this project involve a financial commitment by your organization? Did your organization support the project in other ways?	37a, 37b, 37c, 38
Lack of resources	Were there resources you needed but did not have access to during the project?	39a, 39b, 39c
Formal	Is your organization responsible for seeing that policy requirements are fulfilled? Who is in charge of monitoring the effects of this decision?	1, 2, 7, 26, 34, 36, 37a, 41
Informal	Did your organization support the project in other ways? If [the community became involved], was community involvement part of the formally required process, or was it informal?	3, 4, 5, 6, 21, 38, 40
Reputation of power	Who do you think is viewed by the public as the group primarily responsible for this project? —During this process, if something is important to your group and others disagree, what do you think are your chances of attaining goals important to you?	40, 42

exercises power in each case (Bressers, 2004). Concepts behind power scores can be seen in Table 5.4, with example questions.

RESULTS

Case History

De Alde Feanen is a *laagveenmoeras* habitat, or a fen complex. Fens are wetlands with "mineral-rich peats, typically with significant groundwater inflow, and dominated by sedges and mineral-loving species" (Tiner, 1998, p. 250). A fen is chemically basic and dependent on the water table. De Alde Feanen is a diverse habitat and popular recreation area, including more than 450 plant species, 100 bird species, and 200,000 recreational users per year (MLNV, 2014). It Fryske Gea, a nonprofit nature group, owns approximately 1,500 hectares within the larger fen complex and has since the 1930s managed a portion of the area. This case fits into a larger tapestry of decisions on managing this resource over time.

The long thin bodies of water of De Alde Feanen were formed in the 17th and 19th centuries through peat extraction (MLNV, 2014). Over time lakes formed when the remaining strips of land collapsed from weakening or from pressure during flooding

(MLNV, 2014). In the 1960s, an area not owned by It Fryske Gea was targeted for recreation development in a zoning plan for the municipality of Tytsjerksteradiel. The plan called for the development of approximately 300 holiday houses, but it was not immediately realized. In 1992 the municipality and other stakeholders reignited interest in the holiday house development. It Fryske Gea led other stakeholders in protesting the development, but it was implemented.

After the holiday house development project, stakeholders—particularly It Fryske Gea and the provincial government—thought that collaborative planning should be used in managing the area. A committee formed in 1992, and in 1995 it proposed that this area should be considered for status as a national park. This committee became the *overlegorgaan* in 1995. From 1995 to 2004 the group discussed how the area might be managed if it became a national park. This discussion centered on the controversial issue of balancing nature and recreation within the proposed national park. Each proposed national park area within the Netherlands has its own specific and unique ecological qualities. That being said, national parks are also valued for their recreation component. Actors promoting boating restrictions argued that De Alde Feanen already included many recreation opportunities, such as two large bungalow parks with camping sites and docking harbors, as well as access for sailing, canoeing, kayaking, walking, and biking within the park. This analysis focused on the potential decision to deem core park areas accessible by canoe and kayak but inaccessible by larger watercraft. Deciding which was most important—recreation or ecology—became the defining issue for this committee.

CIT Analysis and Prediction

Table 5.5 shows the scores for motivation, information, and power for all interviewees. It Fryske Gea, not surprisingly, has positive motivation toward the proposed management measure (limiting boating access), whereas De Marrekrite is not motivated about the measure. Both It Fryske Gea and De Marrekrite display positive information levels, though comparatively De Marrekrite's information level is lower. Both De Marrekrite and It Fryske Gea have high, positive power scores, indicating the time and financial support dedicated to the project as a whole and the various areas of control each group maintains. According to this analysis, there is not a great disparity between power scores for De Marrekrite and It Fryske Gea, meaning power is balanced between them.

The two other content-oriented actors, the municipalities of Smallingerland and Boarnsterhim, show a range of motivation about the project. Smallingerland, like De Marrekrite, is not in favor of limiting access, whereas Boarnsterhim is moderately in favor of limiting access. Smallingerland has adequate information, whereas Boarnsterhim exhibits a neutral information score. When considering power, Smallingerland lacks resources but scores high on control, whereas Boarnsterhim has positive scores in both control and resources.

The two process-oriented actors are both in favor of the proposal limiting access and both have adequate information about the project. Both also exhibit positive scores for

Table 5.5

Scores for Interviewees Using Analysis via the Contextual Interaction Theory

	Motivation	Information	Power–control	Power–resources
It Fryske Gea	+22/24 (+91.7)	+17/17 (+100)	+5/8 (+62.5)	+2/3 (+66.7)
De Marrekrite	−17/21 (−81.0)	+5/9 (+55.6)	+4/6 (+66.7)	+2/3 (+66.7)
Municipality of Smallingerland	−11/18 (−61.1)	+6/8 (+75.0)	+2/3 (+66.7)	−2/3 (−66.7)
Municipality of Boarnsterhim	+11/20 (+55.0)	0/10 (neutral)	+3/5 (+60.0)	+2/3 (+66.7)
Province of Friesland	+16/22 (+72.7)	+17/17 (+100)	+4/7 (+57.1)	+3/3 (+100)
Frisian Water Authority	+13/20 (+65.0)	+13/15 (+86.7)	+4/7 (+57.1)	−2/3 (−66.7)

power–control; the Province of Friesland also scores positively for power–resources, whereas the Frisian Water Authority has a negative score for this aspect of power.

In the creation of a hypothesis, the contextual interaction theory, a two-actor model, focuses on It Fryske Gea's and De Marrekrite's scores. Based on these scores, the theory provides the following prediction: "If application of the instrument would contribute positively to the objectives of one actor, while the other actor is negative, and the information of the positive actor is sufficient, then the character of the interaction process will be dependent on the balance of power between actors. A relatively equal balance of power will lead to opposition. Opposition can take the forms of negotiation and conflict" (Bressers, 2004, p. 32).

This case agrees with the theory's prediction. For a number of years De Marrekrite and It Fryske Gea maintained conflicting goals for the management of the park. One constraint in decision making for a national park, likely closely tied to the strong tradition of negotiated agreements in the Netherlands, is that decisions must be made by consensus. In this case, opposition eventually gave way to negotiation. De Marrekrite and It Fryske Gea compromised after many years of deliberation and negotiations. The final vote was to maintain the status quo, with additional monitoring as a part of the management plan.

This one-time analysis does not shed light on how the variables changed over time, but interviews with actors provide more insight. The Marrekrite interviewee reported that It Fryske Gea was initially "better organized" and built early support for its cause. As the Marrekrite interviewee described it, at times the municipality representatives were not communicating with their constituencies, but instead were closely tied to nature interests. During the process, De Marrekrite felt that this link [to nature] for the municipality representatives subjugated the link to those they "should be" representing. The De Marrekrite representative recognized a shift in power toward nature (perhaps even toward what the theory predicts for such a case: forced cooperation). In answer, De Marrekrite began an informal lobbying effort to inform the public about the process and the stakes, as they believed they are not being well represented. They used their resources to inform the public about what was happening within the advisory group for management, design, and monitoring, believing the municipality constituents would align with De Marrekrite's own goals for the area. De Marrekrite had little to lose by informing the public and lobbying for more support. In the end, their strategy was highly effective and showed that in many ways De Marrekrite understood the public's interests. This led to the situation in analysis: neither De Marrekrite nor It Fryske Gea held the balance of power, leading to opposition which eventually channeled into a negotiation process.

DISCUSSION

Despite a decade of meetings about the area, the pro-environment stakeholders were unable to convince other actors to change access within De Alde Feanen. The *overlegorgaan* confirmed the national park borders on April 26, 2006, without reducing access, with the condition that a monitoring plan would take place to better understand the impact of boating access on core park areas.

Trust

Nature managers have historical water quality data for several areas within the site, beginning in 1987. There are also some species lists dating to the late 1950s. It Fryske Gea presented these data to the Advisory Group for Management, Design, and Monitoring to show the changes in the area's ecology over time. Yet, It Fryske Gea was unable to establish a *causal* relationship between the degraded habitat and recreational use. It Fryske Gea felt that the 1950s data in particular gave a clear picture of the area when recreational activity was limited. A causal relationship is difficult to establish, according to one process-oriented actor, because of "other influences . . . in the area like water table management and agricultural pressure." The Marrekrite representative mentioned a lack of trust that "the experts" would present a true picture of the ecological status of the area. This interviewee (from De Marrekrite) clearly stated that they believed these experts were aligned with the nature organization and that influenced perception of the information they share. This lack of trust did not help It Fryske Gea in its quest to establish causality between recreational boat use and ecological impact.

Primary and Secondary Goals

How individuals value nature influences management priorities (Owens, 2008). Some stakeholders and decision makers might support nature for its own sake, whereas others view nature's value only in its capacity to support human activity. Interviewee responses to one question in particular shed light on how they internalized the value of nature (shown in Table 5.6).

It Fryske Gea and the process-oriented actors (Province of Friesland and Frisian Water Authority) valued nature for nature's sake. In contrast, De Marrekrite equated

Table 5.6

Interviewee Responses to Interview Question 19

Interviewee	Do you find wetland restoration benefits your community? If so, how?
It Fryske Gea	"Yes . . . in the first place for the birds . . . also for a lot of people who enjoy birds and also for some other forms of recreation, not only water recreation . . . and a source of employment."
De Marrekrite	"Recreation is economically good; more work, more money, but not always easy for the farmer . . . recreation is a very important part . . . nature is water in Friesland."
Municipality of Smallingerland	"Changing from farmland into wetland with use for recreation, I think, is a good business."
Municipality of Boarnsterhim	"In some way it prevents some plans we have for recreation and tourism . . . in the end we say we must consider the possibility to protect bird and water life; in the end we say it is okay though we are limited."
Province of Friesland	"The intrinsic value of nature. Man or people cannot live without nature, people cannot live in a concrete environment . . . so it has value for nature itself, but also for the people because in Holland people decide they find it important that nature exists."
Frisian Water Authority	"It is more and more clear that nature, natural values and natural areas give distressed people [a place] to spend their free time . . . so it has economic values, it is good for your health to be there, and we have a kind of moral duty to [maintain] . . . biodiversity."

nature with recreation and economic benefits. The representative from the Municipality of Smallingerland answered in a similar way, describing wetlands as a place for recreation and therefore "good business." The Municipality of Boarnsterhim representative depicted a trade-off between the value of nature and recreation's economic benefits, finding that nature might limit recreation. In essence, when the motivations for conserving an area are different, this likely influences the type of strategies one will be willing to use to address perceived policy problems.

Governance Strategies

How can this analysis enlighten those working to balance business and the environment through governance strategies? Garnering support for many projects or policies requires including a range of stakeholders, perhaps including actors with incompatible goals. In this particular case, both De Marrekrite and It Fryske Gea support the environment and its conservation, but the motivations for their support are different, with De Marrekrite supporting nature as it enables recreation and It Fryske Gea supporting nature for its own sake.

One municipality interviewee said it best in this case: "It Fryske Gea wanted to make nature number one and recreation number two, while De Marrekrite wanted to make recreation number one and nature number two." This municipality representative wanted a plan that "tries to make both nature and recreation number one." A compromise of this kind is a valid goal for an actor in a decision-making process, but in this case, one goal (nature or recreation) must subjugate the other.

The case meets some of the criteria of a green alliance, though typically a green alliance avoids governmental influence. Arts (2002) describes the risk of business and NGO green alliance members' opposite worldviews leading to instability. Although the *overlegorgaan* remained stable, the oppositional goals of the key players could not be resolved within the process. The co-production of knowledge likely would have proved beneficial—the very remedy to the lack of trust De Marrekrite showed for It Fryske Gea's expert scientists. Instead, the failed legitimacy of the "experts" allowed actors who did not agree with expert opinions to ignore their assessments.

In this case, I believe it is more accurate to view the *overlegorgaan* less as a green alliance and more as a boundary-spanning tool: a decision-making body that sought to facilitate stakeholder interaction over the creation of De Alde Feanen national park. In this way the *overlegorgaan* spanned the sectors of environment and business (recreation), bringing these actors to the table to make decisions together, in many ways fulfilling the promise of boundary spanning (i.e., facilitative interactive strategies that cross boundaries of business and environment).

The De Alde Feanen case fits firmly into Bressers et al.'s (2009) narrative on negotiated agreements—no radical changes were made, decision makers maintained the status quo, actors achieved only moderate goals, and stakeholders avoided trench warfare (which is no small achievement). It should also be noted that these stakeholders participated in a legitimate and inclusive decision-making process.

An inclusive, consensus-based process (like the Dutch-style negotiated agreement) incorporates the goals and opinions of all relevant groups. The benefit is broad support for the decisions made. The risk is that actors and stakeholders beyond scientists influence policy decisions about important resources. This is a trade-off that may be necessary, particularly to build the political support and viability for a project. In this case it certainly proved to be.

CONCLUSIONS

It Fryske Gea proved unable to convince the *overlegorgaan* members to prohibit access to key areas within the park. Instead, the *overlegorgaan* opted to increase monitoring and, over time, re-evaluate to understand whether boating access causes irreparable harm to the wetland complex. Ideally this safety net will be capable of catching potential ecological problems, guaranteeing the conservation of the ecosystem this national park was developed to protect. It Fryske Gea believed that this is a case of "destroying the goose that lays the golden egg," but agreed to the plan. To merit any changes, It Fryske Gea must prove that boating access harms the park ecology. Proving causation, or linking boating definitively to ecological degradation, may prove an impossible task.

De Alde Feanen provides an example of how one set of political actors struggled with a complex issue—balancing environmental and business goals—and eventually found a solution, though one that was neither easy nor simple.

KEY POINTS

Though this appears to be a case of winners and losers, there are key recommendations that one can take from the assessment:

- Including diverse stakeholders provides a benefit in legitimacy but carries a the risk of watered-down policies or programs.
- Creating a watered-down but politically viable policy may be the best possible solution.
- Co-producing knowledge may allow stakeholders with varying goals to find common ground and build trust; at the very least, the opposite proved true in this case: stakeholders were unlikely to fully value expert information from groups with oppositional goals.

NOTES

1. *De Alde Feanen* translates from the Frisian language as "The Old Marshlands".
2. Image from Google maps www.google.com/maps/@53.1277476,5.9223725,13z
3. Image from Google maps www.google.com/maps?t=m&ll=53.1277476,5.9223725&z=13& output=classic&dg=ntvb
4. Institute for higher education in Food Technology, Environment and Agriculture, located in Leeuwarden, Friesland, the Netherlands
5. Translates into the "Agency for Rural Areas".
6. The Waterboard Lauwerswalden was integrated into the Frisian Water Authority on 31 December 2003.
7. Literally *The Frisian Landscape* in Friese.
8. Representatives from the municipalities of Smallingerland and Boarnsterhim, the Province of Friesland, *De Marrekriet,* and *It Fryske Gea.*

REFERENCES

Arts, B. (2002). 'Green Alliances' of business and NGOs. New styles of self-regulation or 'dead-end roads'? *Corporate Social Responsibility and Environmental Management, 9,* 26–36.

Berg, B. L. (2001). *Qualitative research methods for the social sciences.* Boston: Allyn and Bacon.

Bijker, W. E. (2002). The *Oosterschelde* storm surge barrier: A test case for Dutch water technology, management, and politics. *Technology and Culture, 43,* 569–584.

Bressers, H. T. A. (2004). Implementing sustainable development: How to know what works, where, when and how. In W. M. Lafferty (Ed.), *Governance for sustainable development: The challenge of adapting form to function* (pp. 284–318). Cheltenham: Edward Elgar.

Bressers, H. T. A., & de Bruijn, T. (2005). Conditions for the success of negotiated agreements: Partnerships for environmental improvement in the Netherlands. *Business Strategy and the Environment, 14,* 241–254.

Bressers, H. T. A., de Bruijn, T., & Lulofs, K. (2009). Environmental negotiated agreements in the Netherlands. *Environmental Politics, 18*, 58–77.

Cash, D. W., & Moser, S. C. (2000). Linking global and local scales: Designing dynamic assessment and management processes. *Global Environmental Change 10*, 109–120.

De Clercq, M. (2002). *Negotiating environmental agreements in Europe: Critical factors for success.* Cheltenham: Edward Elgar.

De Marrekrite. (2014). *Recreatieschap de marrekrite.* Retrieved May 1, from www.marrekrite.nl/

Dente, B., Fareri, P., & Ligteringen, J. (1998). A theoretical framework for case study analysis. In B. Dente, P. Fareri, & J. Ligteringen (Eds.), *The waste and the backyard. The creation of waste facilities: Success stories in six European countries* (pp. 197–222). Dordrecht: Kluwer.

Dicke, W. (2001). *Bridges & watersheds: A narrative analysis of water management in England, Wales and the Netherlands.* Amsterdam: Askant.

Edelenbos, J., van Buuren, A., & van Schie, N. (2011). Co-producing knowledge: Joint knowledge production between experts, bureaucrats and stakeholders in Dutch water management projects. *Environmental Science and Policy, 14*, 675–684.

Hemmen, B. (2005). *National Park De Alde Feanen, Beheers- en Inrichtingsplan In Nije Faze (Meeleesversie Januari).* Commissioned by: Overlegorgaan National Park De Alde Feanen.

Huntjens, P., Pahl-Wostl, C., Rihoux, B., Schlüter, M., Flachner, Z., Neto, S., . . . Nabide Kiti, I. (2011). Adaptive water management and policy learning in a changing climate: A formal comparative analysis of eight water management regimes in Europe, Africa and Asia. *Environmental Policy and Governance, 21*, 145–163.

It Fryske Gea. (2014). *It Fryske Gea.* Retrieved May 1, from www.itfryskegea.nl/

Kaijser, A. (2002). System building from below: Institutional change in Dutch water control systems. *Technology and Culture, 43*, 521–548.

Kearney, J., Berkes, F., Charles, A., Pinkerton, E., & Wiber, M. (2007). The role of participatory governance and community-based management in integrated coastal and ocean management in Canada. *Coastal Management, 35*, 79–104.

Kuks, S. (2002). *The evolution of the national water regime in the Netherlands.* Paper prepared for the EUWARENESS project (www.euwareness.nl). Enschede, the Netherlands: University of Twente.

Lukes, S. (2005). *Power a radical view.* Hampshire, UK: Palgrave.

Medd, W., & Marvin, S. (2007). Making water work: Intermediating between regional strategy and local practice. *Environment and Planning D: Society and Space, 26*, 280–299.

MLNV (Ministerie van Landbouw, Natuur en Voedselkwaliteit). (2008). *Estimating the value of nature and landscape: What is the economic value of nature and landscape.* The Hague, the Netherlands.

MLNV (Ministerie van Landbouw, Natuur en Voedselkwaliteit). (2014). *National parks in the Netherlands.* Retrieved May 1, from www.nationaalpark.nl/

Owens, K. A. (2008). *Understanding how actors influence policy implementation: A comparative study of wetland restorations in New Jersey, Oregon, the Netherlands, and Finland.* Enschede, the Netherlands: University of Twente Press.

Owens, K. A. (2010). The Dutch land-use re-ordering process as a multi-stakeholder management strategy. In H. Bressers & K. Lulofs (Eds.), *Governance and complexity in water management: Creating cooperation through boundary spanning strategies* (pp. 114–135). Cheltenham: Edward Elgar.

Owens, K. A., & Bressers, H. (2013). A comparative assessment of how actors implement: Testing the contextual interaction theory in 40 cases of wetland restoration. *The Journal of Comparative Policy Analysis, 15*, 203–219.

Owens, K. A., Hughes, M., & Skoczenski, E. (2013). Testing of the contextual interaction theory in the evaluation of cooperation and collaboration of water management projects in India. In C. De Boer, J. Vinke-de Kruijf, G. Özerol, & H. Bressers (Eds.), *Water governance, policy and knowledge transfer: International studies on contextual water management* (pp. 76–91). Cambridge, UK: Earthscan.

Özerol, G., de Boer, C., & Vinke-de Kruijf, J. (2013). Introduction. In C. De Boer, J. Vinke-de Kruijf, G. Özerol, & H. Bressers (Eds.), *Water governance, policy and knowledge transfer: International studies on contextual water management* (pp. 1–11). Cambridge, UK: Earthscan.

Ramsar. (2014). *Ramsar sites information service.* Retrieved May 1, from www.ramsar.org

Reuss, M. (2002). Learning from the Dutch: Technology, management and water resources development. *Technology and Culture, 43*, 465–472.

Rothstein, B. (1998). *Just institutions matter: Moral and political logic of the universal welfare state.* Cambridge: Cambridge University Press.

Sivapalan, M., Savenije, H. H. G., & Blöschl, G. (2011). Socio-hydrology: A new science of people and water. *Hydrological Processes, 26*(8), 1270–1276.

Star, S. L., & Griesemer, J. R. (1989). Institutional ecology, 'translations' and boundary objects: Amateurs and professionals in Berkeley's Museum of Vertebrate Zoology, 1907–39. *Social Studies of Science, 19*, 387–420.

Tiner, R. (1998). *In search of swampland: A wetland sourcebook and field guide.* New Brunswick: Rutgers University Press.

Winter, S. C., & May, P. J. (2001). Motivation for compliance with environmental Regulations. *Journal of Policy Analysis and Management, 20*, 675–698.

Yin, R. K. (2003). *Case study research: Designs and methods.* London: Sage.

Part III

Economic Development

6

A Collaborative Approach to Innovation-Based Economic Development

The Triple Helix

Jonathan Q. Morgan

INTRODUCTION

In an increasingly knowledge-based economy, innovation and technology are becoming the key drivers of economic growth. Regions that create a local environment that is conducive to innovation will be positioned to prosper in the new economy. A thriving culture of innovation typically requires the major institutional actors within a region to build and support a substantial knowledge infrastructure. The nature of innovation and the resources, capacity, and expertise needed to support it will often necessitate strong collaborative partnerships among local actors, such as businesses and government agencies.

Although alliances between government and business are important in supporting innovation-based economic development, a third institutional actor, the university, is also thought to play a vital role. For some observers, adding the university to government–business alliances forms a so-called "triple helix" that can enhance a region's innovative capacity and make it more competitive for knowledge-based job creation and private investment (Etzkowitz & Leydesdorff, 1997, 2000). The "triple helix" refers to the close interactions and relationships among government, industry, and universities in the innovation process that ultimately lead to increased regional competitiveness and economic development.

This chapter will review the growing literature on the triple helix model of innovation, with a particular emphasis on how it contributes to our understanding of regional competitiveness and economic development. Most of what we know to date about the triple helix model is based on its application in regions outside the U.S., particularly in Europe and Asia (Penska, 2010). This chapter fills a research gap by examining how the framework has been implemented in a major high-tech region located in the U.S. Using the renowned Research Triangle region as a case study, the chapter will explore how the triple helix model can be used as a basis for establishing creative industry-government-university alliances to tackle the complex challenge of innovation-based economic development.

DEFINING THE TRIPLE HELIX

The triple helix is a metaphor for characterizing the dynamic and interactive nature of innovation. The triple helix concept emerged in the 1990s as a framework for conceiving

Figure 6.1   **The Triple Helix Model of Collaborative Innovation**

of a heightened role for universities in the innovation process relative to industry and government (Etzkowitz & Leydesdorff, 1997). For some observers, there is clearly a normative basis for universities to take on a more central role in innovation (Raman, 2005). Historically, innovation was thought to occur primarily within firms or be controlled by a national government. The statist or state-centered model, in which government dominates both industry and higher education, may not be conducive to innovation in a knowledge-based economy (Etzkowitz, 2008). Moreover, the laissez-faire model of relations among industry, government, and university sees the three institutional spheres as separate and independent, with only limited interaction among them. This approach lacks the collaboration and interconnectedness among the three spheres likely needed to support innovation in the new economy.

As depicted in Figure 6.1, the triple helix model produces "a knowledge infrastructure in terms of overlapping institutional spheres, with each taking the role of the other and with hybrid organizations emerging at the interfaces" (Etzkowitz & Leydesdorff, 2000, p. 111). The "capitalization" of knowledge is at the core of the triple helix model, and there is growing recognition about the important role of universities in this process (Etzkowitz, 2010; Farinha & Ferreira, 2013). In a triple helix approach to regional economic development, the boundary lines separating universities, industry, and government become blurred as the desire to promote innovation breaks down barriers. Triple helix alliances form between the "entrepreneurial university" (Etzkowitz, 2004) and the "entrepreneurial state" (Eisinger, 1988), as well as with enterprising firms, in order to grow the regional economy by catalyzing and supporting innovation.

HEIGHTENED ROLE FOR UNIVERSITIES

As universities expand their focus beyond teaching and basic research and begin to place greater emphasis on community engagement, they are positioned to play a much more prominent role in promoting economic development, especially when working in tight collaboration with industry and government (Etzkowitz, 2002). A triple helix approach considers the university role in innovation and knowledge creation to be particularly vital in building and growing a technology-based regional economy. The university can be a central player in helping a region achieve the prerequisites for becoming a technology hub: scientific excellence, new technologies for emerging industries, recruitment of major technology firms, and support for local technology start-ups (Smilor, Kozmetsky, & Gibson, 1988). It is well documented that universities are increasingly assuming new entrepreneurial roles in the economy (Tornatzky, Waugaman, & Gray, 2002) and becoming more involved in technology transfer and commercialization (Smilor & Matthews, 2004). The idea of an engaged entrepreneurial university is a core tenet of the triple helix model, as it envisions a special role for universities in creating spin-off businesses.

Previous research has examined the evolving roles of research universities in transforming regions into prosperous technology hubs, which is relevant to our understanding of how academia fits into the triple helix framework. One study draws a contrast between North Carolina's Research Triangle Park (RTP); San Diego, California; and Austin, Texas, on the one hand and Boston's Route 128 and California's Silicon Valley on the other. More specifically, the study found that RTP, San Diego, and Austin developed into high-tech centers as the result of a systematic and coordinated strategy, whereas Route 128 and Silicon Valley became technology hubs with minimal planning and "sprang up almost by spontaneous combustion" (Smilor, O'Donnell, Stein, & Welborn, 2007, p. 217). According to the study's authors, the approaches used by RTP, San Diego, and Austin represent an intentional and coordinated effort among business, government, and higher education that "depended on a more proactive and regionally engaged research university that served as the nucleus for economic activity, as a magnet for talent in the regions, and as an engine for technological innovation" (Smilor et al., 2007, p. 217).

BOUNDARY SPANNING AND INTERMEDIARY ROLES

Triple helix collaboration among governmental, university, and industry actors can be hindered by differences in values, norms, organizational structures, and operating missions in the three sectors. For example, government's inclination to regulate may run counter to a firm's plans to bring a new product to market. A university's core educational mission may not readily lend itself to the creation of new business enterprises. The tendency toward bureaucracy in government and many university structures may not necessarily be conducive to promoting the innovation that firms and industries desire. At least one study has found that differences in communication, capabilities, and habits between universities and firms are the top barrier to university–industry collaboration (Ranga et al., 2013). This potential dissonance among institutional actors across the three helices can be mitigated when an individual or entity serves in a boundary-spanning role to help reconcile the differences and potential conflicts.

The literature suggests that boundary spanners are an essential component in a triple helix system of innovation (Etzkowitz, 2012; Lundberg, 2013). In her detailed case study of the attempt to implement a triple helix approach in a Swedish region, Lundberg (2013) found that boundary spanners bridged cultural differences, built networks, and helped increase interaction, which led to "new interfaces and new forms of cooperation" across boundaries (p. 222). The case study identified several specific dimensions of boundary spanning, including information brokerage, semantic translation of domain-specific technical knowledge, sense-making, knowledge creation, resource pooling, and activation of interpersonal relationships.

Boundary spanning is made easier when organizational boundaries are permeable, enabling freer movement between sectors and entities. Etzkowitz (2012) found evidence of this sort of "boundary permeability" in his analysis of four prominent high-tech regions. In two of the cases, Boston–MIT and Silicon Valley–Stanford, the boundary permeability between academia and industry was found to be a driving force for innovation-based regional economic development that encompassed significant entrepreneurial spin-off activity from the universities. The boundaries between universities and industry were found to be less permeable, resulting in much less business spin-off activity, in the other two cases, North Carolina's Research Triangle Park and Northeast UK–Newcastle University.

Boundary spanning can be done by intermediary organizations that "operate in the spaces between institutions of higher education, industrial firms, and government agencies" (Metcalfe, 2010, p. 504), such as nonprofits, trade associations, industry consortia, and the like. These boundary-spanning intermediaries bring together the government, business, and higher education sectors in a fashion that is analogous to the interwoven strands of DNA shown in Figure 6.1. Boundary spanning will often involve a brokering function that attempts to make connections between previously disconnected actors (Fleming & Waguespack, 2007). Oettinger and Henton (2013) argue that such "innovation brokers" or intermediaries are an important "fourth strand" of the triple helix model. These brokers are individuals or organizations that accelerate, facilitate, and make connections among the innovation activities in a triple helix system. The term *cooperative research center* has been proposed as a way to define a specific type of innovation-oriented intermediary (Gray, Boardman, & Rivers, 2013). Other examples of formal brokers may include a business accelerator, technology transfer unit, or economic development office that provides financial and technical assistance and other support for entrepreneurs and firms (Oettinger & Henton, 2013). Informal brokering can occur in a variety of social networks through which ideas, information, and resources flow. MacGregor, Marques-Gou, and Simon-Villar (2010) suggest the possibility of a "quadruple helix" with respect to innovation intermediaries and brokers.

TAKING ON THE ROLES OF THE OTHER ACTORS

An expected characteristic of a triple helix innovation system is that the three sectors—university, government, and industry—will respectively begin to assume roles that extend beyond their typical functions and responsibilities (Etzkowitz & Klofsten, 2005; Lundberg, 2013). Universities will begin doing things that were previously done by industry or government. Government will engage in activities that are usually performed by industry or academia, and so forth. For example, triple helix interactions may evolve to the point where government gets involved in creating new markets for products, services, and technologies. Government may also modify regulations in response to industry preferences in order to promote innovation. Another nontraditional role that government could assume is that of venture capitalist, as a way to support the growth of technology companies. Universities may begin producing spin-off businesses, a function traditionally done by the private sector. Industry may get more involved in job training and research, which are typically higher education roles. The idea is that triple helix interactions will eventually transform the sectors such that the government begins to resemble an "entrepreneurial state" and academic institutions become "entrepreneurial universities."

CRITIQUING THE TRIPLE HELIX MODEL

The triple helix model of innovation is not without its critics. Some analysts suggest that the framework is too simplistic and fails to adequately capture the complex nature of the innovation process. They question whether the model takes into account the substantially different and highly localized contexts in which innovation occurs (Coenen, 2007). A related issue has been raised about the applicability of a triple helix framework that is based on exemplary institutions and success cases (Cooke, 2005; Rodrigues & Melo, 2013). The triple helix model has also been criticized for neglecting the crucial role that individual entrepreneurs play in the process of innovation (Brannback, Carsrud, Krueger, & Elfving, 2008).

Other observers take issue with the heightened role for universities that the triple helix model prescribes. There is concern that the model overstates the potential contribution of universities to the innovation process and to regional economic development (Goldstein & Renault, 2004; Lawton Smith, 2007) and tends to minimize the possibility of conflict among the three spheres—university, government, and industry. For some analysts, the growing pressure for universities to be more entrepreneurial and directly involved in promoting regional economic development may be problematic to the extent that it is politically motivated by a desire to reduce public funding for higher education (Christopherson & Clark, 2010; Lawton Smith, 2007). Finally, the empirical evidence that triple helix interactions are effective at producing desired outcomes appears to be largely missing from the literature, leaving the concept vulnerable to charges that it is an unproven theoretical proposition.

COLLABORATIVE INNOVATION AND KNOWLEDGE CREATION AS DRIVERS OF ECONOMIC DEVELOPMENT

Interest in the triple helix model coincides with our understanding of the shifting sources of competitive advantage in a knowledge-based economy. Innovation increasingly provides the competitive edge for firms and regions alike and can fuel economic growth and prosperity. Indeed, empirical research has established a positive relationship between regional innovation activity and regional income levels (Nelson, 1996; Oughton, Landabaso, & Morgan, 2002). It is now widely accepted that innovation is a collaborative process—a team sport, so to speak. The triple helix model's emphasis on collaborative innovation and knowledge creating activities as the drivers of economic development is consistent with some popular contemporary theories of regional growth and development. These include industry clusters, learning regions, and social capital.

Leading advocates of industry cluster–based development, such as Porter (2000) and Rosenfeld (1995, 1997), accentuate the social network aspects of clusters as being a crucial success factor in that approach. High-performing clusters benefit from the presence of supporting institutions/organizations, and the extent of relations among firms, universities, and government agencies is essential (Hendry et al., 1999). The latest thinking about industry clusters tends to emphasize technology-intensive sectors, innovative enterprises, and entrepreneurs (Asheim, Cooke, & Martin, 2006). A consensus now exists within the cluster literature that "knowledge in clusters is created through various forms of local inter-organizational collaborative interaction" (Malmberg & Power, 2006, p. 60).

The idea of learning regions recognizes that innovation is an interactive process involving firms and the local knowledge infrastructure, which includes universities and other parts of the institutional milieu (Christopherson & Clark, 2010; Morgan, 1997; Simmie, 1996). Firms engage in innovation networks and "learn by interacting" in order to reduce the risks and uncertainty associated with the innovation process (Koschatzky, 1999). Social capital contributes to the innovation process by enabling firms to develop sustained interactions with other firms and institutions that result in mutual gains in productivity and innovative capacity. Innovation networks do not necessarily require geographic closeness, but spatially proximate networks may be advantageous in today's innovation-based economy, because they facilitate the collective learning and informal exchange of tacit knowledge that are so crucial to the innovation process (Asheim et al., 1996). These interactions allow firms to more quickly learn about new market opportunities and technologies. Inter-organizational collaboration on innovation can take the form of R&D partnerships with universities and the federal government, joint ventures, industry networks, strategic alliances, and industry consortia (Powell & Koput, 1996).

THE TRIPLE HELIX IN THE RESEARCH TRIANGLE REGION

The Research Triangle region originated in the late 1950s as a coordinated effort to develop a science park that would attract the R&D facilities of corporations and federal labs located mostly outside the state of North Carolina. Though slow going in the early years, Research Triangle Park (RTP) gained steam over time with the location of the R&D facilities of major corporations, such as IBM, Burroughs Welcome (now Glaxo Smith-Kline), and Nortel, and federal agencies, such as the National Institutes of Environmental Sciences (see Figure 6.2). The RTP strategy helped transform a North Carolina economy that had historically been dominated by agriculture and low-wage manufacturing sectors, such as furniture, textiles, and tobacco products.

The Research Triangle's exogenous approach, which focused on the recruitment of external business and research facilities, can be contrasted with the more endogenous approaches taken early on in other high-tech regions, such as Boston's Route 128 and Silicon Valley (Etzkowitz, 2012). Those regions explicitly pursued a regional innovation strategy, at the outset, that emphasized the creation of local start-up firms. The Research Triangle region was slower to incorporate an overt focus on building the

Figure 6.2   **Milestones in the Evolution of the Research Triangle Region**

1950s	1960s,1970s	1980s, 1990s	2000-present
1959-Research Triangle Foundation created	1963-NC Board of Science & Technology	1984-Council for Entrepreneurial Dev.	2012-RTP adopts new Master Plan
1959-Research Triangle Institute (RTI) founded	1965-IBM locates in RTP	1984-NC Biotechnology Center	2012-Research Triangle Cleantech Cluster formed
	1973-Burroughs Wellcome locates in RTP	1989-NC State Centennial Campus opens	2014-NCSU to lead new mfg. innovation center
	1975-Triangle Univ. Ctr. for Advanced Studies	1990-Research Triangle Regional Partnership	
	1976-SAS founded at NC State (NCSU)	1991-First Flight Venture Center established in RTP	

capacity to support and accelerate business start-up activity. When it eventually did, the shift in focus was part of a larger effort to take better advantage of the tremendous knowledge and innovation assets that exist within the region, an effort that continues in full gear today.

This chapter will use the triple helix model to examine how the nexus of industry, government, and universities supports innovation-based economic development in the Research Triangle region of North Carolina. The Research Triangle region, which is anchored by three top research universities, has recently started using the triple helix concept as part of its marketing brand. The region's lead economic development organization, the Research Triangle Regional Partnership (RTRP), asserts that the triple helix model manifests itself within the region through

- A dense network of researchers who continuously innovate
- Entrepreneurs and investors who turn discoveries into products and companies
- Government agencies that structure intellectual property, regulatory, and tax systems to enable new companies and industries to thrive
- A tightly linked, integrated, and collaborative economic development community, which provides the connective tissue that keeps business, government, and academic resources aligned and focused on business success (www.researchtriangle. org/assets/triple-helix)

This chapter employs a case study research design to gain a deeper understanding of how the triple helix model of innovation-based economic development plays out in the Research Triangle region. The triple helix dimensions shown in Table 6.1 are of particular interest. The analysis is exploratory in nature and relies primarily on structured interviews with key stakeholders in the region's triple helix and a review of the relevant

Table 6.1

Triple Helix Dimensions

Heightened role for universities
Overlapping spheres of activities
Hybrid organizations at the interfaces
Boundary spanning
Taking on the roles of other actors

Source: Adapted from Etzkowitz & Leydesdorff 2000; Etzkowitz 2012; and Lundberg 2013

literature and existing documents, such as strategic plans for economic development. Targeted interviews were conducted in order to verify and get elaboration on the data and information reported in previous research and existing planning documents. Interview respondents included representatives from the region's major universities, the lead regional economic development organization, and the NC Department of Commerce. The interviews addressed the following questions:

1. What is the specific nature and extent of relations, interactions, and alliances among actors within the triple helix for economic development in the region?
2. What are the specific roles of the various institutional actors in the region's triple helix for economic development? To what extent do the triple helix actors take on the roles of each other across the three spheres as suggested by the theoretical framework?
3. What are the tangible organizational mechanisms, programs, and policy tools used to implement the triple helix approach within the region?
4. How does the triple helix model of collaboration contribute to the region's success in promoting innovation-based economic development? How is success measured?

IMPLEMENTING THE TRIPLE HELIX IN THE RESEARCH TRIANGLE

A cursory review of economic development websites and news media within the Research Triangle shows that the triple helix idea is becoming a part of the lexicon and marketing strategy for the region. The triple helix certainly appears to be a high-level source of inspiration for the region's innovation-based economic development efforts and marketing brand. But how deeply embedded is triple helix thinking in the region's economic development efforts? To what extent is the triple helix being used as a substantive and explicit framework for implementing a collaborative approach to innovation-based economic development? The interviews with individuals representing key organizational actors within the region's triple helix shed some light on this question.

The interview respondents suggested that the triple helix model is a useful way to describe and illustrate the intertwined nature of innovation-based economic development in the Research Triangle region and that it has encouraged even higher levels of regional interaction. The model serves as a framework for bringing together a variety of organizational actors in order to leverage their distinctive strengths to make the region stronger as a whole.

There is a sense that the triple helix has been a part of the region's DNA for years, because it fits what the region has been doing—government, private sector, and universities working together to promote economic development. According to interview respondents, the triple helix facilitates collaboration among the region's key institutions and helps organizations address challenges, resolve issues, and secure major research grants. The model helps the region differentiate itself and provides a competitive edge, as many other regions do not have this level of cooperation and partnering. It involves the idea of interdependency between science and government. The interview respondents consider the Research Triangle to be one of the more dynamic triple helix regions in the world in terms of the level of interactions among the various actors. Due to the presence of Research Triangle Park and the three major research universities, interviewees think it is hard to find a more robust and complex innovation ecosystem.

Interview respondents asserted that the triple helix model generates firms and jobs in the region that would not otherwise exist. They cited North Carolina State's Centennial Campus as a prime example of the kind of development that would not be in the region but for leveraging the strengths of the various triple helix actors. The data analytics software firm SAS was mentioned as another good example of what the triple helix has produced for the region. SAS grew out of work that its founder, Jim Goodnight, did while a professor at North Carolina State University and was spun out from that campus. In the case of SAS, university research led to the creation of what would become a major technology firm for the region. When triple helix interactions enable firms like SAS to start up and stay in the region, the firms will hire talent from the universities, providing high wage jobs for students without them having to leave the area.

The triple helix gets credit for helping to create a diversified and resilient innovation economy in the Research Triangle region that has many sources of competitive advantage. As a state commerce department official observed,

> The region would not be what it is without the Triple Helix. Technology and innovation drive economic development in the region and, because of this, the region withstood the recession better than many regions, in that it did not suffer as badly and bounced back quicker.

While there was unanimity among interview respondents about the tremendous value of the triple helix model as a broad framework for regional collaboration on innovation-based economic development, some questioned the model's clarity and how explicitly it was being used within the region. A representative from one the research universities stated that the triple helix is "not a well-elaborated model." A respondent from the state commerce department commented that

> We don't use the Triple Helix term much. But we use terms and language that effectively refer to it. So, we talk about connecting industry, universities, and government all the time.

Despite any internal concerns about the clarity of the model and its explicit use, the region has attracted external interest in and recognition for its triple helix interactions. Interview respondents noted that people travel to the region to study the triple helix model for economic development purposes. The International Cleantech Network asked the Research Triangle Regional Partnership organization to join the group, in large part because of the region's triple helix approach to supporting cleantech industries.

THE ORGANIZATIONAL ACTORS AND THEIR ROLES IN THE RESEARCH TRIANGLE TRIPLE HELIX

The Triple Helix model has been in place in the Triangle for decades, but operationalizing the model means making sure the leadership of the various sectors (private, government, and universities) is engaged in the process in order to leverage the respective strengths that each organizational actor brings to bear. The primary actors are the

Figure 6.3   **Key Organizational Actors and Roles in the Research Triangle's Triple Helix**

Universities	Government	Industry	Regional Intermediaries/ Brokers

•North Carolina State
•UNC-Chapel Hill
•Duke
•North Carolina Central
•**Roles include:**
  •Research
  •Tech transfer
  •Business spin-offs
  •Technical assistance
  •Talent development
	•NC Dept. of Commerce
	•NC Board of Science & Technology
	•Local governments
	•Federal Government
	•**Roles include:**
	  •Convener
	  •Facilitator
	  •Master planner
	  •Regulator
	  •Funder
		•Information technology
		•Telecommunications
		•Biopharmaceuticals
		•Advanced medical care
		•Nanoscale technologies
		•Gaming
		•Cleantech
		•**Roles include:**
		  •Entrepreneur
		  •Innovator
		  •Job creator
		  •Wealth creator
			•Research Triangle Foundation
			•NC Biotechnology Center
			•Council for Entrepreneurial Dev.
			•Research Triangle Regional Partnership
			•Cleantech Cluster
			•TUCASI
			•NCSU-ORIED
			•**Roles include:**
			  •Facilitator
			  •Connector
			  •Broker
			  •Boundary spanner
			  •Developer

Research Triangle region's research universities (University of North Carolina–Chapel Hill, Duke, and North Carolina State), companies, government, and several important intermediary organizations. It is important to identify the specific organizational actors that comprise the region's triple helix, examine their respective roles, and consider how they contribute to and benefit from this regional innovation system.

THE UNIVERSITIES

The three universities that anchor the Research Triangle—UNC–Chapel Hill, North Carolina State, and Duke University—are fully engaged in the region's triple helix. Despite taking a passive role in recruiting technology businesses during the early years of Research Triangle Park, the universities are now partners in that process. Each institution has its own strengths and expertise and fills a distinctive niche. For example, North Carolina State provides science and technology expertise and talent for the area. Whenever firms need support for aviation, aerospace, and automotive engineering, North Carolina State is involved and works with the North Carolina Commerce Department to assist in recruiting or expanding those activities in the Triangle region. In addition to scientific research and education, UNC and Duke provide medical, legal, and humanities-based knowledge.

The Research Triangle universities contribute to triple helix–based innovation by playing many of the roles suggested by the literature, including technology transfer, creation of entrepreneurial spin-offs, entrepreneurship education and support, and inter-disciplinary, industry-relevant research. These are in addition to the traditional university roles of teaching, talent development, and research. Interview respondents pointed out that university-based extension services are also vital aspects of the region's triple helix. It was noted that the industrial and agricultural extension programs at North Carolina State are an important interface through which many companies interact with the triple helix. Another important area to consider is contract research at universities, in which they contract with firms to do research. Duke does some biomedical research on behalf of companies, for example. Another area of university involvement is the consulting that university faculty, staff, and researchers do for firms and industries. Also consistent with the literature, boundary-spanning activities are readily evident in many of the university interactions with industry and government within the Research Triangle region's triple helix. Boundary spanning among the three universities has occurred in substantive ways that have enhanced the region's culture of innovation. For example, high-level technology transfer brokers have rotated in key positions among the three campuses, producing a "cross-pollination" of administrators that lessened unhelpful rivalries and facilitated the exchange of best practices (Smilor et al., 2007, p. 207).

The universities participate in triple helix innovation activities in proportion to the size of their interest in R&D and in commercializing their research and technologies, which means that Duke, UNC, and North Carolina State are almost always engaged in one way or another. The universities have data and technical assistance capabilities and will often ask the Department of Commerce for help in identifying potential users or purchasers of their technology and research.

The region's triple helix began with UNC, Duke, and North Carolina State, but it has expanded to include other local universities, such as North Carolina Central, which is a historically African American campus located in Durham. Many of the businesses located in Research Triangle Park engage in the triple helix and make vital linkages with the universities that are often centered on research and technological innovation.

North Carolina State's position within the region's triple helix is unique due to its land-grant status and its strengths in engineering and technology-related disciplines. As a land-grant institution, North Carolina State has always emphasized community outreach and engagement, an ethos that shapes its involvement in triple helix interactions. Many of its innovation activities are coordinated through the Office of Research, Innovation, and Economic Development (ORIED). ORIED is led by the Vice Chancellor for Research, Innovation, and Economic Development; it coordinates research activities across campus and performs boundary-spanning activities with external actors through a number of interfaces. It serves as the university's primary point of contact and portal for industry, entrepreneurs, and small businesses; government agencies; and nonprofit organizations. ORIED units handle research administration, intellectual-property issues, technology transfer, and venture development. ORIED has an Associate Vice Chancellor for Partnerships and Alliances who builds and supports alliances with industry and cultivates economic development partnerships. Several interdisciplinary research centers and institutes are administered through ORIED.

ORIED facilitates a specialized set of triple helix interactions through its unit that forges partnerships with the Centennial Campus. North Carolina State's Centennial Campus is a next-generation version of the Research Triangle Park concept, designed to facilitate interaction and collaboration among university, industry, and government partners in ways that promote innovation-based economic development. It is currently billed as a "living lab where research rocks, ideas collide, and partnerships matter" (Centennial Campus web site). The Centennial Campus enables industries and firms to work in close proximity to university and government researchers. Unlike its predecessor, Research Triangle Park, the Centennial Campus is a mixed-use university property that includes labs, office space, residential units, classrooms, and recreational amenities. This sort of spatially proximate live, work, study, and play physical layout is thought to be highly conducive to collaborative innovation.

As a vehicle for implementing triple helix interactions, the Centennial Campus model looks very promising. This university research park and technology campus has grown to span more than 1,200 acres, with 65 partner companies and organizations, and houses 11,000 employees and students. The campus has three million square feet of space, which is 99% occupied. Two major North Carolina State academic units, the College of Textiles and the College of Engineering, as well as a number of research centers and institutes, have relocated from the main campus to the Centennial Campus. A major research center located on the Centennial Campus is the Nonwovens Institute; one of the largest such centers in the U.S., it is organized as a consortium supported, in part, by industry membership fees (Tornatzky & Rideout, 2014). The Nonwovens Institute itself represents a triple helix model in that it operates at the nexus of academia, industry, and government in order to promote innovation in the development and application of engineered nonwoven fabrics.

UNC-Chapel Hill's involvement in the region's triple helix is largely driven by its innovation roadmap dubbed "Innovate@Carolina." Adopted in 2010, this innovation roadmap provides a strategic framework for accelerating innovation across the campus. In this effort, UNC-Chapel Hill defines innovation broadly as creating solutions for pressing problems in a variety of sectors, including health, education, energy, government, and business. Although the innovation roadmap does not explicitly reference the region's triple helix by name, it certainly recognizes the importance of what it calls the "RTP entrepreneurial ecosystem." The Innovate@Carolina roadmap calls for greater coordination among Duke, North Carolina State, and UNC in making university labs and research facilities more accessible to innovators within the Research Triangle region. It also proposes to incentivize more collaboration among RTP universities and key partners more generally to promote innovation.

The Chancellor's Office of Innovation and Entrepreneurship was established in 2010 to facilitate implementation of the innovation roadmap at UNC–Chapel Hill. In 2015, the university created a new position, Vice Chancellor of Commercialization and Economic Development, to lead campus innovation efforts. One promising new economic development initiative to come out of UNC–Chapel Hill's renewed focus on promoting collaborative innovation is the Blackstone Entrepreneurs Network. UNC–Chapel Hill brought Duke University, North Carolina Central University, North Carolina State University, and the Council for Entrepreneurial Development together to form the Blackstone Entrepreneurs Network as a way to expand the pipeline of potential high-growth start-up firms in the region. The network recruits successful veteran entrepreneurs to mentor and assist start-up companies with marketing, business development, strategy, and securing possible funding through their own investor networks.

GOVERNMENT

The literature suggests that government's role in a triple helix system is to help promote interactions across sectors, modify regulatory and incentive policies to create an environment more favorable to innovation activities, and possibly invest in public venture-capital funds (Lundberg, 2013). In the U.S., the federal government establishes the "rules of the game" with respect to patenting, trademarks, and intellectual property, which can influence the technology transfer process and encourage university–industry collaborations on R&D activities (Etzkowitz, 2003, p. 301).

Beyond the substantial federal research dollars that flow into the region, the government role in the Research Triangle's triple helix is fulfilled primary by the state of North Carolina and local governments, and most often takes the form of convener, facilitator, master planner, regulator, and funder. The historical involvement of state government in what is now Research Triangle Park dates back to the 1950s and the public-sector leadership of Governor Luther Hodges, who coordinated with a number of key private-sector and university actors in planning for the eventual implementation of this transformational idea. In 1961, Governor Terry Sanford convened a group of university scientists from UNC, North Carolina State, and Duke who came up with the idea of creating the North Carolina Board of Science and Technology, which the General Assembly would formally establish in 1963 (Hardin & Feldman, 2011). State government would help propel Research Triangle Park and innovation-based economic development during the 1980s under the leadership of Governor Jim Hunt, who was instrumental in getting the North Carolina Biotechnology Center created (discussed below).

The state government apparatus continues to play a convening role in bringing together the region's universities, industries, and public-sector agencies. In the view of one interview respondent representing a university, "Government is the chief economic developer for the state of North Carolina, and good government involvement and relationships are important for a successful triple helix." The North Carolina Department of Commerce (NC Commerce) and the Governor's Office work closely together to promote economic development generally and innovation-based development in particular. NC Commerce takes the lead on marketing North Carolina and recruiting technology firms to the state.[1] The agency also administers the Board of Science and Technology through its Office of Science and Technology (OST). OST uses data-driven analysis to inform strategic planning and policymaking in support of technology-based economic development. OST also administers technology commercialization grant programs and works with other NC Commerce staff to help recruit and retain high-growth technology industries. Cultivating nanotechnology-related sectors in North Carolina is a current focus for OST.

Local government involvement in the region's triple helix includes planning and zoning functions, as well as providing funding for innovation-based local and regional economic development efforts. Planning and zoning issues are currently in play for Research Triangle Park as it seeks to incorporate higher density, mixed-used development in order to attract technology workers and facilitate more informal face-to-face interaction among tenants. Interview respondents indicated that local governments in the region embrace regionalism and understand that a business locating in a neighboring county can benefit their respective counties. So, if a business goes to one county, neighboring counties will tend to be supportive because they will enjoy spillover effects and be positioned to attract a similar firm looking to locate near related firms or suppliers.

Interview respondents also noted that the cities and counties in the Research Triangle recognize that the spin-off firms and growth from Research Triangle Park proper will inevitably extend beyond its boundaries. For example, certain manufacturing and production activities that are spawned from Research Triangle Park or university innovation may not fit within Research Triangle Park, but could be located in Chatham County or another nearby area with the land and zoning for it. It was suggested that cities and counties within a 60-mile radius of Research Triangle Park could benefit from the innovation of the Research Triangle's triple helix if they effectively position themselves as an ancillary business location and possible home for some Research Triangle

Park and other technology workers. This is exactly the strategy of four counties located just north of Research Triangle Park that have formally joined forces to create a network of development-ready business and industrial parks (Morphis & Pearson, 2011). These rural county governments located outside the urban core—Franklin, Granville, Vance, and Warren—hope that their multi-county collaborative effort, called "Triangle North," will attract companies wanting to be near the innovation hub of Research Triangle Park, but not necessarily directly within it due to costs or other factors.

INDUSTRY

The industry role in triple helix collaboration will typically be as entrepreneur, innovator, job creator, and wealth creator. The primary industries stimulated by the Research Triangle's triple helix are parts of technology clusters. However any cluster or industry that needs aspects of the triple helix to succeed, such as government support, an ecosystem of collaborative innovation, and research and talent from universities, will benefit from being engaged. The most prominent industries in the region's triple helix are information technology, telecommunications, and biopharmaceuticals. Other regional specialties include agricultural biotechnology, pervasive computing, advanced medical care, analytical instrumentation, nanoscale technologies, and informatics. Advanced gaming, defense technologies, and clean/green technologies are emerging clusters that are gaining traction within the region. These industries play off the triple helix partners' strengths and institutional expertise. For example, medical device and biomedical firms connect to strengths at Duke, North Carolina State and UNC. Vaccine production is another example in which R&D comes out of the Research Triangle universities, although some of the related manufacturing may end up locating outside the region.

Interview respondents pointed to clean/green technology as an example of an industry cluster that engages the universities and activates the triple helix model. One respondent credited the region's triple helix collaboration for helping to convince a prospective cleantech business to locate in the area. North Carolina State University and some private firms drove the process, with the Research Triangle Regional Partnership (RTRP) convening all of the important regional stakeholders. As discussed below, RTRP has organized clean/green technology firms into a formalized industry cluster organization in order to optimize triple helix interactions.

REGIONAL INTERMEDIARIES AND BROKERS

A triple helix system of collaborative innovation is supposed to give rise to "new interfaces and new forms of cooperation across sectoral boundaries" (Lundberg, 2013, p. 222). In many cases the organizational mechanism through which this happens is an intermediary organization that serves as an innovation broker and boundary spanner, bridging the divides between universities, government, and industry. These intermediary organizations help connect industries, firms, and entrepreneurs to the ideas, knowledge, services, financing, talent, and networks needed to thrive in a competitive global economy (Oettinger & Henton, 2013). Many of these intermediary organizations now exist in the Research Triangle and are instrumental actors in the region's triple helix approach to innovation-based economic development.

Among the region's core triple helix intermediaries is the Research Triangle Foundation (RTF), which is a private, nonprofit organization that was founded in the late 1950s to manage Research Triangle Park. RTF has functioned as a real-estate development intermediary of sorts by purchasing land on which to develop Research Triangle Park and serving as an interface for private developers and industry. RTF is primarily responsible for the physical development of Research Triangle Park, but it also helps attract and retain companies. RTF's land acquisitions for Research Triangle Park grew from an initial 4,400 acres in 1959 to 5,500 acres in 1979, and now includes nearly 7,000 acres. By most counts, Research Triangle Park is considered the largest research park in the U.S., with more than 170 companies, nearly 40,000 technology workers, and 22.5 million square feet of built space. RTF's long-time role in building and managing Research Triangle Park is an instructive example of how an alternative organizational form can be put in place to mediate innovation-based economic development in a region.

One of the early research and innovation intermediaries created in Research Triangle Park is the Triangle Universities Center for Advanced Studies, Inc. (TUCASI). The idea for TUCASI came from Archie Davis, who in 1975 headed up the Research Triangle Foundation (Tornatzky & Rideout, 2014). Davis decided to allocate a large tract of land (120 acres) in Research Triangle Park to provide a home within the park for the three founding universities. TUCASI facilitates collaborative research activities among UNC, North Carolina State, and Duke and interfaces with RTF on larger projects that advance Research Triangle Park. The TUCASI campus has helped attract a number of major tenants to Research Triangle Park, including the National Humanities Center, MCNC (a nonprofit provider of advanced networking technologies), NC Biotechnology Center, and the National Institute of Statistical Sciences.

The region's lead economic development organization is the Research Triangle Regional Partnership (RTRP). RTRP is a public–private partnership that works to market and promote economic development within the larger 15-county region in which Research Triangle Park is located. RTRP explicitly uses the triple helix in its marketing pitch to prospective companies and touts the concept as a critical regional asset. RTRP works with prospective companies to find real estate and labor/talent solutions within the region. RTRP plays an important intermediary role in bringing together multiple counties within a 60-mile radius of Research Triangle Park, which are all represented on its board of directors, to devise and implement a regional approach to economic development that meets the varying needs of the different localities. Although the urban counties most proximate to Research Triangle Park have the assets needed to support a dynamic knowledge-based economy, many of the outlying counties are rural and economically distressed. RTRP convenes the counties and other public, private, and university stakeholders every five years to prepare a formal strategic plan to guide the region's economic development efforts. The latest strategic plan, titled "The Shape of Things to Come," centers on growing existing and emerging technology clusters; enhancing the region's quality of life, infrastructure, and competitive business climate; and promoting greater regional collaboration.

Interview respondents pointed to RTRP's work in supporting regional industry clusters as another example of its role as an important intermediary and boundary spanner within the triple helix. RTRP recently created a hybrid structure to use in formally organizing the businesses and supporting institutions that comprise the region's "Cleantech Cluster." The Research Triangle Cleantech Cluster (RTCC) is a nonprofit entity that facilitates collaboration among firms, institutions, and government in order to grow emerging sectors focused on renewable energy, smart grid, water efficiency, waste reduction, and smart transportation solutions. RTRP staff members administer the RTCC, which is supported by membership fees. The founding members of the RTCC Board of Directors include ABB, Cisco, Duke Energy, RTI International, SAS, and Siemens. The RTCC's program of work is about (1) branding the cluster and promoting the region as a competitive location for cleantech firms, (2) building connections among cluster firms and to related activities that support cleantech, (3) accelerating innovation and fostering entrepreneurial ventures, and (4) promoting workforce development and attracting talent. In the spirit of the triple helix, the RTCC working group on entrepreneurship is led by the point person for venture development at North Carolina State University, reflecting the kind of cross-pollination that spurs regional innovation.

The region's assets, knowledge infrastructure, and triple helix collaborations in support of cleantech industries are having a snowball effect. The growing list of specialized research and innovation assets that are forming in the region include the NC Solar Center and the Advanced Transportation Energy Center, both at North Carolina State University, and the Energy Frontier Research Center located at UNC–Chapel Hill. The region's approach to and focus on cleantech received major affirmation in early 2014, when President Barack Obama traveled to Raleigh to announce that North Carolina State would lead a new $140 million manufacturing innovation institute that will develop cost-effective ways to produce energy-efficient semiconductors. True to triple helix form, this new institute is a consortium of 18 companies and 6 universities, with half of the funding being provided by the U.S. Department of Energy. Moreover, one of the institute's corporate partners is Cree, a Durham-based firm specializing in LED lighting that utilizes a technology that originated in a lab on the North Carolina State campus in the 1980s. As another sign of the momentum building around cleantech, the Research Triangle is one of only two U.S. regions that have been invited to join the International Cleantech Network.

During its first couple of decades, promoting entrepreneurship was not a primary focus for Research Triangle Park and the Research Triangle region. That began to change with the formation of the Council for Entrepreneurial Development (CED) in 1984. CED's mission is to support the start up and expansion of high-growth companies and to strengthen the entrepreneurial culture of the Research Triangle and the state of North Carolina. This important intermediary organization provides networking opportunities and connects entrepreneurs to the expertise, knowledge and financial capital needed to start and grow a business enterprise in key sectors of the regional economy. CED provides value-added services to its more than 700 member companies through an extensive network of mentors and partners. CED services include face-to-face events, customized mentoring, and web-based networking forums. As a nonprofit organization, CED fulfills its educational mission by offering a variety of training workshop and seminars. The creation of CED has enhanced the regional entrepreneurial ecosystem and boosted the ability of the region's triple helix interactions to produce home-grown technology firms, particularly spin-offs from the universities (Smilor et al., 2007).

A highly specialized triple helix intermediary within the Research Triangle region is the North Carolina Biotechnology Center (Biotech Center). The Biotech Center was established in 1984 to help jump start what was at that time an emerging industry cluster in the state. Since the Biotech Center's inception, North Carolina's biotechnology sectors have grown significantly. The state's biotech sectors develop technologies that are used in agriculture, pharmaceuticals, biomanufacturing, biofuels, regenerative medicine, and vaccines. The Biotech Center is a private, nonprofit organization that receives most of its funding from state government. It is a statewide hub for the commercialization of the life sciences and performs several intermediary and boundary-spanning roles in advancing the biotechnology cluster. The Biotech Center provides low-interest loans to biotech start-ups and helps connect firms with venture-capital funds and potential angel investors. While it does not have labs on site or directly incubate firms, the Biotech Center funds faculty research and university–industry partnerships, supports university technology transfer offices, and sponsors training workshops for biotech entrepreneurs. The Biotech Center works with a variety of partners to improve and expand the workforce that is available to the region's biotech companies. Finally, it collaborates with CED to offer bi-monthly "Biotech Forums," which feature expert panel discussions and social networking opportunities. According to one interview respondent, "The NC Biotech Center is an example of the Triple Helix in itself . . . [it's] the Triple Helix at play."

THE NATURE AND EXTENT OF INTERACTIONS AND ALLIANCES

There is no centralized, overarching coordination of the Research Triangle region's triple helix. It is not implemented in a top-down and formally organized manner throughout the region. Formal coordination tends to occur within specialized domains on the campuses, such as technology transfer; in university–industry research partnerships; and through targeted industry cluster efforts.

All interview respondents described the region's triple helix interactions and relationships as being highly organic. There are no formal agreements or contracts for roles in the triple helix. Instead, the various actors embrace the spirit of collaboration in the region and work together informally to promote innovation-based economic development. Interview respondents view the creation and evolution of Research Triangle Park as the source of the collaborative spirit that is at the heart of the region's triple helix interactions.

The universities, Research Triangle Park, partner organizations like RTRP, and government participants communicate with each other frequently and through many different venues. People interact both electronically and face to face. One interview respondent said the region benefits from this collaborative ethos in ways that areas outside the Triangle that lack the triple helix model do not. Those areas may not have the university presence and collaborative spirit needed to foster triple helix interactions. In those areas, neighboring counties tend to compete a lot more with each other. The triple helix model encourages a more regional approach to economic development, whereby multiple counties, universities, and governments work together with private firms to increase jobs, with the idea that the region wins and loses together. The region's triple helix, though, is mostly informal and organic, and based on numerous long-term personal relationships that have been cultivated over time.

As another example of the collaborative spirit within the region, one interview respondent mentioned that each part of the triple helix knows the strengths of the others and will hand off projects or assist others with certain projects when it makes sense to do so. In one specific instance, UNC gave North Carolina State a proposed project because the project was a better fit for North Carolina State, given its strengths and expertise.

According to interview respondents, Research Triangle Park reflects the triple helix because it demonstrates the complex interactions of different sectors collaborating on innovation-driven economic development. One respondent thought the term innovation "ecosystem" was an equally if not more applicable way to describe the region's culture of and support for innovation. He went on to express some concern about a gap in the region's triple helix that local leaders now recognize as an area in need of improvement:

> We have an above average ecosystem for innovation, but there is not enough velocity of interaction between different firms in the area. People don't live in [Research Triangle Park] itself, and doing so would greatly increase the interaction between various people in tech[nology] and innovation. The communities of the Triangle are spread out, and so there is not a seamlessness amongst them, which would help the triple helix.

MEASURING SUCCESS IN THE REGION'S TRIPLE HELIX

The consensus view among interview respondents was that measuring the success of the region's triple helix interactions was somewhat of a challenge. For example, while Research Triangle Park boasts the creation of 1,800 start-up firms since 1970, attributing such outcomes directly to any individual triple helix actor can be difficult. Maybe that is the point: the success comes from collaborative synergy rather than the isolated efforts of individual organizations. Still, as interview respondents observed

> The [return on investment] on the triple helix is difficult to measure. You can look at companies that work together and see when business, academic, and government

partners worked together to land a business or help one expand. Grants are also another one, such as a climate hub grant for the region.

It's hard to measure directly. You know it when you see it. But it is hard to directly attribute anything to the triple helix specifically. But look at individual companies and see if they thrive from or require an ecosystem. You can also look at the various relationships around the region and who is connected to and working with whom.

An anecdotal example of the success of the triple helix is how Glaxo came to the Triangle area and helped spur growth and development in outlying rural areas, such as Franklin County, and helped attract new facilities to the region. This growth was possible because of the NC Biotech Center, which was also instrumental in attracting Merck to Durham.

A university official suggested that a detailed industry cluster analysis may shed some light on the how the triple helix contributes to the region's economic prosperity, but he acknowledged the methodological and analytical challenges of doing so:

Cluster research may offer more answers on this. The synergies of the triple helix model and this region are so complex. You can look at job growth, but really parsing out the effects of all these interactions and spin offs would be very difficult.

CONCLUSIONS AND KEY POINTS

The Research Triangle, fueled by Research Triangle Park, is generally viewed as an exemplary case study of how to promote innovation-based economic development within a region. This chapter has examined how the triple helix framework helps us understand this process, with a focus on the collaboration and interaction among universities, government, and industry. The case study analysis reveals some key lessons and take-aways that will be instructive to public officials and local leaders who may be interested in using a triple helix approach to address the challenges of creating jobs and wealth and enhancing regional competitiveness in an increasingly knowledge-based economy.

1. **Triple helix ecosystems are complex.** As the Research Triangle case study shows, a high-performance triple helix involves a lot of moving parts. Because innovation is a team sport, multiple actors interface across sectoral boundaries in ways that are not always easy to discern. The triple helix provides a framework and inspiration for collaboration and interactions to occur, but there is no mandate to work together. In the case of the Research Triangle region, the interactions and relationships are mostly organic in nature and rooted in long-term personal connections. Yet, is also clear from the case study analysis that critical public- and private-sector decisions and investments can influence the level of formal and informal interaction and collaboration that occur.

Keeping triple helix actors involved in the region's innovation ecosystem can be a challenge over the long-term. One important consideration has to do with the different incentives that may drive the various triple helix actors to engage and to what extent at different points in time. This can be an issue for new industry partners, who may be reluctant to participate and invest financially unless they see a clear return to the bottom line of corporate profit. Most government agencies, nonprofits, and universities are confronting fiscal challenges and budgetary constraints that can shift priorities and affect their ability to participate fully in triple helix interactions. Then there is human nature and the fact that people are self-interested. Engaging in the triple helix requires organizational actors to consider the collective good and act on it. That can be difficult to do without appropriate incentives that connect self-interest to the collective interest in promoting regional economic development.

Another possible concern is that the complexity of triple helix systems can lead to fragmentation of services and other governance and accountability issues. As mentioned in the case study analysis, measuring success and attributing outcomes directly to the triple helix is not necessarily straightforward. In certain regional contexts, these sorts of governance and accountability issues will likely need to be addressed in order to secure and maintain the support of key investors and stakeholders.

2. **Strategic alignment of university assets can make a difference.** The universities that anchor the Research Triangle are fully engaged in the region's efforts to promote innovation-based economic development. Consistent with the literature, these academic institutions are indeed becoming more entrepreneurial and taking on a heightened role in the region's triple helix approach to innovation. North Carolina State University has strategically organized its research, innovation, and commercialization activities and aligned them with the region's technology industries and other triple helix partners. North Carolina State has organized itself internally to enable stronger and more substantive linkages to the region's innovation ecosystem. UNC-Chapel Hill is using its Innovate@ Carolina roadmap to identify the university's innovation assets and better connect them to the region's triple helix. This sort of strategic alignment and focusing of the university role is important given the realization that academic institutions face constraints and may not, and perhaps should not, be able to fulfill all of the expectations placed on them as promoters of economic development (Christopherson & Clark, 2010).

3. **Collaboration begets collaboration.** The Research Triangle case study demonstrates how triple helix–inspired collaboration can result in additional collaborative activity, new forms of interacting, and new ways of working together. The organic nature of the region's triple helix interactions provides a flexible and adaptive framework for bringing actors together. The region has avoided instituting a top-down, highly circumscribed approach to forming partnerships

and collaborations. It has instead created an environment that is conducive to decentralized, organic collaborative innovation that tends to feed on itself.

4. **Regional intermediaries matter.** The potential game changers in the triple helix system are the intermediary organizations. The case study analysis illustrates the indispensable brokering and boundary-spanning roles that these entities play in supporting and accelerating the process of innovation-based economic development. It is these hybrid organizations operating at the interfaces among universities, industry, and government that implement the Research Triangle's triple helix through programming and support for key industry clusters, technology firms, entrepreneurs, and collaborative research projects. This suggests that an effective triple helix strategy will need to identify and support effective intermediary organizations and create new ones, if necessary.

5. **"Triple helix" can be more than a mere marketing slogan.** A lot has been written about the triple helix model of collaborative innovation. It might be tempting to use the triple helix as a convenient marketing slogan that resonates with prospective technology firms without much substantive application. This was not the case in the Research Triangle region. Triple helix is very much a part of the region's marketing brand, but it also provides inspiration for many of the collaborative efforts in support of innovation-based economic development. The level of triple helix consciousness varies from one actor to another, depending on the respective role, but very few deny the concept's implicit influence in shaping the region's innovation culture. If nothing else, the triple helix is a useful metaphor for thinking about the interdependencies and connections that can matter so much for innovation within a region.

NOTE

1. Starting in 2014, the NC Department of Commerce will contract with a newly created nonprofit entity to perform the state's marketing and recruitment activities.

REFERENCES

Asheim, B. T. (1996). Industrial districts as "learning regions": A condition for prosperity. *European Planning Studies, 4*(4), 379–401.

Asheim, B., Cooke, P., & Martin, R. (2006). *Clusters and regional development: Critical reflections and explorations.* London: Routledge.

Brannback, M., Carsrud, A., Krueger, N., & Elfving, J. (2008). Challenging the triple helix model of regional innovation systems: A venture-centric model. *International Journal of Technoentrepreneurship, 1*(3), 257–277.

Christopherson, S., & Clark, J. (2010). Limits to 'the learning region': What university-centered economic development can (and cannot) do to create knowledge-based regional economies. *Local Economy, 25*(2), 120–130.

Coenen, L. (2007). The role of universities in the regional innovation systems of the North East of England and Scania, Sweden: providing missing links? *Environment and Planning C: Government and Policy, 25*(6), 803–821.

Cooke, P. (2005). Regionally asymmetric knowledge capabilities and open innovation: Exploring "Globalisation 2"—A new model of industry organisation. *Research Policy, 34*(8), 1128–1149.

Eisinger, P. K. (1988). *The rise of the entrepreneurial state.* Madison, WI: University of Wisconsin Press.

Etzkowitz, H. (2002). *The triple helix of university-industry-government: Implications for policy and evaluation.* Working Paper, Science Policy Institute.

Etzkowitz, H. (2003). Innovation in innovation: The triple helix of university-industry-government relations. *Social Science Information, 42*(3), 293–338.

Etzkowitz, H. (2004). The evolution of the entrepreneurial university. *International Journal of Technology and Globalisation, 1*(4), 64–77.

Etzkowitz, H. (2008). *The triple helix: University-industry-government innovation in action.* London: Routledge.

Etzkowitz, H. (2010). A company of their own: Entrepreneurial scientists and the capitalization of knowledge. In R. Viale & H. Etzkowitz (Eds.), *The capitalization of knowledge: A triple helix of university-industry-government* (pp. 201–217). Cheltenham: Edward Elgar.

Etzkowitz, H. (2012). Triple helix clusters: Boundary permeability at university-industry-government interfaces as a regional innovation strategy. *Environment and Planning C: Government and Policy, 30,* 766–779.

Etzkowitz, H., & Klofsten, M. (2005). The innovating region: Toward a theory of knowledge-based regional development. *R&D Management, 35*(3), 243–255.

Etzkowitz, H., & Leydesdorff, L. (Eds.). (1997). *Universities and the global knowledge economy: A triple helix of university-industry-government relations.* London: Pinter.

Etzkowitz, H., & Leydesdorff, L. (2000). The dynamics of innovation: From national systems and "mode 2" to a triple helix of university–industry–government relations. *Research Policy, 29,* 109–123.

Farinha, L., & Ferreira, J. (2013). *Triangulation of the triple helix: A conceptual framework.* Working Paper, Triple Helix Association.

Fleming, L., & Waguespack, D. M. (2007). Brokerage, boundary spanning, and leadership in open innovation communities. *Organization Science, 18*(2), 165–180.

Goldstein, H., & Renault, C. (2004). Contributions of universities to regional economic development: A quasi-experimental approach. *Regional Studies, 38,* 733–746.

Gray, D., Boardman, C., & Rivers, D. (2013). The new science and engineering management: Cooperative research centers as intermediary organizations for government policies and industry strategies. In C. Boardman, D. O. Gray & D. Rivers (Eds.), *Cooperative research centers and technical innovation* (pp. 3–33). New York: Springer.

Hardin, J., & Feldman, M. (2011). North Carolina's Board of Science and Technology: A model for guiding technology-based economic development in the South. In D. Gitterman & P. Coclanis (Eds.), A way forward: Building a globally competitive south. (pp. 120–123). Chapel Hill: University of North Carolina Press.

Hendry, C., Brown, J., DeFillippi, R., & Hassink, R. (1999). Industry clusters as commercial, knowledge and institutional networks. In A. Grandori (Ed.), *Interfirm networks: Organization and industrial competitiveness.* London: Routledge.

Koschatzky, K. (1999). Innovation networks of industry and business-related services: Relations between innovation intensity of firms and regional inter-firm cooperation. *European Planning Studies, 7*(6), 737–757.

Lawton Smith, H. (2007). Universities, innovation, and territorial development: A review of the evidence. *Environment and Planning C: Government and Policy, 25*(1), 98–114.

Lundberg, H. (2013). Triple Helix in practice: The key role of boundary spanners. *European Journal of Innovation Management, 16*(2), 211–226.

MacGregor, S. P., Marques-Gou, P., & Simon-Villar, A. (2010). Gauging readiness for the quadruple helix: A study of 16 European organizations. *Journal of the Knowledge Economy, 1*(3), 173–190.

Malmberg, A., & Power, D. (2006). True clusters: A severe case of conceptual headache. In B. Asheim, P. Cooke, & R. Martin (Eds.), *Clusters and regional development: Critical reflections and explorations* (pp. 50–68). London: Routledge.

Metcalfe, A. (2010). Examining the trilateral networks of the triple helix: Intermediating organizations and academy-industry-government relations. *Critical Sociology, 36*(4), 503–519.

Morgan, K. (1997). The learning region: Institutions, innovation, and regional renewal. *Regional Studies, 31*(5), 491–503.

Morphis, C., & Pearson, E. (2011). Creating economic opportunity: Multi-jurisdictional parks as a product development tool. *Economic Development Journal, 10*(2), 28.

Nelson, R. R. (1996). *The sources of economic growth.* Cambridge, MA: Harvard University Press.

Oettinger, J., & Henton, D. (2013). *The role of innovation brokers in a knowledge economy: The fourth strand to triple helix.* Collaborative Economics, paper submitted to the Triple Helix XI International Conference, London, July 2013.

Oughton, C., Landabaso, M., & Morgan, K. (2002). The Regional Innovation Paradox: Innovation policy and Industrial Policy. *Journal of Technology Transfer, 27*(1) 97–110.

Penska, J. (2010). *A triple helix within the triple helix: A case study of a university-government-industry network.* (Doctoral dissertation). The Graduate School of the State University of New York at Buffalo.

Porter, M. E. (2000). Location, competition, and economic development: Local clusters in a global economy. *Economic Development Quarterly, 14*(1), 15–34.

Powell, W., & Koput, K. (1996). Interorganizational collaboration and the locus of innovation: Networks of learning in biotechnology. *Administrative Science Quarterly, 41*(1), 116–146.

Raman, S. (2005). Institutional perspectives on science-policy boundaries. *Science and Public Policy, 32*(6), 418–422.

Ranga, M., Hoareau, C., Durazzi, N., Etzkowitz, H., Marcucci, P., & Usher, A. (2013). *Study on university-business cooperation in the U.S., final report.* LSE Enterprise: London School of Economics.

Rodrigues, C., & Melo, A. (2013). The triple helix model as inspiration for local development policies: An experience-based perspective. *International Journal of Urban and Regional Research, 37*(5), 1675–1687.

Rosenfeld, S. A. (1995). *Industrial strength strategies: Regional business clusters and public policy.* Washington, DC: The Aspen Institute. Retrieved from www.aspeninstitute.org/sites/default/files/content/docs/pubs/Industrial-Strength-Strategies.pdf

Rosenfeld, S. A. (1997). Bringing business clusters into the mainstream of economic development. *European Planning Studies, 5*(1), 3–24.

Simmie, J. (Ed.). (1996). *Innovation, networks and learning regions?* London: Jessica Kingsley Publishers.

Smilor, R. W., Kozmetsky, G., & Gibson, D. (Eds.). (1988). *Creating the technopolis: Linking technology commercialization and economic development.* Cambridge, MA: Ballinger Publishing Company.

Smilor, R., & Matthews, J. (2004). University venturing: Technology transfer and commercialization in higher education. *International Journal of Technology Transfer and Commercialization, 3*(1), 111–128.

Smilor, R., O'Donnell, N., Stein, G., & Welborn, R. S. (2007). The research university and the development of high-technology centers in the United States. *Economic Development Quarterly, 21*(3), 203–222.

Tornatzky, L., & Rideout, E. (2014). *Innovation U 2.0: Reinventing university roles in a knowledge economy.* http://innovation-u.com/InnovU-2.0_Links.pdf

Tornatzky, L., Waugaman, P. G., & Gray, D. (2002). *Innovation U.: New university roles in a knowledge economy.* Research Triangle Park, NC: Southern Growth Policies Board.

7

Improving Administrative Outcomes through Collaborative Governance

Evidence from the City of Tallahassee

Carrie Blanchard Bush and Karen Jumonville

INTRODUCTION

Increasingly, public administrators are called upon to organize and participate in collaborative structures to meet a variety of community needs. While previous research demonstrates the power of collaboration in areas such as the delivery of public services (Silva, 2011), overcoming barriers to collective action (Ostrom, 1990), and achieving specific policy objectives (Agranoff & McGuire, 2003), less is known about how collaboration can improve administrative outcomes within a public organization. The purpose of this chapter is to explore how one local government leveraged collaborative governance in order to achieve improved administrative outcomes that yield both internal and external benefits to the organization. The collaboration examined involves the City of Tallahassee's Growth Management Department and private stakeholders, including developers, engineers, neighborhood members, and community advocates located in Tallahassee, Florida.

Growth Management: An Arena for Conflict?

Because localities offer a rich venue to pursue development and economic activity, the implementation of growth management is one of the most important responsibilities of local government. Growth management covers a range of regulatory practices that affect how, what, and where specific development may occur. As a result, the practice of growth management at the local level involves balancing the interests of both public and private stakeholders, while working toward a development plan that coincides with the community's vision of growth. In this combined role of facilitator and regulator, growth management is an arena for potential conflict, where opposing groups express divergent views about how a community develops (Feiock, 2004). Disputes over development issues are common in local communities because of differing expectations among interested parties that have a stake in the outcome of land-use decisions (Beatley, 1989). As a result of these tensions, divergent interests may find themselves at odds with each other, as well as at odds with the public entities that seek to implement and enforce local growth-management policies.

The Role of Collaborative Governance

For a locality that oversees growth-management functions, the question may arise as to how to mitigate conflict and seek consensus in regulatory arenas. In addition, the locality may also seek to improve its own administrative processes related to departmental functions. Here the role of collaborative governance provides insight into ways to both pursue conflict mitigation and achieve organizational improvements. Before addressing the specific roles of collaborative governance, a working definition of what is meant by *collaborative governance* must first be established. According to Purdy (2012), the concept of collaborative governance refers to "processes that seek to share power in decision-making with stakeholders in order to develop shared recommendations for effective, lasting solutions to public problems" (p. 409). This definition serves to ground the overarching purpose for employing the collaborative governance perspective adopted in this case.

Next, we will provide an overview of previous literature in the field of public administration that describes the structure and roles of collaborative governance. Collaboration often requires a leader or leading organization to spearhead a collaborative effort. In convening a stakeholder group, a public organization may serve as both the organizer as well as a participant in the joint effort. In such a capacity, the public entity has a responsibility to pay attention to how the collaboration is structured, including who participates, how frequently the group meets, and what outcomes are sought (Purdy, 2012). Research suggests that several factors influence the success of collaboration, including whether there is the opportunity for face-to-face interaction among group members, whether a shared understanding of objectives has been established, and whether a history of cooperation or conflict exists among group members (Ansell & Gash, 2008). As initiators and leaders of collaboration, public organizations may wish to focus on creating an environment that is conducive to building trust and on establishing open lines of communication.

Once the collaborative structure is initiated, collaborative governance may serve to move combative relationships beyond confrontation and toward cooperation (Ansell & Gash, 2008; Cooper, Bryer, & Meek, 2006). The literature suggests that increased interaction among stakeholders may help to build trust and commitment, which in turn reduces the barriers to cooperation and eventually results in progress toward shared goals (Agranoff & McGuire, 2003; Ostrom, 1990). Applied to a growth-management context, if tensions related to development exist within a local community, the engagement of various stakeholders through collaborative governance may play a role in building consensus related to the overarching goals of community development.

Another purpose of collaborative governance may be the pursuit of outcomes or results, including less tangible outcomes, such as consensus building, or more tangible outcomes, such as the provision of public services. The collaborative governance

Table 7.1

Purposes of Collaborative Governance

Purpose	Author(s)
Building consensus in the pursuit of shared goals	Agranoff and McGuire (2003)
	Ostrom (1990)
Addressing complex issues	McGuire (2006)
Increasing the legitimacy of public action	Purdy (2012)
Transforming adversarial relationships by developing trust	Cooper et al. (2006)

literature suggests that collaborative networks are useful in addressing complex issues that any one single organization may be challenged to confront (McGuire, 2006). By spanning organizational and sectoral boundaries, cooperating organizations may benefit from extending beyond the reach of their own limited supply of information, resources, and capacity. Further, collaboration presents an alternative to traditional management practices, which may increase the perceived legitimacy of public action (Purdy, 2012). Increased legitimacy is achieved by replacing a closed decision-making process with a participatory approach that is based on building shared commitment and trust. In such an approach, information and knowledge exchange is an outcome of collaboration that may lead to new courses of action or adjustments to existing practices and policies (Agranoff, 2006). Finally, another purpose of collaboration is to transform adversarial relationships by encouraging interaction and communication, which develops a positive feedback loop of trust among the partners and results in obtaining shared goals and objectives (Cooper et al., 2006). Following the previous literature, the purposes of collaborative governance are outlined in Table 7.1.

While several depictions of collaborative governance are available in the extant literature (Emerson, Nabatchi, & Balogh, 2011; Morse & Stephens, 2012; Purdy, 2012), here we adopt the model of collaborative governance put forth by Ansell and Gash (2008). Ansell and Gash depict a comprehensive model of collaborative governance by conducting a meta-analysis of 137 case studies that span programmatic disciplines as well as international contexts. As illustrated in Figure 7.1, their model emphasizes the following elements of collaborative governance: starting conditions, facilitative leadership, institutional design, collaborative processes, and outcomes.

As described by Ansell and Gash (2008), the starting conditions of the collaboration involve the incentives that stakeholders have for participating in the collaboration, the balance of power among group members, and the previous interactions that enable or discourage trust among the participants. For instance, whether the participants have a past history of cooperation and respect for one another versus a history of conflict and mistrust will influence whether the collaborative effort is successful. Next, the leadership aspect of collaborative governance encompasses who is responsible for bringing together and

Figure 7.1   **Governance Goals of Organizations Incorporated in the U.S.**

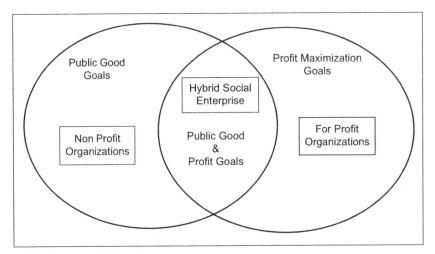

leading the engagement of participants in order to achieve shared objectives. In addition to who leads the effort, institutional design—or the rules and procedures that govern the collaboration—are necessary to determine whether the collaborative structure is perceived to be transparent and inclusive across a broad group of participants. Further, the collaborative process itself is viewed as a cyclical, reinforcing phenomenon whereby integral components of the collaboration are created and strengthened. Specifically, Ansell and Gash depict the collaborative process as facilitated by having face-to-face interaction, building trust and commitment between participants, obtaining intermediate outcomes, and developing a shared understanding of what the group can collectively achieve. Finally, the group will experience outcomes as a result of collaborative governance. As previously discussed, these results may be either tangible or less tangible outcomes. The model, however, depicts that the obtainment of such outcomes is influenced by the preceding elements of starting conditions, institutional design, leadership, and the collaborative process.

Building on this model of collaborative governance, this chapter highlights an example of a local government that utilizes collaborative governance in order to facilitate tangible administrative outcomes in growth management. Following Ansell and Gash's model, this case focuses on the starting conditions, leadership, institutional design, and collaborative processes employed by the public–private collaboration in order to achieve those administrative outcomes. Next, an in-depth examination of the collaboration is presented and the outcomes of the initiative are discussed.

COLLABORATION STARTING CONDITIONS

In response to the economic crises of 2007–2009, the municipal government of the City of Tallahassee (hereafter referred to as "the City") sought programs designed to stimulate the local economy through development and construction. One such program, which is the focus of this chapter, Private Sector Fast Tracking, was created to streamline or "fast track" private-sector development efforts by improving local growth-management processes. Instead of making the Private Sector Fast Tracking project solely a government effort, the City took a collaborative approach by inviting private stakeholders to identify and formulate recommendations for efficient growth-management practices that would also benefit the local economy (City of Tallahassee Commission Agenda Item, 2011; City of Tallahassee Growth Management, 2013).

According to Ansell and Gash, the ability to engage in successful collaborative governance is influenced by the starting conditions that are present for the collaboration. In the City of Tallahassee example, group participants reported being aware of each other either through involvement in local civic institutions, such as the Chamber of Commerce, or as competitors in the development arena. Thus, a previous history of interaction and familiarity was a starting condition that assisted in developing trust among the participants. Further contributing to the starting conditions of collaboration were impressions taken from previous public–private collaboration, which were described as "limited and painful." It was suggested by interviewees that in past experiences with public–private collaboration, "There were a lot of words, but there wasn't the commitment behind the words to get things done." This previous lack of commitment left some participants feeling uncertain about their involvement with this initiative. However, as described by the interviewees, one point of distinction in the collaboration at hand was the City's sincerity and desire to make administrative improvements in the growth-management arena. This authenticity and willingness for organizational change helped to overcome the history of negative associations with public–private collaboration taken from previous experiences.

FACILITATIVE LEADERSHIP

In terms of the collaborative governance model, here the City assumes the facilitative leadership role of bringing together participants and beginning the engagement process. With the support of the City Manager and Commission, city staff identified potential participants from the private sector that had direct experience with the local growth-management process ad that would represent a diversity of perspectives. For instance, individuals with experience in land development and construction, engineers, marketers, and citizens were all solicited to provide context and insight into various aspects of the existing growth-management procedures and policies. The specific individuals were selected based on their reputation with staff and the City Manager as respected leaders and technical experts in the development community who are also active participants in broader community issues. Participants who met these criteria and were deemed by staff as representative of all segments of the development community were recommended by staff to the City Manager for final selection.

The private-sector participants initially held varying opinions about their involvement in the collaboration, with one individual describing his reaction as "tentative," while others "thought it was great" and "appreciated the opportunity" to collaborate. Although divergent opinions initially existed about the collaboration, the city ultimately maintained the facilitative leadership role in order to encourage a meaningful dialogue about the local land-development process.

INSTITUTIONAL DESIGN

To begin this dialogue among participants, procedures for the collaboration were established. Namely, city staff initiated face-to-face meetings with citizens, developers, contractors, and civic organizations. During these meetings a broad range of feedback was solicited on both the barriers and opportunities related to local growth-management practices. Participants reported having common and yet also diverse experiences with the local growth-management process: "there's different-sized projects, different experiences, different examples yet . . . everybody certainly had throughout their career with working through growth management." This shared direct experience coupled with a diversity of angles or perspectives speaks to the inclusiveness of the collaboration's institutional design.

In the later stages of the collaboration, input, feedback, and discussion were obtained virtually from participants. These virtual meetings also provided an opportunity for staff to share the intent of the regulations and ask for feedback on ways that growth-management functions could be redesigned to be more effective in achieving a smooth development review process. The structure of these face-to-face and virtual interactions allowed for a transparent and inclusive approach that helped affirm the group's perceived openness and legitimacy.

COLLABORATIVE PROCESSES

Next, we will explore the collaborative processes that facilitated administrative outcomes. As discussed above, initially face-to-face meetings were used as a forum for staff to hear about the experiences the participants had with the permitting process and to get suggestions for improvement. This supports Ansell and Gash's model of collaborative governance in which face-to-face dialogue builds a reinforcing cycle of trust among participants and ultimately leads to developing a shared understanding of what the group can accomplish. As a result of these conversations, a shared understanding of the goals for the collaboration were arrived at by the group, including reducing the review time for private-sector projects; changing the role of city staff from regulators to facilitators, while still protecting the community's quality of life; and improving customer service. To achieve these goals, participants outlined recommendations that could be made to the City's growth-management functions immediately, in the short term, and in the long term.

During the collaborative process phase, interviewees indicate that disagreement did occur at times; however, mutual trust and open communication allowed the collaboration to continue. One factor that appears to contribute to this reinforcing cycle of commitment is the trust and respect that group members developed throughout the collaboration: "We all respect each other and our opinions . . . we didn't agree on everything, but we could debate things. Pretty much we agreed that it's ice cream, we just debated on which flavor it is." Another interviewee stressed the importance of continuing communication and involvement: "The lines of communication need to stay open and absolutely I think whenever there's a change that could impact economic development in a community, it needs to be broadcast, it needs to be shared and vetted very carefully before it's adopted." Thus, common themes from interviewees confirm that certain elements of the process, such as building trust and developing shared understandings, are crucial in facilitating a successful collaboration. The next section examines specific administrative outcomes and improvements in local growth management that resulted from this public–private collaboration.

RESULTS FROM COLLABORATIVE GOVERNANCE: OBTAINING OUTCOMES

According to Ansell and Gash's model of collaborative governance, outcomes are a final result of collaboration. This collaboration resulted in 26 recommendations to city staff and the City Commission to improve administrative outcomes. The recommendations were categorized into process improvements, code improvements/ordinance changes, organizational improvements, and information improvements. The City Commission ultimately approved the committee's slate of recommendations, and these improvements still persist today. A description of the substantive changes in each category of administrative outcomes is described below.

Process Changes

A fundamental process improvement was the adoption of multi-departmental performance standards. Prior to this change, there were no defined performance standards for resubmittals, and there were no multi-departmental defined performance standards for new applications. Strict review timeframes for staff across all city departments were adopted so that environmental permit and site plan resubmittals were required to be reviewed by staff within seven working days. Environmental permit review times were also reduced.

Another important process change was adding a representative from the electric utilities department to the development review team to facilitate coordination between the placement of utilities and the preservation of environmental features at the earliest point in the permitting process. Prior to this change, developers often expressed frustration over learning about conflicts late in the process. Another notable process change was developing a conflict-resolution protocol that would allow members of the City's development review team to internally resolve what would otherwise be competing or contradictory conditions that would adversely affect the development. Other process changes included improving staff and applicant communication on project resubmittals and creating a simultaneous site plan and rezoning process. Overall, these process changes served to create more accountability and certainty in the development review process.

Code and Ordinance Changes

The group also submitted recommendations for improvements to the land development code to streamline the permitting process. Three significant ordinance changes were adopted by the City Commission based on the group's recommendation. The first ordinance change was to the site plan review thresholds for development projects. A site plan review is the process of reviewing documents that detail the proposed land use and activities of the development in accordance with existing ordinances to ensure that a proposal meets local zoning standards as well as state statutes. There are two levels of review for site plan applications: Type A and Type B. Type A site plans have a one-week review time and are reviewed through an informal process by a staff committee. Type B site plans have a one-month review time and are reviewed by a more formal administrative body, the Development Review Committee. Prior to the ordinance change, the determination of whether a project was subject to a Type A or a Type B review depended on the size of the project, the zoning district in which the project was located, and whether variances to zoning standards were needed. The ordinance recommended by the committee revised the development review thresholds so that all projects are subject to Type A site plan review unless a variance is required. This creates an incentive for developers to meet the regulations and not seek variances in order to reduce the review time.

The second ordinance change was based on the committee's recommendation to modify the environmental review procedures required through the Natural Features Inventory process. This change provided greater flexibility in defining the area of the site subject to the environmental survey requirements to correspond only to the area where development will occur, rather than corresponding with the entire parcel boundary. This change saves developers time and money by reducing surveying costs without sacrificing the quality of the environmental reviews and the protection of features. As a result of these collective ordinance modifications, the timeframes for reviewing development applications were reduced considerably. A summary of the changes in the review timeframes associated with the environmental permitting and site plan review processes is presented in Table 7.2.

The third ordinance recommended by the committee and adopted by the City Commission revised regulations that required design review through an Urban Design Commission for minor projects. The ordinance authorized staff to conduct the design reviews for minor projects, which saves time and reduces steps in the development review process, while still requiring projects to adhere to the same high-quality architectural standards. Overall, these improvements were designed to create regulatory incentives for compliance with the land development code by reducing the review timeframe for projects that meet the adopted community standards, better align the

Table 7.2

City of Tallahassee Growth Management Permitting Timelines, Pre and Post Fast Tracking

Application Type	Prior to Fast Tracking	Actual Average, Post Fast Tracking	Percent Time Reduction
Standard Environmental Permit	Up to 100 days	52 days	(–48%)
Type A Site Plan Process	Up to 120 days	75 days	(–37%)
Type B Site Plan Process	Up to 135 days	73 days	(–46%)

Source: City of Tallahassee Commission Agenda Item, 2011

environmental surveying requirements to only the affected areas, and delegate decision-making authority for design review to staff for minor projects.

Information Improvements

The committee also recommended a number of information improvements, ranging from enhancing growth management's web presence to the development of a customer service "top ten" list of deficiencies that staff sees with permit applications and ways to avoid them. Another significant information improvement was the development of a "post permitting" electronic customer survey designed to provide staff with feedback on specific projects immediately upon completion of permitting so that customers had a simple way to provide feedback and so staff could learn where improvements were needed. An additional information improvement was the development of a Process Improvement Working Group to share ideas about the permitting process and make recommendations about potential ordinance and process changes needed for continuous improvement. These informational improvements serve both to provide effective feedback to the public organization and to facilitate the development process for private stakeholders.

Organizational Improvements

The committee further recommended that staff adopt a new role of customer advocacy and customer-friendly facilitation of development. The group felt that staff should use their expertise and creativity to better assist customers in designing projects that are consistent with the adopted community standards in the most efficient manner. The change, as recommended by the committee, was essentially a cultural change in which the role of staff would shift from regulator to facilitator. As reported by one interviewee, the cultural change has been tangible and significant: "They (growth management staff) literally took me into the back room, sat down, and helped me do everything I'm supposed

Table 7.3

Summary of Major Administrative Improvements Recommended by Committee

Process Changes	Adopting multi-departmental performance standards Increasing coordination among city departments and addition of a conflict-resolution mechanism in the development review process
Code Improvements/ Ordinance Changes	Increasing use of Type A site plan reviews to reduce review time Aligning the environmental surveying requirements to only the affected areas Delegating decision-making authority for design review to staff for minor projects
Information Improvements	Developing an electronic post-permitting customer survey feedback process Establishing continuous information exchange through standing work group
Organizational Improvements	Shifting organizational culture to support customer advocacy and a facilitation orientation

to do, led me like a lamb and made it happen. It was, to me, the way it should be. I felt like a customer and not like I was imposing on somebody." Shifting an organization's culture can be a challenge; however, receiving feedback from the stakeholders of a public agency can serve as an effective impetus for change.

Table 7.3 provides an overview of the committee's major recommendations to modify growth-management functions in the City of Tallahassee across the four key areas.

Numerous projects have benefited from the changes that were adopted as part of the fast-tracking initiative. For example, a former grocery-shopping center was left with few tenants after the grocery anchor relocated; however, the site has been recently redeveloped into a thriving shopping center under the new growth-management protocols. The redevelopment site is over 17 acres and located at the intersection of two of Tallahassee's major roadways in the central part of town. The site benefited from the Type A site plan review, which reduced review time from one month to one week, as well as from resubmittal review timeframes of seven days, reduced from a previously undefined standard. Furthermore, the redevelopment was subject to the significant benefits associated with the Natural Features Inventory review changes, which reduced on-site environmental surveying requirements and consulting fees substantially.

Similarly, a logistics distribution center of approximately 125,000 square feet on over 16 acres was able to utilize the Type A site plan process with a one-week review time, rather than one month, based on the fast-tracking ordinances. Using a comparable approach to the grocery center example, this site also benefited from the changes to the Natural Features Inventory and site plan review processes. Both of these projects demonstrate the ongoing benefit of the public–private collaboration and the solutions that were put forward and actualized in the community. As a result, both redevelopment and growth objectives for the city are being achieved in a reduced timeframe and at less expense, without compromising environmental features or the quality of review. In Figure 7.2, a conceptual map of Tallahassee's collaborative governance structure is depicted following the Ansell and Gash model.

Figure 7.2   **Tallahassee's Collaborative Governance Conceptual Map**

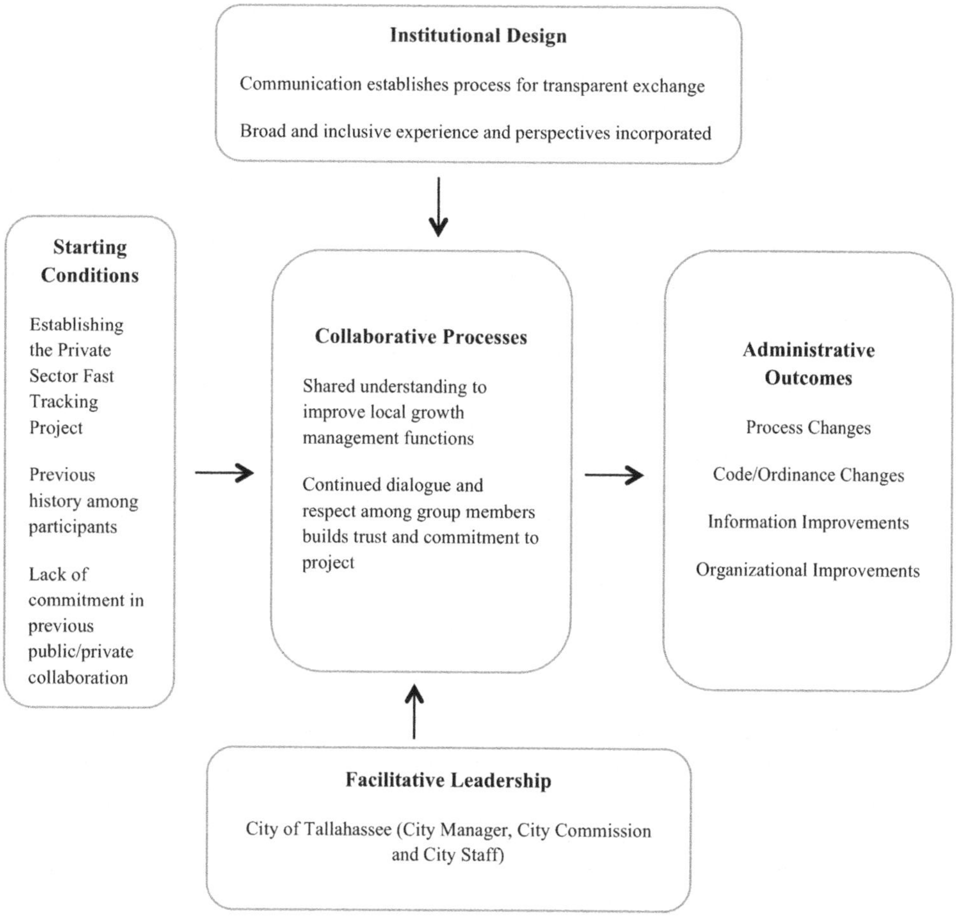

Institutional Design

Communication establishes process for transparent exchange

Broad and inclusive experience and perspectives incorporated

Starting Conditions

Establishing the Private Sector Fast Tracking Project

Previous history among participants

Lack of commitment in previous public/private collaboration

Collaborative Processes

Shared understanding to improve local growth management functions

Continued dialogue and respect among group members builds trust and commitment to project

Administrative Outcomes

Process Changes

Code/Ordinance Changes

Information Improvements

Organizational Improvements

Facilitative Leadership

City of Tallahassee (City Manager, City Commission and City Staff)

Note: This model is adapted from the work of Ansell and Gash, 2008.

In their entirety, the administrative outcomes produced through this example of collaborative governance have several implications for development regulation in Tallahassee, namely, more accountability and certainty in the development review process, a reduction of review timeframes, a cultural shift to be customer-centric, and increased empowerment for staff to make decisions on minor projects. Finally, interviewees indicate that they found this to be a successful effort and they would participate in future collaborations, so long as the effort embodies a sincere desire for action and results. This suggests that achieving shared goals in one collaborative effort may contribute to the positive starting conditions needed to fuel future collaborative processes. Next, we will conclude with a list of general recommendations that other public organizations may wish to consider when establishing collaborative governance mechanisms to achieve administrative outcomes.

CONCLUSIONS AND KEY POINTS

It is well-known that public and private organizations gravitate toward different purposes, and thus their perspectives in achieving their objectives may also vary. However,
providing the opportunity for meaningful interaction through collaboration is a cross-
cutting strategy that can benefit both public and private stakeholders. Although the
Private Sector Fast Tracking program originated as a response to the economic crisis,
the administrative outcomes achieved ensure that the improvements continued well after
the immediate threat of economic crisis had subsided. As reported in participant interviews, the City has been able to attract new investment and capital to the community, in
part because "local government has become much more willing to sit down and work
through the (development) process." In this sense, the City has been successful in meeting its goal of making lasting improvements to administrative functions that also benefit
community stakeholders.

In this case, the Ansell and Gash (2008) model of collaborative governance provides a lens through which we can understand the dynamics that lead to successful
collaborative governance. Although the case described here examines a public–private
collaboration undertaken by the City of Tallahassee, the insights gleaned from this
example extend beyond just a single jurisdiction or functional area of public administration. The generalizable insights into creating successful public-private collaboration
include the following:

- *Seek broad participation and inclusiveness in designing collaborative governance.* When pursuing a public–private collaboration, diverse perspectives within a
shared experience matters. Utilizing a "360-degree" approach to receive input and
feedback will not only yield valuable information as to how different stakeholders
view an experience, but can also increase the perceived transparency of the collaboration. Further, by engaging citizens and private stakeholders in problem solving,
new solutions to existing challenges may be discovered. Soliciting varied perspectives of direct experiences will enhance the information exchange of the group and
may increase the overall depth, relevance, and effectiveness of the outcomes.
- *Develop a shared understanding and be prepared for action.* Sincerity and a commitment to make meaningful improvements help to develop trust among participants, and eventually lead to a shared understanding of the goals of collaborative
governance. Participants should feel open in communicating their expectations
of the collaboration, and once a shared understanding of the overarching goals is
reached, participants should be prepared to follow through with action. By obtaining improved outcomes in one collaborative effort, a positive trust-building loop
may encourage participation in future collaborative activities.
- *Public organizations can (and should) lead the way to collaboration.* Do not under-
estimate the potential role of the public sector in leading collaborative efforts. Public organizations should proactively seek opportunities for collaboration by serving
in the role of a facilitative leader. By investing the time and effort in collaboration,

an organization may experience significant results that are both tangible and less tangible. For instance, initiating a collaborative effort is a low-cost way to increase the perceived openness and legitimacy of government action, but it can also produce tangible administrative outcomes. Thus, proactively seeking public–private interaction may lead to improved organizational and societal outcomes, in addition to garnering good will among stakeholders going forward.

As the convener of a collaborative effort, a public organization must be aware of how the process of collaboration is structured. In this case, the City of Tallahassee was able to improve the delivery of local growth-management functions by reframing the exchange between government and the private sector as participatory and inclusive. A potential consequence of public organizations failing to engage in collaborative strategies is the promulgation of rules and policies that are not connected to the experience of those who are most directly affected by said policies. Additionally, a lack of collaboration may also threaten the perceived legitimacy of public action as governments work to implement public policies. Although many public organizations embrace values of fairness, transparency, and democracy, they might consider that responsiveness, innovation, and collaboration are also expectations among their stakeholders.

Further, collaboration may assist in establishing critical communication channels that span multiple organizations and perspectives. The establishment of such communication channels is one way for public organizations to receive critical feedback on the impact and effectiveness of policies and may lead to reforming certain public institutions and processes. Finally, as seen in the City of Tallahassee example, a cooperative approach can minimize potential conflict in the regulatory process by proactively obtaining consensus regarding reasonable recommendations for public processes, as well as by connecting individuals across sectors. This case can be seen as one example of how to create collaborative opportunities among public and private stakeholders. Such collaborations counter the popular narrative of discord between the sectors and demonstrate that collaboration can create win-win situations for government organizations and the stakeholders that they serve.

The Tallahassee example presented in this research has broad applicability to other jurisdictions as a model of both administrative reform and general public–private collaboration to solve problems. From the regulatory perspective, Tallahassee is not unique in its challenges to effectively balance land-use regulation and preservation of community character with the desire for economic development and job creation. This example offers a framework that other communities can adopt to create partnerships with public and private stakeholders to help balance the interests of development and overall community and improve outcomes in the arena of land use. Tallahassee's example also provides a more general model of collaboration that has broad applicability as a method for addressing problems in government administration that span such service areas as public works, solid waste, storm water, planning, code enforcement, and economic development, in order to produce positive administrative outcomes and results in the community.

REFERENCES

Agranoff, R. (2006). Inside collaborative networks: Ten lessons for public managers. *Public Administration Review, 66,* 56–65.

Agranoff, R., & McGuire, M. (2003). *Collaborative public management: New strategies for local government.* Washington, DC: Georgetown University Press.

Ansell, C., & Gash, A. (2008). Collaborative governance in theory and practice. *Journal of Public Administration Research and Theory, 18,* 543–571.

Beatley, T. (1989). The role of expectations and promises in land use decision-making. *Policy Sciences, 22*(1), 27–50.

City of Tallahassee Commission Agenda Item. (2011). *Development review improvements and customer service initiative (Private sector fast tracking).* Authored by Karen M. Jumonville, Director of Growth Management, City of Tallahassee.

City of Tallahassee Growth Management. (2013). *City of Tallahassee development review fast tracking and customer service initiative.* Retrieved September 25, 2013, from www.talgov.com/growth/growth-fasttracking.aspx

Cooper, T. L., Bryer, T. A., & Meek, J. W. (2006). Citizen-centered collaborative public management. *Public Administration Review, 66,* 76–88.

Emerson, K., Nabatchi, T., & Balogh, S. (2011). An integrative framework for collaborative governance. *Journal of Public Administration Research and Theory, 22,* 1–29.

Feiock, R. C. (2004). Politics, institutions and local land-use regulation. *Urban Studies, 41*(2), 363–375.

McGuire, M. (2006). Collaborative public management: Assessing what we know and how we know it. *Public Administration Review, 66,* 33–43.

Morse, R. S., & Stephens, J. B. Teaching collaborative governance: Phases, competencies, and case-based learning. *Journal of Public Affairs Education, 18*(3), 565–583.

Ostrom, E. (1990). *Governing the commons.* Cambridge: Cambridge University Press.

Purdy, J. M. (2012). A Framework for assessing power in collaborative governance processes. *Public Administration Review, 72*(3), 409–417.

Silva, C. (2011). Collaborative governance concepts for successful network leadership. *State and Local Government Review, 43*(1), 66–71.

Part IV

Finance and Innovation

8

Public–Private Collaboration and Trust Funds of the U.S. States

Joshua Franzel and Ryan Gregory

U.S. state public employee retirement funds and other public trusts continue to play important roles in managing state assets accumulated from public employee and employer retirement contributions, the sale and rental of public lands, revenues generated from the extraction of natural resources, and investment returns, among other sources. Realized investment income and (sometimes) principal are used to pay for the retirement income and health care of public employees, supplement funding for state initiatives, underwrite infrastructure projects, and provide direct and indirect subsidies to state residents, among other purposes.

Although the terms of fund establishment, types of revenues, financial and governance structures, broad investment policies, and purposes of the generated investment revenue are determined by public elected and appointed officials through constitutions, statutes, and other related policies, states and their funds often work closely with private-sector, quasi-governmental, and nonprofit firms in administering the funds and their assets. The nongovernmental organizations involved manage assets, provide financial analyses, prepare key reports, and, more generally, provide management consulting and organizational support services to state entities ultimately responsible for overseeing the funds. These multi-sector arrangements have not been the focus of much academic or practitioner research, yet they play important roles in states' ability to effectively manage their assets, both in the short and long term.

To describe and provide context to the public-private-nonprofit relationships that have been established to manage a range of public trust funds, this chapter will start by covering previous research themes about state trusts and investment pools. It will then provide a brief overview of state public pension structures, investments, and the organizations involved in fund management and administration. Similarly, the non-pension trusts, such as funds that have been established to invest natural resource revenues and employee and employer contributions for future retiree health care, will be described. The chapter will then conclude with three brief case descriptions of trusts that use some form of public-private-nonprofit arrangement to manage fund assets and inform fund administration: the Texas Permanent University Fund, the Ohio Public Employees Retirement System, and the Colorado Local Government Liquid Asset Trust. These case descriptions have been selected due to their variations in purposes, structures, revenue sources, geography, and other attributes. The research of this chapter aims to advance the understanding of how multi-sector organizational relationships are used to manage important and complex public initiatives, such as public trusts.

STATE TRUSTS/INVESTMENT POOLS AND PUBLIC–PRIVATE PARTNERSHIPS

There has been a range of previous literature written about governmental trusts, including their establishment, challenges, and potential. The previous literature described below and, more generally, this chapter overall is offered as a descriptive piece. It is important to keep in mind that all funds have been established in unique policy environments and for a range of purposes. There is not one best way to structure and manage these funds.

Public pension funds, are public trust funds for the specific purpose of providing retirement income to government employees. The funds receive income from employer and (often) employee contributions, as well as investment income. Portions of the funds' assets are and will be used to provide payments to public retirees "as an exact dollar amount, such as $100 per month at retirement. Or, more commonly, it may calculate a benefit through a plan formula that considers such factors as salary and service."[1] Public pension funds are managed with the oversight of a board of trustees or some other committee.[2] This structure is similar to how private pension funds are run. However, private pension funds are governed by federal law as part of the Employee Retirement Income Security Act of 1976, whereas public pensions are typically subject to the state or local laws in which the pension fund is located.[3]

Public non-pension funds, for the sake of discussion within this chapter, are defined as those public funds not involving pensions (or retiree health care) of public employees. They are also frequently called public purpose trust funds. These funds can take a variety of forms and serve a variety of purposes, and they are created through legislation for specific policy objectives.[4] In the case of non-pension funds, their creation came about, in part, from the recognition of the unutilized potential of cash balances retained[5] or large revenue increases realized by state and local governments. In 1968, J. Richard Aronson estimated that forgone interest earnings could exceed $100 million annually.[6] Adjusted for inflation, using U.S. Bureau of Labor Statistics estimates, Aronson's 1968 number of $100 million equates to just under $675 million in today's dollars.[7] In the face of diminishing revenues and a reduced ability to raise taxes, governments recognized that they needed to find innovative ways to generate additional revenues.[8] Also, some governments needed an effective way to manage and save portions of revenue spikes and/or sustained increases in income from their natural resource assets.

At the local level, a common example of these funds is state investment pools. This arrangement began in the mid-1970s as state and local governments began to feel the effects of high inflation, which made investing entirely in traditional ways, such as treasury bonds, not ideal.[9] This was due to the inflation rates outpacing any such yields received. The pools also arose, in part, due to an increased interest among state governments in providing oversight and assistance to local governments' management of their cash funds.[10] The intent of these pools continues to be to provide local governments with "an attractive and relatively safe investment option."[11] The pools offered local governments the ability to recognize the benefits of economy of scale and achieve higher rates of return than if they invested on their own. These pools are also typically administered by officials with high levels of investment expertise.[12]

Some concerns exist regarding trust funds' lack of direct, democratically elected oversight. Legislative and constitutionally enacted limitations to the funds' uses remove the ability for elected representatives to use the funds for general purposes.[13] Alternatively, these constitution-level limits can be viewed as a firewall against instances of legislative "raids" of the funds.[14] These concerns come at the same time that others view the existing transparency and oversight layers of the funds as inefficient. The "burden" of answering to elected officials and the public, along with various state oversight policies, dampen the ability of these pools to maximize their rates of return.[15] Political pressure has also been noted to influence investment decisions of public trust funds.[16]

More generally, the move toward engaging the private sector in the management of public funds can be viewed as part of the larger movement to reinvent government and new public management.[17] These movements espouse the efficiencies found in the private sector and advocate for government to adopt more characteristics of the private sector. This includes a variety of measures, such as referring to citizens as customers and a rise in outsourcing of public services to private companies for service delivery.

Although some of the literature on investment pools focuses on the downside of these funds, benefits exist.[18] As mentioned previously, investment pools came about in part due to the need for local governments to find innovative ways to generate revenue in environments where raising taxes is not a realistic option. These investment pools hold the potential to generate revenue without the addition of new or increased taxes and fees.[19] Investment pools, particularly during periods of economic downturn or recession, have been found to potentially serve as the best and safest investment option for local governments.[20] Certain types of funds generally enjoy greater and easier support than others. The wider the direct or indirect benefit distribution among the population, the greater support the funds enjoy.[21] When an individual or organization sees a benefit, be it a cash payout or some other obvious direct or indirect benefit, such as the financing of school structure improvements, they are more likely to support a fund's existence.

Why U.S. State Governments Established Funds

Governments have established public trusts for a variety of reasons. Many funds have been established to manage and invest public employer and (often) employee contributions used to pre-fund all or portions of future benefit costs for public workers. As an example, the Ohio Public Employees Retirement System will be described later in this chapter. Another, separate reason is a preference by the public to restrict the funds' access by government officials. The funds are earmarked for specific purposes and with limited access by officials. Many times, the fund is managed by separate entities, with oversight of government bodies, such as state legislatures or city councils (Anderson,

2002). This is the case with the Texas Permanent University Fund, which will be discussed later in the chapter. Another reason for some funds' establishment centers on the need to invest idle cash reserves. In the case of the government investment pools, they were formed to raise revenue from idle cash without having to increase taxes in an anti-tax environment (Aronson, 1968; Coe, 1988; Hayes, 1999; Kearns, 1995; Modlin & Stewart, 2012). These investment pools are intended to provide relatively safe options for primarily local governments to invest this idle cash (Bunch, 1999; Modlin & Stewart, 2013). As an example, the Colorado Local Government Liquid Asset Trust will be described later. Finally, in addition to other reasons, these funds may exist as part of the outsourcing movement of New Public Management governance efforts—the belief that private financial managers could operate with lower costs while achieving higher investment returns relative to their public counterparts. The funds' segregation from the general funds of government operation and oversight more easily allow for such privatization to occur. An example of this move is the Texas municipal investment pool, called TexPool. This fund, under the administration of the Texas State Comptroller, made a move to outsource many of its functions to private companies through a public bidding process (Bunch, 1999).

States Attempting to Increasing Funds' Potential through Public–Private Collaboration and Aggregating Available Monies

These trusts typically offer higher rates of returns than when governments invest on their own (Bunch, 1999; Coronado, Engen, & Knight, 2003; Thompson, 1988). The reasons for this come down to two major factors. One is the professionally trained financial investors administering the pool and the generally superior investment skills they bring to the table. This expertise gap between government and the investment pool can hold particularly true for smaller governments. A second factor is simple economies of scale. The investment pools are a collection of tens, hundreds, or even thousands of member governments, with collectively large amounts to invest. This permits, for example, the purchase of high-denomination bonds producing higher yields (Bunch, 1999; Thompson, 1988).

An additional distinction and potential benefit is the de-politicization of the funds' management (Coronado et al., 2003). The segregation of these dollars from the direct political process and general funds can lead to more efficient fund management. Proponents of this view argue this de-politicization means decisions on the funds' management are not based on elected officials' desires for reelection, but rather on what constitutes a good investment or management move for the fund. These goals can pose challenges and will be the focus of the next section.

States Balancing Efficiency with Accountability and Transparency

A classic dichotomy within public administration applies to public trust funds. The balancing of the values of efficiency with accountability and transparency are frequently in contrast. Borrowing from Rubin (1996), accountability of public funds comes in four major facets: (1) responding to authority within the government bureaucracy or hierarchy, (2) expenditure reporting to the public, (3) responsibility of elected officials for budget outcomes, and (4) citizens' direct control of government. Conversely, seeking maximum efficiency within public trust funds means seeking the highest return on investment for the lowest administrative cost possible. According to Rubin (1996), this push for efficiency has led to policy changes that allow for relaxed investment policies and less oversight of these funds. Although this allows for more entrepreneurial investment strategies and fewer restrictions, it may reduce the public's ability to monitor and evaluate the practices of these funds. Also, elected officials and other government staff, by design, may be kept away from the funding decisions of these trusts (Anderson, 2002). It can be a challenging balance between flexibility and public accountability. Public trust funds may be at least one step removed from direct oversight of the public, with many of their functions contracted out to private entities (Anderson, 2002; Bunch, 1999). Although potential benefits include the de-politicization of the fund's management (Bunch, 1999), the ability of the public to weigh in on the fund's management may also be limited.

Recognizing the efficiency and accountability/transparency dichotomy and its effects is critical for the public administrator when making decisions related to public trust fund management. Past research has suggested that providing oversight in the form of guidelines for investment and limitations as to the type of investments allowed should be strongly considered (Hayes, 1999) and may serve as a balance to complete autonomy of these funds.

U.S. STATE GOVERNMENT PENSION, RETIREE HEALTH CARE, AND NON-RETIREMENT U.S. STATE FUNDS: THE CURRENT ENVIRONMENT

U.S. State Pension Systems and Retiree Health Care Trusts

According to the U.S. Census Bureau's Annual Survey of Public Pensions, there are approximately 222 state and almost 3,200 local government retirement systems[22] across the U.S., which often cover the range of state workers, including general, education, and public-safety employees, among other groups. These systems came into existence in all states between the 1930s and mid-1970s.[23] As of the third quarter of 2013, these systems held about $3.7 trillion dollars in assets.[24] The systems' assets historically (1982–2011) have been composed of a combination of government employer contributions (26%), employee contributions (13%), and investment earnings (61%).[25] In the aggregate, as of 2012, these pension funds had an asset allocation of 48% in equities, both domestic and international; 24% in fixed income, both domestic and international; 7% in real estate; 2% in cash and short term; and 17% in alternative and investments, such as private equity, private infrastructure, commodities, etc.[26] The sponsoring government may limit the asset classes within which a fund can invest and/or limit the amount invested within an asset class, among other restrictions.

Depending on the legal and policy environment, size of the system, and other factors, some combination of the following constituencies make up the retirement systems' governing boards: retirees, current employees, elected officials, citizens, management, appointed officials, union representatives, and others.[27] Among other responsibilities, these boards determine the systems' investment strategies and asset allocations, often in coordination with an investment committee, state investment board, and/or government officials.[28] The systems and their boards may contract with private-sector consultants for advice, money management, administration, actuarial services, and other services. Specifically related to asset management, depending on the system, all assets may be managed internally, all assets may be managed externally, or a mix of internal and external management may be used; the majority of the main state systems use a mixed approach.[29] Although there are a range of reasons for outsourcing certain components of fund asset management, often it is done to allow the fund to acquire external knowledge and expertise—needs that evolve over time, both by subject matter and level—without the public fund entity having to expand internal organizational capacities.

Aside from pension trusts, state and local governments (and possibly employees) may set aside and invest funds to cover future retiree health care liabilities. Although there has been an uptick in the number of states setting funds aside, most state and local governments have not or have not done so at a rate that will allow them to fully prefund the benefit.[30] That said, examples of states that have set funds aside are the Alaska Retiree Health Care Trust, which has $5.9 billion in assets (as of 6/30/13), with an FY13 asset allocation of 66% fixed income and 34% domestic and international equities,[31] and has its assets managed both internally and externally,[32] and the Ohio Public Employees Retirement System Health Care Plan, which has $12.8 billion in invested assets (as of 12/31/12), with an FY12 asset allocation of 37.5% in fixed income and 53.9% in equities, with the rest in a combination of private equity, derivatives, hedge funds, short-term, and cash.[33] The Ohio Public Employees Retirement System Health Care Plan has internal and external advisors and investment managers.[34]

Non-Retirement U.S. State Funds

Between the mid-1800s and 2011, several U.S. states established trusts to manage and invest revenues they receive from the sale and rental of public lands and severance taxes and fees associated with the extraction of state natural resources. Portions of the investment gains are used for a range of public purposes, from dividends paid to state residents to education programs to infrastructure projects to more general state expenditures. Examples include the Alaska Permanent Fund, which held $50 billion in assets at the end of FY13;[35] Permanent Wyoming Mineral Trust Fund, which held $6 billion in assets at the end of FY13;[36] and North Dakota Legacy Fund, which held $1 billion in assets at the end of FY13.[37] The largest eight U.S. funds manage over $122 billion in assets.[38] These and other U.S. funds invest in a combination of equities, fixed income, real estate, cash/short term, and alternatives. Some of the U.S. funds manage most or all of their assets internally, whereas others contract with external asset managers, or nongovernmental/

quasi-public entities have been created to manage the funds in coordination with the sponsoring governments. Often these governments have fund boards that provide fund oversight and guidance while also setting and/or ensuring the implementation of investment policy.

CASE DESCRIPTIONS

Public–private collaboration takes many forms within the trust funds of the U.S. states. To provide some additional detail, three case descriptions are offered that describe the public-private-nonprofit arrangements that have been established to manage fund assets and inform fund administration: The Texas Permanent University Fund, the Ohio Public Employees Retirement System, and the Colorado Local Government Liquid Asset Trust. These case descriptions range in terms of fund purpose, internal and external organizational structures, sources of non-investment income, geography, and other characteristics.

The Texas Permanent University Fund (PUF) was created through the state constitution in 1876. Between its creation and 1883, over two million acres of Texas land were appropriated to the fund.[39] Aside from investment earnings, the fund receives revenue from the sale of public lands under its control and from severance and rental charges on natural resource extraction, such as oil, gas, and water, from public lands.[40] Income from grazing and a certain portion of non-principal investment income are provided to the two university systems.[41]

The Board of Regents of the University of Texas system is responsible for overseeing the fund and in 1996 contracted with the University of Texas Investment Management Company (UTIMCO), a 501(c)(3) entity, to manage and invest the fund's capital.[42] UTIMCO manages other funds for the board as well. UTIMCO is overseen by a board composed of at least three appointees, three members of the University of Texas system board and the system's chancellor, and two members of the Texas A&M system board.[43] UTIMCO employs investment staff and contracts with external consultants to manage and invest the fund's assets with the objective of maintaining the real value of PUF assets, given inflation, while also distributing funds to the university systems (at the end of calendar year 2013, the rate was 4.75%).[44] The public–nonprofit arrangement was designed to provide public oversight to fund governance, while allowing non-public finance expertise to manage and invest the fund assets.[45] At the end of FY13, PUF held $15.3 billion in assets, which were invested in investment funds ($10.5 billion), equity securities ($1.9 billion), cash ($1.2 billion), debt securities ($814 million), and other categories, such as preferred stock, convertible securities, purchased options, and physical commodities.[46] In FY13 the fund distributed $644 million to the state university systems.[47]

The Ohio Public Employees Retirement System (OPERS) has two funds: the defined benefit pension plan, established in 1935, and the Health Care Preservation Plan, established in 2004. These funds receive revenue from state (and local) government employer and employee contributions, in addition to asset investment returns, and will ultimately be used to pay for public employee pensions and a portion of retiree health care.[48] As of the end of calendar year 2012, the pension plan held $67.6 billion in assets, and the health-care plan held $12.8 billion. These assets were invested in a combination of fixed income (27% for the pension plan and 38% for the health-care plan) and domestic and international equities (44% for the pension plan and 54% for the health-care plan), with the rest in private equities, real estate, derivatives and hedge funds, and cash.[49] The funds are overseen by the OPERS board, an 11-person board of individuals elected by employee groups and the appointees of state-elected officials; more broadly, the state legislature governs the retirement system through the Ohio Retirement Study Council.[50] Aside from general system management, guided by state statute, the OPERS board is responsible for the funds' oversight and for setting investments policies that seek to maximize returns while working within certain risk parameters. To help achieve these goals, OPERS has an investment division composed of around 60 staff members who manage some of the assets internally and monitor external brokers and private sector firms that manage public market, private equity, and real estate investments.[51] The staff members also identify, hire, and oversee private-sector investment advisors, actuaries, and other professionals.[52] More specifically, as the OPERS Defined Benefit Fund and Health Care Fund "Investment Objectives and Asset Allocation Policy" reports outline, the system's "Board may appoint Advisors unaffiliated with OPERS" to evaluate the annual investment plans and proposals, review portfolio guidelines and benchmarks, monitor investments and independently report on performance, conduct special projects requested by OPERS, provide staff support, and perform other duties.[53] Independent actuaries also work with the system to provide asset and liability forecasts and to recommend interest rate, inflation, investment, mortality, turnover, medical/health care inflation cost, and other assumptions to be considered and potentially adopted by the OPERS board.[54] Estimates from 2014 offer that about 34% of assets are managed internally and 66% managed externally. The OPERS investment plan notes that internal management comes as a lower cost due to lower salaries, more of the assets being managed passively, the absence of a profit motive, and the efficiencies that come from OPERS larger, centralized organization.[55]

The Colorado Local Government Liquid Asset Trust (ColoTrust) was created in 1985 as a way for Colorado local governments to temporarily pool their cash for investment purposes.[56] Local governments eligible to participate in ColoTrust as members include municipalities, counties, school districts, and special districts. Currently, over 1,200 local government entities participate in the trust, and the Trust controls assets of over $3 billion.[57] The fund is statutory and follows strict state statutes allowing its creation.

The trust is governed by not only the Colorado state statutes but also the articles set forth in ColoTrust's Indenture of Trust, which serves as the trust's bylaws or charter.[58] The trust is overseen by a board of trustees and officers made up of representatives from trust members. These members are high-level staff, such as finance directors or elected officials from the member organizations. That board appoints and hires an administrator, who hires and oversees professional staff and counsel to manage the trust on behalf of the members. Currently, through an agreement for services, a private company, Public Trust Advisors, serves as the administrator of the Trust.[59] The range of services provided by the private company, as administrator, includes asset allocation, management, and reporting. In addition, a private legal firm serves as legal counsel to advise the trust and a private audit firm provides independent audits. Therefore, in the case of ColoTrust, the fund is completely managed day-to-day by private companies.

CONCLUSION

Across the U.S., a variety of fund types exist and play important roles in providing capital to pay for the pension liabilities of states and localities; managing natural resource revenues so that they may benefit many generations of state residents; and helping governments pre-fund retiree health-care obligations, among other roles. Intertwined in the public roles of these funds are the subject-matter expertise and organizational support capacities brought via arrangements with private and nongovernmental firms. These arrangements, although important, have received little attention in research. This chapter is offered as a descriptive piece to provide information about the current U.S. pension, retiree health trust, and non-retirement U.S. state fund sectors, and the public-private-nonprofit relationships that have been established for the purpose of managing the funds, along with three brief case examples: the Texas Permanent University Fund, the Ohio Public Employees Retirement System, and the Colorado Local Government Liquid Asset Trust. How these and similar arrangements are structured and implemented will continue to be one of the central determining factors for how effective and successful the funds will be today, tomorrow, and well into the future.

KEY POINTS/TAKEAWAYS

- Across the U.S., states have established a variety of funds to manage and invest billions of dollars, portions of which ultimately pay for public employee benefits, public services, and infrastructure, among other public needs.
- Although some states mostly or completely manage these funds in-house, other states have established public–private arrangements for this purpose.
- When nongovernmental organizations are involved in fund administration, they may manage and invest assets, provide financial analyses, prepare key reports, and, more generally, provide management consulting and organizational support services to state entities responsible for overseeing the funds.
- It is important for elected and appointed officials to be mindful of the challenges that come with the balance between allowing for fund efficiency and ensuring fund accountability/transparency.
- All funds have been established in unique policy environments and for a range of purposes. There is not one best way to structure and manage these funds, be it mostly insourced or outsourced.

NOTES

1. United States Department of Labor Web Site (2014).
2. Coronado, Engen, and Knight (2003).
3. Coronado et al. (2003).
4. Anderson (2002).
5. Aronson (1968).
6. Aronson (1968).
7. Bureau of Labor Statistics, www.bls.gov/data/inflation_calculator.htm
8. Hayes (1999); Kearns (1995).
9. Hayes (1999).
10. Coe (1988).
11. Bunch (1999).
12. Bunch (1999).
13. Anderson (2002).
14. Anderson (2002).
15. Modlin and Stewart (2012).
16. Coronado et al. (2003).
17. Kearns (1995).
18. Modlin and Stewart (2013).
19. Modlin and Stewart (2012).
20. Modlin and Stewart (2013).
21. Anderson (2002).
22. United States Census Bureau (2014).
23. Clark, Craig, and Sabelhaus (2011).
24. Board of Governors of the Federal Reserve System (2013), p. 82.
25. National Association of State Retirement Administrators (2013a).
26. Author calculations of SLGE and BC-CRR Public Plans Database (2012 preliminary data); National Association of State Retirement Administrators (2013b) 'Roll Call of the States'.
27. United States Government Accountability Office (2010).
28. Ibid.
29. National Association of State Retirement Administrators (2013b) 'Roll Call of the States'.
30. Franzel and Brown (2013).
31. KPMG (2013).
32. State of Alaska, Department of Administration, Division of Retirement and Benefits (2013).
33. Ohio Public Employees Retirement System (2012).
34. Ohio Public Employees Retirement System Web Site (2014a) and Ohio Public Employees Retirement System (2014a).
35. Alaska Permanent Fund Corporation (2013).
36. Wyoming State Treasurer (2013)
37. North Dakota Retirement and Investment Office (2013).
38. Author calculations of fund documents and Sovereign Wealth Fund Institute Fund Rankings (2014).
39. University of Texas Investment Management Company Web Site (2014b).
40. Texas State Historical Association Web Site (2014).
41. ibid and University of Texas Investment Management Company (2013a).
42. University of Texas Investment Management Company Web Site (2014a) and University of Texas Investment Management Company (2013a).
43. University of Texas Investment Management Company Web Site (2014a).
44. University of Texas Investment Management Company (2013a).
45. University of Texas Investment Management Company Web Site (2014a).

46. University of Texas Investment Management Company (2013b) (p. 8).
47. University of Texas Investment Management Company (2013b).
48. Ohio Public Employees Retirement System Web Site (2014b).
49. Author calculations of Ohio Public Employees Retirement System (2012), p. 97 and p. 101.
50. Ohio Public Employees Retirement System Web Site (2014b).
51. Ohio Public Employees Retirement System (2014b), pp. 26–32.
52. Ohio Public Employees Retirement System (2014c), pp. 8–11.
53. ibid, p. 10.
54. ibid, p. 11.
55. ibid, p. 30.
56. Colorado Local Government Liquid Asset Trust (2012).
57. Colorado Local Government Liquid Asset Trust Web Site (2014).
58. Colorado Local Government Liquid Asset Trust (2009).
59. Colorado Local Government Liquid Asset Trust (2012).

REFERENCES

Alaska Permanent Fund Corporation. (2013). *2013 Annual report*. Retrieved from www.apfc.org/_amiReportsArchive/FY2013AnnualReport.pdf

Anderson, J. (2002). The Alaska permanent fund: Politics and trust. *Public Budgeting and Finance, 22*(2), 57–68.

Aronson, J. R. (1968). The idle cash balances of state and local governments: An economic problem of national concern. *The Journal of Finance, 23*(3), 499–508.

Board of Governors of the Federal Reserve System. (2013). *Z.1 financial accounts of the United States flow of funds, balance sheets, and integrated macroeconomic accounts fourth quarter 2013*. Retrieved from www.federalreserve.gov/releases/z1/Current/z1.pdf

Bunch, B. (1999). TexPool's experiences in the 1990s: Policy implications for other state investment pools. *Public Budgeting & Finance, 19*(4), 21–34.

Center for Retirement Research at Boston College, Center for State and Local Government Excellence, and National Association of State Retirement Administrators. *Public plans database.*

Clark, R. L., Craig, L. A., & Sabelhaus, J. (2011). *State and local retirement plans in the United States*. Northampton, MA: Edward Elgar.

Coe, C. K. (1988). The effects of cash management assistance by states to local governments. *Public Budgeting & Finance, 8*(2), 80–90.

Colorado Local Government Liquid Asset Trust. (2009). *Indenture of trust*. Retrieved from www.colotrust.com/uploads/Indenture_of_Trust.pdf

Colorado Local Government Liquid Asset Trust. (2012). *Information statement*. Retrieved from www.colotrust.com/uploads/COLOTRUST%20Information%20Statement%2012–7–2012.pdf

Colorado Local Government Liquid Asset Trust Web Site. (2014). *About colotrust*. Retrieved from www.colotrust.com/about

Coronado, J. L., Engen, E. M., & Knight, B. (2003). Public fund and private capital markets: The investment practices and performance of state and local pension funds. *National Tax Journal, 56*(3), 579–594.

Franzel, J., & Brown. A. (2013). *Retiree health care benefits for state employees in 2013. Center for state and local government excellence and national association of state retirement administrators.* Retrieved from http://slge.org/wp-content/uploads/2013/06/OPEB-Spotlight-06176.pdf

Hayes, Jr., V. R. (1999). The dangers of relying on a legal list: A case study of the West Virginia consolidated investment fund. *Public Budgeting & Finance, 19*(4), 49–64.

Kearns, K. P. (1995). Accountability and entrepreneurial public management: The case of the Orange County investment fund. *Public Budgeting & Finance, 15*(3), 3–21.

KPMG. (2013). *State of Alaska retiree health fund—Financial statements—June 30, 2013 and 2012.* Retrieved from http://doa.alaska.gov/drb/pdf/ghlb/retiree/fs2013rhf.pdf

Modlin, S., & Stewart, L. S. M. (2012). Cash management practices among southeastern county governments: Proper utilization or excessive caution. *Public Finance and Management, 12*(2), 100–119.

Modlin, S., & Stewart, L. S. (2013). Assessing participation in the state-sponsored local government investment pool during the recession: An examination of North Carolina counties. *Public Budgeting & Finance, 33*(4), 90–107.

National Association of State Retirement Administrators (2013a). *Public pension plan investment return assumptions.* Retrieved from www.nasra.org/files/Issue%20Briefs/NASRAInvReturnAssumptBrief.pdf

National Association of State Retirement Administrators. (2013b). *Roll call of the states.* (ongoing annual series, established in 2005).

North Dakota Retirement and Investment Office. (2013). *Financial statements June 30, 2013 and 2012.* Retrieved from www.nd.gov/rio/tffr/Publications/Financial%20Audit/FinalAuditReport2013.pdf

Ohio Public Employees Retirement System. (2012). *Comprehensive annual financial report for the years ended December 31, 2012 and 2011.* Retrieved from www.opers.org/pubs-archive/investments/cafr/2012-CAFR.pdf

Ohio Public Employees Retirement System. (2014a). *Investment objectives and asset allocation policy health care fund.* Retrieved from www.opers.org/pdf/investments/policies/HC-Investment-Policy.pdf

Ohio Public Employees Retirement System. (2014b). *2014 investment plan.* Retrieved from www.opers.org/pubs-archive/investments/inv-plan/2014_Investment_Plan.pdf

Ohio Public Employees Retirement System. (2014c). *Investment objectives and asset allocation policy defined benefit fund.* Retrieved from www.opers.org/pdf/investments/policies/db-investment-policy.pdf

Ohio Public Employees Retirement System Web Site. (2014a). *Health care total assets.* Retrieved from www.opers.org/investments/health-care/total.shtml

Ohio Public Employees Retirement System Web Site. (2014b). *History & background.* Retrieved from www.opers.org/about/history/

Rubin, I. (1996). Budgeting for accountability: Municipal budgeting for the 1990s. *Public Budgeting & Finance, 16*(2), 112–132.

State of Alaska, Department of Administration, Division of Retirement and Benefits. (2013). *Comprehensive annual financial report fiscal year ended June 30, 2013.* Retrieved from http://doa.alaska.gov/drb/pdf/pers/cafr/2013PersCafr.pdf

Sovereign Wealth Fund Institute Web Site. (2014). *Fund rankings.* Retrieved from www.swfinstitute.org/fund-rankings/

Texas State Historical Association Web Site. (2014). *Permanent university fund.* Retrieved from www.tshaonline.org/handbook/online/articles/khp02

Thompson, F. (1988). Taking full advantage of state investment pools. *Journal of Policy Analysis and Management, 7*(2), 353–372.

United States Census Bureau. (2014). *Annual survey of public pensions: State & local data.* Retrieved from www.census.gov/govs/retire/.

United States Department of Labor Web Site. (2014). *Retirement plans, benefits & savings—Types of retirement plans.* Retrieved from www.dol.gov/dol/topic/retirement/typesofplans.htm

United States Government Accountability Office. (2010). *State and local government pension plans: Governance practices and long-term investment strategies have evolved gradually as plans take on increased investment risk.* Retrieved from www.gao.gov/assets/310/308867.pdf.

University of Texas Investment Management Company—UTIMCO. (2013a). *Permanent university fund semiannual report.* Retrieved from www.utimco.org/Funds/Endowment/PUF/PUFSemiAnnual201312.pdf

University of Texas Investment Management Company—UTIMCO. (2013b). *Permanent university fund—Financial statements—Years ended August 31, 2013 and 2012*. Retrieved from www.utimco. org/Funds/Endowment/PUF/PUF2013AuditedFinancials.pdf

University of Texas Investment Management Company—UTIMCO Web Site. (2014a). *About us*. Retrieved from www.utimco.org/scripts/internet/about.asp

University of Texas Investment Management Company—UTIMCO Web Site. (2014b). *PUF Timeline*. Retrieved from www.utimco.org/scripts/internet/puf_timeline.asp

Wyoming State Treasurer. (2013). *Annual report—For the period July 1, 2012 through June 30, 2013*. Retrieved from http://treasurer.state.wy.us/pdf/annualweb2013.pdf

9

The Public Good in the Accountability of Businesses

The Functions and Uses of Benefit Corporations

Quintus Jett and Arturo E. Osorio

INTRODUCTION

In recent years, the public sector in the U.S. has created governance options to support businesses in the simultaneous pursuit of profit generation and the public good. One of these options is a legal entity called the benefit corporation. When a business incorporates as this organizational form, social purpose is legally embedded in its governance. Thus, its managers are responsible for achieving and reporting social performance on a variety of dimensions. This is a revolutionary development in business law within the U.S., and it occurs through the government's statuary powers to define and regulate the functioning of organizations (Battiliana, Lee, Walker, & Dorsey, 2012; Cummings, 2012).

It has been 60 years since federal law in the U.S. enacted the 501(c) category of tax-exempt organizations, which are now a standard legal entity through which nonprofit charitable activities are performed. Within the 501(c) category, the 501(c)(3) (i.e., charitable, tax-exempt) organization has been the preferred form of incorporation for groups that do social good. The 501(c)(3) is supported and regulated by the Internal Revenue Service (IRS) to function through government tax incentives. This form of organization is required to pursue (and is restricted to) charitable purpose and forbidden from distributing its financial surplus to those who manage it; the organization (and its donors) receive tax-reduction benefits. However, since 2008, new legal entities have been enacted by state governments throughout the U.S. that create an alternative approach for private organizations to contribute toward (and be accountable for) public benefits. These newly conceived legal forms are hybrids between for-profit and charitable, tax-exempt entities, and they offer businesses greater flexibility to use market-oriented practices for charitable and social purposes while still generating profit (Mickels, 2009).

This chapter focuses on the benefit corporation, the most prevalent of these new hybrid legal entities that bind the public good with the accountability of businesses. Our intent is to provide practitioners and students of public administration with a clear understanding of the functions and uses of benefit corporations. The chapter addresses four main points:

1. The benefit corporation is intended to facilitate a business locking into a legal commitment to the public good, without having the legal restrictions associated with being a nonprofit.
2. Benefit corporations and B-Corps are related but distinct solutions for businesses to demonstrate commitment to the public good.
3. Benefit corporations are one of several public-sector solutions that address a business's combined pursuit of profits and social purposes.
4. Benefit corporations are a public-sector solution limited to the U.S., and their future and broader relevance should be interpreted accordingly.

We organize the chapter into five sections in which we discuss these four main points as well as an example. In section 1, we address benefit corporations as a new legal entity available to businesses (point 1). In section 2, we explain the relationship between benefit corporations and B-Corps (i.e., B-certified companies) (point 2). In section 3, as an interlude, we use the King Arthur Flour Company to illustrate the transition of a long-standing business to a benefit corporation. In section 4, we compare benefit corporations to other new legal entities that aim to serve similar functions (point 3). Finally, in section 5, we suggest how to interpret the relevance and future of benefit corporations, given that they are legal entities conceived and enacted within the public-administration environment of the U.S. (point 4).

BENEFIT CORPORATIONS: A NEW ALTERNATIVE FOR BUSINESSES

The benefit corporation is intended to facilitate a business locking into a commitment to the public good, without having the legal restrictions associated with being a nonprofit.

The benefit corporation is a legal hybrid between for-profit and charitable, nonprofit entities. A benefit corporation commits a business to the simultaneous pursuit of profit and public benefit. The pursuit of public good includes multiple dimensions, achieving positive impacts on communities, on the natural environment, and for the business's employees. Under U.S. law, a benefit corporation departs from other legal forms for conducting business in two critical ways. First, it has social and environmental missions formally incorporated into its governance, such that managers are legally accountable for fulfilling the public good in addition to maximize profits. Second, it requires the business to publish an assessment of its social and environmental impacts by an independently verified source. This social and environmental assessment is to be released as part of the business operation's report that includes the financial standings of the venture.

The Statuary Power of the Public Sector

The creation of benefit corporations further illuminates the statutory (and other) authority that the public sector has over all private organizations. The public sector's fundamental functions include defining and enforcing what constitutes a formal organization, that is, establishing specific legal classifications of organizations with their associated purposes and requirements, as well as establishing the governing processes by which different classifications of organizations are regulated and otherwise held accountable (including the adjudication processes for disputes between organizations). The public authority for these functions is distributed across different branches of government (principally legislative and judicial) and across public oversight and regulation agencies at different levels of government (e.g., federal, state, local).

Overall, benefit corporations illuminate a significant constraint that inhibits a business from addressing social interests, as a charity may do: businesses have the fiduciary responsibility, codified in U.S. law, to solely focus on maximizing the profits of their shareholders. The benefit corporation provides a solution to this profit-maximizing constraint as it offers a hybrid legal entity that can include other non-economic goals (Battiliana et al., 2012). As a hybrid entity, the benefit corporation enables owners to lock social and environmental missions into the legal governance of the business, thus committing the business to consider the social and public benefits of its future decisions (Cummings, 2012). This commitment holds true even when there is a change in ownership, as the dual mission is part and parcel of the incorporation status of the organization.

Business Entities under U.S. Law

In the U.S., government statutes and subsequent case-law judicial decisions and interpretations provide two significant precedents involving incorporation. First, incorporating organizational activities as a legal entity provides liability protection. Second, as applied to business entities, managers have a fiduciary duty to maximize profits. Businesses must comply with public regulations, and they are restricted from inflicting particular social or environmental damages that public authorities have specified, but they have no general accountability to serve the public good beyond the legal minimum requirements and may do nothing more if doing so would result in a reduction of profits.

When a business incorporates in the U.S., its managers have a fiduciary duty to its stakeholders to maximize profits to optimize the economic return on their investment. This money-making duty is legally binding and has defined over the last 100 years the culture and institutional forces under which U.S. businesses operate. Under this framework, managers are required, to the best of their ability, to make decisions that will fulfill the profit-driven goals of the business. This responsibility was first construed in U.S. law in 1919 in the seminal case of *Dodge v. Ford Motor Co.*, 170 N.W. 668 (Mich. 1919), in which the Michigan Supreme Court held that "a business corporation is organized and carried on primarily for the profit of the stockholders. The powers of the directors are to be employed for that end. The discretion of the directors is to be exercised in the choice of means to attain that end, and does not extend to . . . other purposes." More recently, in the state of Delaware, where more than half of U.S. publicly traded companies and 64% of the Fortune 500 are registered, 2014 case law has confirmed this fiduciary duty (Delaware Division of Corporations, 2014). Delaware's case law states that "directors of a for-profit Delaware corporation cannot deploy a [policy] to defend a business strategy that openly eschews stockholder wealth maximization—at least not consistent with the directors' fiduciary duties under Delaware law" (*EBay Domestic Holdings, Inc. v. Newmark*, 16 A.3d 1 (Del. Ch. 2010)).

Benefit Corporations: Legal Hybrids between For-Profit and Nonprofit

Corporate law and governance in the U.S. has traditionally established different sets of restrictions for business corporations and charitable, nonprofit organizations. Benefit corporations are fundamentally a public-sector solution to enable a bridge: the application of entrepreneurial business initiative and financing methods toward social purposes.

In the U.S., a constitutional principle of the law is explained by the statement "everything which is not forbidden is allowed." Managers of a business entity may neglect social and public good to maximize profits, as long as their business activities remain legal. In comparison, managers of nonprofit entities may accumulate financial surplus from organizational operations, as long as this surplus is not considered a profit and is not distributed among the financial contributors to the organization (e.g., not distributed

Table 9.1

Comparison of Business Corporations, Charitable Nonprofit Organizations, and Benefit Corporations in the U.S.

	Business Corporations	Charitable, Nonprofit Organizations	Benefit Corporations
Restrictions	Must prioritize *profit* mission	Must prioritize *social* mission	Mandates emphasis of *both* profit and public benefit in managerial decisions
Required reporting	Annual financial reporting to investors and regulating public agencies	Annual reporting of finances and activities to federal tax agency (Internal Revenue Service)	Same as business corporation plus a third-party assessment of public benefit
Taxable	Profits taxed	Donations, assets, and income associated with mission-related activities are generally *not* taxable	Same as business corporation
Common funding sources	Debt and equity	Gifts and grants	Generally same as business corporation
Governance	Owners or Board of Directors	Board of Directors	Board of Directors
Basic succession procedures	Transferable ownership through stock transfer	Transfer of assets	Same as business corporation

among donors as a compensation for their donations or gifts). Thus, the surplus in a nonprofit entity must remain dedicated to the mission that the nonprofit has adopted in its governance.

As a hybrid organization, a benefit corporation is a distinct legal entity that mandates a business to incorporate purposes beyond profit maximization (André, 2012). It does so by integrating public benefit objectives in the organization's corporate governance. As a result, managers of the benefit corporation may be considered to have a more complex accountability system to follow, as they have a dual governance mandate: the attainment of profits while achieving public good. Thus, even when actively pursuing public good, a benefit corporation is still in essence a standard business corporation and follows business rules, including the need to generate profits to distribute among investors and the obligation to pay taxes on those profits. Consequently, in contrast to a charitable, nonprofit entity, under U.S. law, the benefit corporation can receive investments (not donations) like a business, and it does not qualify for tax-exempt status (Bromberger, 2011), even when actively pursuing the public good.

A benefit corporation is not only allowed to pursue both profit and social goals; it is legally mandated to do both at the same time. Managers of a benefit corporation are bound by the organization's governance to incorporate a triple bottom-line perspective, that is, a simultaneous consideration of the economic, social, and environment impact in managerial decision making. This holistic view of organizational goals is a contrast to other forms of incorporation, where either a mandated economic priority produces neglect toward social or environmental impacts (a for-profit entity) or a mandated social mission priority produces additional barriers to financial flexibility and the organization's economic survival (a nonprofit entity).

BENEFIT CORPORATIONS & B-CERTIFIED COMPANIES

Benefit corporations and B-Corps are related but distinct solutions for businesses to demonstrate commitment to the public good.

The benefit corporation is a legal form enacted by law, whereas B-Corps is a brand certification (B Lab, 2015). Both serve to increase business accountability for public benefit and social purposes. However, the B certification is a private-sector solution, a goodwill commitment by a business to achieve standards higher than normally regulated for the company's environment, employees, community, and governance. The benefit corporation, as previously discussed, is a public-sector solution (i.e., a form of business incorporation), executed as a binding legal commitment in the governance of a business to concurrently generate profit and public benefit. To understand what benefit corporations are, what they are intended to do, and how they are different from a B-certification, it helps to see the role of the B Lab organization—the originator and leading advocate for both B-certifications and benefit corporations.

B Lab is a registered charitable tax-exempt organization in the U.S. Since its founding in 2006, it has led the widespread adoption of both B certifications and benefit corporation status, guided by a principle to support businesses in elevating their purpose and accountability (i.e., not to become "best *in* the world," but to become "best *for* the world"). B Lab developed the B certification, owns the associated trademarks, and facilitates the brand certification's adoption and use by companies in the U.S. and throughout the world. It is also the lead advocate for public-sector adoption of benefit corporations as a legal business entity throughout the U.S. Simultaneously through the private-sector mechanism of brand certification and the public-sector mechanism of legal incorporation, B Lab is on a mission to add public benefit (in general and specific terms) to the purpose, operations, and accountability of for-profit businesses.

B-Certified Companies

B Lab established B-certification in 2007 as a third-party standard for assessing the general and specific public benefits achieved by a business. As of 2014, businesses across 60 different industries and in more than 30 countries have become B-certified. B Lab supports businesses in learning how to meet the certification's standards, and it revisits the definition and validity of standards over time. It further offers benefits with achieving certification, such as exclusive access to its information services, professional consultants in specialized fields (e.g., finance, human resources, operations), and access to a private network of other B-certified companies. Businesses meeting certification standards are often popularly referred to as "B-Corps" or B-corporations.[1] Many B-certified companies are leaders in their industries on social and environmental issues, in that their associated practices often exceed the mandated minimum compliance of government regulations. The B certification is a development standard for businesses to raise their commitment to public benefit and social purposes. It is also a branding signal, alerting the public (e.g., consumers, investors) to a business achieving high standards of social responsibility.

The B certification does *not* involve a change in the governance structure of a business. To become B certified, a business must successfully complete B Lab's four-step assessment review process. First, the organization must complete an initial assessment focusing on the company's overall impact on its stakeholders. Second, B Lab reviews the assessment with the company, to ensure there was proper interpretation of questions by the company and to help B Lab gain a better understanding of the company's particular circumstances and practices. Third, if the company scores at least 80 of the 200 possible points, B Lab invites the company to provide support documentation for 8–12 randomly selected questions. The collection of support documentation is a collaborative process to ensure the company's responses reflect its operational realities and results. Finally, B Lab invites the company to confidentially disclose any sensitive practices, fines, and sanctions that might affect the company's ability to create public benefit. After these four steps are completed, the board of B Lab reviews the company's case and decides whether to offer B certification. After initial certification, the B certification is reviewed every two years, as a company's particular circumstances and practices may vary with time. When companies fail to be certified after a first assessment, B Lab can help them address problem areas before undergoing another review process.

Table 9.2

Overall Scorecard Categories Reported for B Certification

Category		Target Area
Environment	This section evaluates a company's environmental performance in its facilities; materials, resource, and energy use; and emissions. Where applicable, it also considers a company's transportation/distribution channels and the environmental impact of its supply chain. This section also measures whether a company's products or services are designed to solve an environmental issue, including products that aid in the provision of renewable energy, conserve resources, reduce waste, promote land/wildlife conservation, prevent toxic/hazardous substance or pollution, or educate, measure, or consult to solve environmental problems.	Environmental products and services (e.g., renewable energy, recycling) Environmental practices Land, Office, Plant Energy, Water, Materials Emissions, Water, Waste Suppliers and Transportation
Workers	This section assesses the company's relationship with its workforce. It measures how the company treats its workers through compensation, benefits, training, and ownership opportunities provided to workers. It also focuses on the overall work environment within the company in terms of management/worker communication, job flexibility and corporate culture, and worker health and safety practices.	Compensation, Benefits, Training Worker ownership Work environment
Community	This section assesses a company's impact on its community. It evaluates a company's supplier relations, diversity, and involvement in the local community. It also measures the company's practices and policies around community service and charitable giving. In addition, this section includes whether a company's product or service is designed to solve a social issue, including access to basic services, health, education, economic opportunity, and arts, and increased flow of capital to purpose-driven enterprises.	Community products and services Community practices Suppliers and distributors Local Diversity Job creation Civic engagement and giving
Governance	This section evaluates a company's accountability and transparency. It focuses on the company's mission and stakeholder engagement, as well as overall transparency of the company's practices and policies.	Accountability Transparency

Note: A company must score at least 80 points (out of 200 total points across all areas) to be considered for B certification.

Benefit Corporations

When a business becomes B certified, it is *not* a benefit corporation. To become a benefit corporation, a business must be registered in one of the states that has enacted this new legal entity. In the U.S., business incorporation is a function authorized at the state-government level. Federal authority (e.g., laws, regulations, and agencies) generally supersedes state-government authority when there is a conflict between federal and state law or a conflict in law between two states. As a result of these (and other) features of the U.S. constitutional system, the statutory power to create new organizational entities normally starts at the state-government level;[2] from there it may become federally recognized and regulated.

B Lab has been the leading advocate for benefit corporations being legally enacted across U.S. states (Benefit Corp, 2014). It has developed and shares a general legislative template for state governments to consider, refine, and adopt. In all, B Lab serves as a coordinator for the widespread enactment of benefit corporations by more than half of the nation's 50 states since 2010. The first state to enact the benefit corporation was Maryland; its prescribed mission and definition for benefit corporations is "to have a material positive impact on society and the environment as measured by a third party standard through activities that promote a combination of specific public benefits" (State of Maryland, 2010). Other states that have enacted benefit corporations have adopted missions and definitions in similar terms, as they share a common advocate: B Lab.

Table 9.3

Comparison between B-Certified Company and Benefit Corporation

	B-Certified Company ("B-Corps")	Benefit Corporation
Nature	Private-sector solution Brand certification (worldwide)	Public-sector solution Option for legal incorporation (United States)
Function and Use	Goodwill commitment to public benefit Internal development standard to elevate public benefit in business decisions External signal of public benefit purposes(s)	Legal commitment to public benefit Internal lock-in of public benefit(s) in corporate identity External signal of public benefit purpose(s)
Authorization Authority	B-Lab, a registered nonprofit organization in the U.S.	State government where the business is registered The state must have enacted legislation establishing benefit corporation as a legal option for business operations.
Accountability	Certification by B Lab (renewal every two years)	Third-party assessment of public benefit Public benefit adopted in corporate by laws A benefit director on corporation's board (required in many states)

In contrast to a B certification, which is just a report of how an organization does business, benefit corporation status is a legal commitment to do business in a certain manner. A benefit corporation is a legal commitment for a business to incorporate both profit and public benefit in its formal governance, shaping future decisions by the corporation's managers as well as the corporation's formal legal identity. One standard feature of the benefit corporation across states is the formal adoption of public benefit (generally and specifically) in the business's corporate bylaws. The other standard feature is a mandated third-party assessment of the corporation's general and specific contributions to public benefit. Which third-party standard and assessor must be used is not commonly specified. Although B Lab originated and takes an active role in state adoptions of benefit corporations, we have not found legislation in any state that names B Lab as either a required or exclusive third-party assessor. There are states that also mandate creation of a benefit director, a specific role on the corporation's board of directors, whose responsibility is to ensure transparency and accountability for public benefit in the corporation's business decisions. Having a required external audit of public benefit (and its required reporting) serves critical accountability functions. These monitoring and reporting procedures ensure that public-benefit goals are part of managerial decision making (Cummings, 2012), while also in theory protecting managers from legal liability (i.e., shareholder lawsuits) when the pursuit of public benefit impairs profitability (Bromberger, 2011).

EXAMPLE: A BUSINESS BECOMES A BENEFIT CORPORATION

Businesses incorporating as benefit corporations are legally bound and accountable to equally pursue profit and public benefit, for as long as the corporation exists—even after changing ownership.

The benefit corporation is a standard form of business incorporation, with accountability for public benefit added to corporative governance. Thus, it legally commits managers of the business to pursue both profit and public benefit in perpetuity. A business's form of legal incorporation and corporate bylaws define its formal purpose and governance in ways that determine its legal identity in terms of public regulations and economic transactions. More broadly, the form of legal incorporation establishes, directs, and signals an organization's corporate identity. In addition to defining general elements of formal organizational structure and administration, it also defines informal organizational features, such as how organizational participants and stakeholders conceive performance and their expectations of how the organization should behave.

In order to illuminate these issues with respect to benefit corporations, we provide a real example of the King Arthur Flour Company.

Becoming the King Arthur Flour Company

The King Arthur Flour Company is a long-standing business that has produced premium baking flour for over 200 years, but its current ownership structure and name are relatively new. The company was founded in 1790 as an importer of fine British flour to the newly independent American colonies (King Arthur Flour Company, 2016). There have been numerous changes in its business since (e.g., changes in flour-production technologies, changes in consumer preferences and uses of baking flour, broader societal changes in marketing and distribution). However, during the past 30–40 years the company has undergone significant changes, greatly altering how the company makes business decisions and how it operates.

One major change for the company was its transition from family ownership to employee ownership. This change in ownership had results that made the company's later incorporation as a benefit corporation unsurprising and consistent with the company demonstrating culture and values beyond profit maximization. The transition to employee ownership began with the company's owners (Fred and Britta Sands) deciding to postpone their retirement in the 1980s. The company had been family-owned for many generations under the name of Sands, Taylor, & Wood (ST&W), but there was no evident succession in the family to run the company.

Rather than retire immediately and sell the company, Fred and Britta Sands took an active role in shaping what the company's succession would be after they retired. The Sands relocated and re-registered the company from Massachusetts, where the business had operated for generations, to Vermont, where they planned to retire. They adopted as company practice Open Book Management: a management philosophy that entailed disclosing more financial information about the company's operations to employees and further training employees in the use of this information so they can have greater participation in business decisions. Then to facilitate their retirement and the company's leadership succession, Fred and Britta Sands decided to make the company employee owned.

The U.S. public sector has defined employee ownership of corporations in a specific way not common to the rest of the world. At the federal level, it has enacted the option referred to as an Employee Stock Ownership Plan (ESOP). ESOP is a complex legal and financial instrument that gives employees ownership of a company by having them become shareholders through a specifically designed employee retirement fund. Under the ESOP transition process, moving from family ownership to employee ownership became a matter of property transfer. The transfer process enabled the Sands to cash in the value of their company by selling their family-owned stocks to the designated employee fund, which would issue stocks among current employees over time as part of the workforce compensation package. After initiating this process in the mid-1990s, the company became 100% employee owned over a period of several years. Throughout this process, the business remained a standard business corporation. However, as the company became employee owned, the business was formally renamed as the King Arthur Flour Company.

King Arthur Flour Becoming a Benefit Corporation

The King Arthur Flour Company was to be among the earliest benefit corporations in the U.S., in one of the earliest states to adopt benefit corporations as a legal form. What started as a quest to find a governance mechanism that would ensure commitment to employees (when the family owners retired) set the ground for the company's larger legal transformation. The company's legal incorporation and the fiduciary responsibilities of its managers was to expand from employees to broader commitments of social purpose and public benefit.

The King Arthur Flour Company became a benefit corporation in 2010, months after the state legislature in Vermont enacted the benefit corporation as a legal entity. Relative to the legal and financial complexities of converting from family ownership to employee ownership, the transition to benefit corporation was more straightforward. King Arthur Flour became one of the early B-Corps through B Lab certification. It further participated in establishing the benefit corporation as a legal option in Vermont. Once the state's legislature enacted the benefit corporation, King Arthur Flour made the legal transition to become one. It added the benefit corporation's additional requirements of public benefit purpose, accountability, and transparency into its corporate bylaws. Otherwise, its other legal attributes, including its employee ownership structure and its tax status, remained the same. Although a business having B-certification and its being a benefit corporation are distinct attributes, the King Arthur Flour Company can claim both.

ALTERNATIVES TO BENEFIT CORPORATIONS

Benefit corporations are one of three public-sector solutions that address a business' combined pursuit of profits and social purposes.

The benefit corporation is not the only U.S. incorporation alternative for businesses that want to combine greater social accountability to profit. To foster public accountability in businesses, U.S. state governments have enacted, in addition to the benefit corporation, two other kinds of legal entities: limited liability corporations (L3Cs) and social purpose corporations (SPC).

As is the case with the benefit corporation, the other two choices are also relatively new legal entities approved by individual state legislatures. The L3C emerged first. The benefit corporation emerged second. The SPC emerged most recently.

Hybrid "Social Enterprise" Entities

For many years entrepreneurs trying to establish sustainable social ventures that did not require ongoing fundraising or depend on grant writing for funding, often relied on so-called dual business models in which the operations of the social venture (nonprofit) were paid for or subsidized by the profits of a for-profit partner organization. This early arrangement, although well established and operationally sound, is complicated to manage and expensive to execute as it requires the coordination of at least two distinctively different organizations with two opposite goals (i.e., social versus economic).

Hybrid corporations are business entities that are legally committed (and allowed) to pursue social purposes as part of their for-profit operations. The three different types of social-purpose business incorporations provide for different levels of emphasis on social purposes and profit focus. L3Cs have a charitable purpose run through business methods where the attainment of profits is secondary. The benefit corporation is a business where the mandate to focus on social and environmental requirements must be balanced with the maximization of profits. The SPC is a business with a self-defined social impact that comes second to its profitability goals.

Hybrid social enterprises also illuminate the structural challenges in the nonprofit sector's ability to foster innovation and entrepreneurship. For example, 501(c)(3) organizations have barriers on income generation and distribution, which can hinder bold efforts to make breakthrough leaps in models for social purposes. In comparison, the legal forms available for hybrid organizations offer capital flexibility (more diverse sources and access to higher levels of financing; greater flexibility to distribute capital for either operational efficiency or as incentives to organizational participants).

Hybrid Entities and Social Investing

Because of their profit-driven goals, most of the financing for these types of organizations comes from traditional sources in the form of equity and debt. Yet, their social purposes allows them to access program-related investment (PRI) funds as well. Nonprofit organizations may attain operational financing from donations, grants, and PRI,[3] as well as to a lesser degree from its own operations (IRS, 2015). As they do not generate profits but only working capital, and they solely focus on social or environmental purposes, nonprofit organizations have tax incentives to encourage their operations. On the other side of the spectrum, traditional businesses have access to equity and debt financing but are taxed on their profits as their attainment of profits is the purpose and motivation for their operations. Hybrid organizations, with their dual goals, are located at the intersection of financial opportunities and operational motivations. Thus, as businesses, hybrid organizations have access to debts and equity financing, while being allowed to use PRI because of their social and/or environmental purposes. Also, as businesses pursuing profits, the profits generated by hybrid organizations are subject to taxation.

Specific Alternatives to Benefit Corporations

Low-profit, Limited Liability Corporations (L3Cs)

The low-profit, limited liability corporation (L3C) is a variation on the traditional limited liability corporation (LLC). Whereas the LLC focuses its business operations on profit maximization, while ensuring the limited liability of its owners, the L3C uses the same liability protection to achieve a self-sustained social purpose as it relegates profits to a secondary goal (yet does not ignore them). Relegating profits to a secondary goal makes difficult the financing of operations, as there is no interest in attaining high returns for investors. To compensate for this operational handicap, the L3C follows two concurrent funding strategies.

Table 9.4

U.S. Hybrid Legal Entities to Address Dual Purpose of Private Profit and Public Benefit

	Low-Profit, Limited Liability Corporation (L3C)	Benefit Corporation	Social Purpose Corporation (SPC)
First legislation enacted	2008 State of Illinois	2010 State of Maryland	2012 State of Washington
Percentage of states where enacted in law	20% 10 states	56% 28 states	6% 3 states

First, L3Cs are "designed primarily to enable companies to access investment from tax-exempt sources such as foundations" (Battilana, Lee, Walker, & Dorsey, 2012). These foundation sources mainly include PRI funding as foundations are mandated by the IRS to allocate no less than 5% of their investment income toward a charitable purpose. Second, L3Cs actively seek private investors that share the social mindset at the core of the L3C organization's operations. Thus, funding members and managers target investors who are willing to forego the principle of profit maximization, but not profits altogether.

To ensure that social goals are preserved as new investors come into place, L3C organizations explicitly set both economic and non-economic targets as part of their status of incorporation. Despite of their strong social emphasis and a legal structure allowing fundraising tied to lower returns on investments, as well as the intense lobbying of the Americans for Community Development Group, L3Cs have not gained much traction and are only available in 10 states in the U.S.

Social Purpose Corporations (SPCs)

Another alternative to benefit corporations is the social purpose corporation (SPC). The SPC enables a business to formally include particular social or environmental goals as part of its legal corporate purpose and governance. Yet it does not make those goals the primary goals of the business. This form of incorporation "requires boards and management to agree on one or more social and environmental purposes with shareholders, while providing additional protection against liability for directors and management" (Battiliana et al., 2012). This form of incorporation enables a company to focus narrowly on a specific social or environmental goal. The SPC, unlike a benefit corporation, does not need to identify a broad, general public or social benefit to pursue. Instead, this legal form requires a business only to identify one or more special purposes, besides its economic goals, as described in the statute. Also, unlike a benefit corporation, SPCs are not required to assess or report against any independent or third-party standard.

Table 9.5

Comparison of U.S. Hybrid Entities

	Low-Profit, Limited Liability Corporation (L3C)	Benefit Corporation	Social Purpose Corporation (SPC)
Public-sector action to support dual purpose	Specified kind of limited liability corporation whose purpose is defined consistent with the federal tax system's list of activities for program-related investments (PRIs)	Mandated formal adoption of public benefit in corporate bylaws and governance Mandated third-party assessment of public benefit	Mandated formal adoption of one or more particular social purpose (or environmental) goals in corporate bylaws Corporation defines own social purpose goal(s)
Public-sector authorization and compliance authority	State government where corporation is registered Federal tax authority (Internal Revenue Service)	State government where corporation is registered	State government where corporation is registered
Additional accountability and reporting	Annual report if there are shareholders or the corporation uses PRIs	Annual report to corporation's shareholders includes benefit report Benefit report includes third-party assessment of corporation's public benefit	Annual report to corporation's shareholders includes social purpose report Social purpose report accessible to the public at no charge

THE FUTURE OF BENEFIT CORPORATIONS

Benefit corporations are a public-sector solution limited to the U.S., and their future and broader relevance should be interpreted accordingly.

Benefit corporations (and other hybrid entities, such as L3Cs and SPCs) are solutions created by the U.S. public sector to bridge the gap between the functions and uses of for-profit and charitable, nonprofit organizational entities. However, these are new solutions enacted by state governments; benefit corporations have been permitted only since 2010. One can expect developments to occur at different levels and in various branches of the public sector, with uncertainty as to the levels of significance. The broader system of the U.S. constitutional government has yet to exercise its authority in addressing the uncertainties and conflicts that will inevitably arise with the creation of a new organizational entity. Further, the creation of benefit corporations (and other hybrid entities) arose from the particular political and institutional environments of the U.S., so interpretations of the function and use of benefit corporations should be viewed accordingly.

U.S. Public-Sector Responses to Benefit Corporations

In the U.S. constitutional system, there are at least two sources of public-sector response to emerging benefit corporations. One source is the state government (variation). The other is the federal government.

State-level Adaptations

At the state level, particular states can revise their formal definitions and requirements for benefit corporations, and/or increase the variation and complexity of what benefit corporations are when comparing among states. For example, when the state of Delaware enacted benefit corporation legislation, it named it a "public benefit corporation" and mandated a different level of accountability than most other states; it required biannual (not annual) reporting of public benefit, and it designated the use of third-party assessment of public benefit as an option (not mandated). Considering that a high percentage of U.S. corporations choose to register in Delaware, this divergence from the standard features of benefit corporations adopted by other states may have significant implications. In rare cases, a state might also repeal legislation that has created a new legal entity. For example, North Carolina enacted the L3C as a legal form in 2010; then a subsequent session of the state legislature repealed the L3C legislation in 2014.

Federal Resolutions

Variation in the adoption or legislation across states will inevitably lead to a significant response from sources of authority within the U.S. federal government, if this variation produces a significant threshold of conflict, uncertainty, or complication to warrant scrutiny to resolve (legislatively, judicially, or administratively through a federal regulating agency).

The required verification for benefit corporations is not an audit from a regulating authority. The benefit corporation is more similar to how the Generally Accepted Accounting Principles (GAAP) are applied to financial reporting, used solely as a verification standard for a company to measure its own performance and to allow for comparisons with other companies. Overall, the verification and reporting help to ensure the organization's commitment to fulfilling the public good on a variety of dimensions (Bromberger, 2011).

Social Enterprises in Comparative Perspective

The benefit corporation as a hybrid legal form (combining public benefit and private profit) is an option limited to the U.S. The political system of each country determines the different kinds of formal organizations that can legally operate, including the particular purposes and restrictions associated with each kind of organization and the processes

Table 9.6a

U.S. Hybrid Entity Adoption for Each of 50 States Plus the District of Columbia

No	Name	Abbreviation	Benefit Corp	L3C	SPC
1	Alabama	AL			
2	Alaska	AK			
3	Arizona	AZ	•		
4	Arkansas	AR	•		
5	California	CA	•		•
6	Colorado	CO	•		
7	Connecticut	CT	•		
8	Delaware	DE	•		
9	Florida	FL	•		•
10	Georgia	GA			
11	Hawaii	HI	•		
12	Idaho	ID			
13	Illinois	IL	•	•	
14	Indiana	IN			
15	Iowa	IA			
16	Kansas	KS		•	
17	Kentucky	KY			
18	Louisiana	LA	•	•	
19	Maine	ME		•	
20	Maryland	MD	•		
21	Massachusetts	MA	•		
22	Michigan	MI		•	
23	Minnesota	MN	•		
24	Mississippi	MS			
25	Missouri	MO			

for changing the definition and regulations of these organizations. In some nations, there is a legal federal entity to enact organizational forms. In other nations, such as the U.S., there is considerable legal and jurisdictional complexity and historical precedents affecting what constitutes a formal organization, what different kinds of organizations are possible, and the restrictions and accountability that govern them. Thus, other nations have their own particular circumstances involving hybrid organizations that can be similar or dissimilar to what is happening in the U.S. with benefit corporations and other hybrid business forms.

Table 9.6b

U.S. Hybrid Entity Adoption for Each of 50 States Plus the District of Columbia

No	Name	Abbreviation	Benefit Corp	L3C	SPC
26	Montana	MT			
27	Nebraska	NE	•		
28	Nevada	NV	•		
29	New Hampshire	NH	•		
30	New Jersey	NJ	•		
31	New Mexico	NM			
32	New York	NY	•		
33	North Carolina	NC			
34	North Dakota	ND		•	
35	Ohio	OH			
36	Oklahoma	OK			
37	Oregon	OR	•		
38	Pennsylvania	PA	•		
39	Rhode Island	RI	•	•	
40	South Carolina	SC	•		
41	South Dakota	SD			
42	Tennessee	TN			
43	Texas	TX			
44	Utah	UT	•	•	
45	Vermont	VT	•	•	
46	Virginia	VA	•		
47	Washington	WA	•		•
48	West Virginia	WV	•		
49	Wisconsin	WI			
50	Wyoming	WY		•	
51	District of Columbia	DC	•		

CONCLUSION

The benefit corporation is a solution enacted by the public sector, through its unique power to define the normative and administrative environments in which all private formal organizations are constituted and must conduct operations. It is a government solution that enables businesses to pursue a dual purpose of profit and public benefit, through a hybrid legal entity that aims to combine the advantages of profit and charitable entities. Benefit corporations have the flexibility to make business commitments with consideration of general and specific benefits to the public, without the risk of lawsuits by financial investors (André, 2012). Yet, benefit corporations remain, in essence, business corporations, so they can receive investments like a business (with neither the investment restrictions nor the tax exemptions of a charitable nonprofit) (Bromberger, 2011).

Benefit corporations belong to a new sector of hybrid legal entities in the U.S. that are simultaneously nongovernmental and non-profit maximizing (André, 2012). The benefit corporation is the most commonly adopted of these new forms. However, benefit corporations (and other hybrid entities) are relatively new creations, since the year 2008. Changes in the defining requirements and accountability may occur in individual states, producing excessive variation and complication concerning benefit corporations across the nation as a whole. There may also be proactive or reactive responses from federal authorities, and these responses might significantly augment or weaken the functions and uses of benefit corporations. Further, because of the nature of the U.S. constitutional system, case law interpretations and judgments arising from court cases involving benefit corporations (and other entities) might either increase their adoption or illuminate new complex issues, problems, and directions.

KEY POINTS AND LESSONS LEARNED

The benefit corporation is a new option for incorporation only available in the U.S. This new legal form is a public-sector solution, addressing longstanding distinctions in law separating the for-profit and nonprofit sectors. The following points summarize the benefit corporation's significance:

1. The benefit corporation facilitates a business having greater legal flexibility to combine the public good and the pursuit of profits, without having the legal restrictions associated with being a nonprofit.
   a. Starting (or becoming) a business that is a benefit corporation involves formal adoption of public benefit into corporate governance.
   b. Including public benefit in governance legally binds corporate managers to consider public benefit in their business decisions.
   c. Benefit corporations are also required to have third-party assessment of their operations.
2. Benefit corporations and B-Corps are related but distinct solutions for businesses to demonstrate commitment to the public good.
   a. Benefit corporations are a legal form of incorporation designed to allow the concurrent and balanced pursuit of public good and profits
   b. B-Corps certification is a global standard, confirming the pursuit of public good as part of the business operations.
   c. B Lab is the nonprofit organization that manages the B-Corps certification standard and processes, and acts as the main lobby agent for promoting the benefit corporation (and providing model legislation for its adoption) throughout the U.S.

3. Benefit corporations are one of three kinds of hybrid organization: public-sector solutions that facilitate a business's concurrent pursuit of profits and the public good.

   a. The low-profit, limited liability corporation (L3C) is the earliest form of possible hybrids found in the U.S.

   b. The social purpose corporation (SPC) is the most recent to emerge.

   c. The benefit corporation is the most prevalent of the three in state adoption throughout the U.S.

4. Benefit corporations are a relatively new public-sector solution limited to the U.S.

   a. Hybrid organizations are relatively new in the United States. The earliest hybrid form became a legal option in 2008; benefit corporations have existed since 2010.

   b. Developments within the U.S. public sector (legislative, judicial, regulatory branches) may alter the requirements and accountability structures for benefit corporations in the future.

   c. Other nations have their own challenges and public-sector solutions with respect to businesses incorporating the public good into their governance and operations.

NOTES

1. We use the term B-certified companies to maintain clarity of B certification as a brand, not a form of legal incorporation.

2. In the U.S., enactment of state law generally occurs after the state's congress passes the law and its governor (i.e., the state's highest level government executive) signs to approve. However, there are special conditions, such as when the government rejects the approved law or delays signing, and the specifics of legislative process and approval can vary by each state.

3. According to IRS rules, Program-Related Investments (PRI) are those in which: the primary purpose is to accomplish one or more of the foundation's exempt purposes; production of income or appreciation of property is not a significant purpose, and influencing legislation or taking part in political campaigns on behalf of candidates is not a purpose.

REFERENCES

André, R. (2012). Assessing the accountability of the benefit corporation: Will this new gray sector organization enhance corporate social responsibility? *Journal of Business Ethics, 110*(1), 133–150.

Battilana, J., Lee, M., Walker, J., & Dorsey, C. (2012). In search of the hybrid ideal. *Stanford Social Innovation Review, 10*(3), 50–55.

Benefit Corp. (2014). *Benefit Corporation information center*, Vol. 2014.

B-Lab. (2015). *Benefit Corp vs. Certified B Corp*, Vol. 2015.

Bromberger, A. R. (2011). A new type of hybrid. *Stanford Social Innovation Review, 9*(2), 48–53.

Cummings, B. (2012). Benefit corporations: How to enforce a mandate to promote the public interest. *Columbia Law Review, 112*(3), 578–627.

Delaware Division of Corporations. (2014). *Facts and myths*, Vol. 2014.

IRS. (2015). *Program-related investments*, Vol. 2015.

King Arthur Flour Company. (2016). Company history: King Arthur Flour. Retrieved from www. kingarthurflour.com/about/history.html

Mickels, A. (2009). Beyond corporate social responsibility: Reconciling the ideals of a for-benefit corporation with director fiduciary duties in the U.S. and Europe. *Hastings International & Comparative Law Review, 32*, 271–304.

State of Maryland. (2010). *Corporations—Benefit Corporations.* Session, Department of Legislative Services: 2010. In Maryland General Assembly. House Bill 1009, Chapter 98. Approved by the Governor, April 13, 2010.

10

Sorting Out Social Impact Bonds

Daniel E. Bromberg and Jonathan B. Justice

Over the past 35 years government has transitioned from working primarily through traditional hierarchical structures to relying increasingly on networked provision of goods and services (Phillips, 2004; Salamon, 2002; van Bueren, Klijn, & Koppenjan, 2003). Discussions of networked government, or *governance networks*, can be found throughout the public administration literature. The premise is that public goals are no longer simply achieved by traditional bureaucratic structures and traditional coercive means or direct service provision, but by an array of public and private actors utilizing multiple techniques. This perspective asserts that "governance is accomplished through decentralized networks of private and public actors associated to international, national and regional institutions" (Dedeurwaerdere, 2005, p. 2).

One argument favoring this shift is that the public sector is faced with many challenging problems that cannot simply be divided into independent issues—they must be dealt with through innovative comprehensive structures (O'Toole, 1997). For example, dealing with complex socio-economic challenges such as poverty reduction, gainful employment, and prison recidivism are better addressed as interrelated phenomena and require collaborative efforts to reach sustainable solutions. Due to both the complexity of the issue and the economic ramifications, one organization—or agency—is insufficient to deal with these challenges in a traditional hierarchical sense. Governments, therefore, rely on networks of actors and multiple policy tools to solve complex problems.

Unlike traditional hierarchical or market relationships, networks are based on ideals of "complementary strengths" and resolve conflicts through relations of reciprocity (Lowndes & Skelcher, 1998). Within networks, governments may utilize various "tools of public action" to accomplish a public goal (Salamon, 2002, p. 19). Salamon (2002) suggests that to analyze the pursuit of public purposes, one must redirect attention from the specific organization or program to the specific "tool" being employed by the public entity (p. 9). The dynamic nature of organizational relationships in networks has made utilizing the organization as a unit of analysis very challenging; therefore, studying the tool employed provides a more static unit of analysis. Salamon (2002) labels this approach "the new governance" (p. 8) and defines a tool of public action as: "An identifiable method through which collective action is structured to address a public problem" (p. 19).

In this chapter we describe the social impact bond (SIB) as a newly developed tool of public action through which public-sector agencies can encourage entrepreneurial private-sector design, management, and financing of preventive social services. SIBs involve government commissioners of services working with teams of investors and service providers to develop, finance, and implement social interventions that take the form of investments in human and/or social capital. Common objectives of SIB projects include preventing recidivism by ex-offenders and helping disadvantaged labor-market entrants to secure employment. Services of this type can be framed as investments in human capital, since they are expected to provide both private benefits, such as helping service recipients generate income or avoid incarceration, and social benefits, by reducing the future financial and economic costs of providing remedial services, transfer payments, or incarceration. Service providers are paid up front for their work by the investors, who will recover their financial capital plus an agreed-upon profit margin in cases where the results of the policy intervention meet or exceed stipulated measures of effectiveness in accomplishing the program objectives. The SIB device, it is clear, is very much at the center of a network collaboration and activates a number of actors.

Proponents claim that SIBs bring the innovativeness of nongovernmental social entrepreneurs and inter-organizational networks to bear on technically and politically challenging problems that call for significant investment in human and social capital through social-service interventions. In principle, the SIB structure allows social entrepreneurs and governments to work together to overcome political obstacles to investing in preventive social services, and to share the long-term savings resulting from successful investments. Finally, proponents assert, SIBs are virtually a free lunch for the public-sector partners: The archetypal SIB design calls for some or all of the financial risks of success or failure to be borne by the social entrepreneurs and their financial backers, rather than by governments. Thus, if the SIB-financed program is successful, both government and investors win, but if it fails, the private-sector investors will bear most or all of the downside.

In this chapter, we seek to begin answering several questions about SIBs (but with the understanding that this is an emerging policy tool and that continuing experience in several countries will in time provide information to support more complete answers). First, what are they, what familiar and novel policy instrument-design features do they incorporate, and what problems do they have the potential to solve? Second, in what ways do SIBs in practice fulfill their proponents' promises of innovation? Third, under what circumstances do they appear likely to fulfill the promises of delivering significant cost savings or value for money to governments? Fourth, what implications does the use of the SIB structure to overcome political obstacles to investing in human and social capital have for the accountability and political-responsiveness goals of democratic public administration?

In the next section, we begin by describing SIBs and providing a brief history and description of their use. That is followed by two illustrative case studies. The UK's Peterborough Prison recidivism-reduction project is the world's first SIB and has begun to generate measurable results. In the U.S., the Massachusetts recidivism-reduction project is a high-visibility and potentially replicable model. We then assess the promises of innovation and fiscal benefits in light of our case studies and work by other researchers.

Finally, we conclude with some key points for decision makers and policy analysts to bear in mind when evaluating proposed or existing SIB arrangements.

INTRODUCING SOCIAL IMPACT BONDS

The terms "social impact bonds," "payment by results," and "pay for success" broadly refer to a novel, privatized method of designing and financing investments in preventive social services. The generic SIB model involves outsourcing the design, management, and initial financing of social-service interventions that can be framed as investments in human or social capital, the long-term benefits of which are great enough to justify significant short-term expenditures. The interventions themselves are financed by equity investments in and/or loans to a special-purpose organization, which in turn contracts with a government commissioner to deliver the services in return for future payments based on the effective accomplishment of agreed-upon objectives. Early programs have featured efforts such as recidivism-reduction and job-readiness and placement schemes.

Nicholls and Tomkinson (2013) portray SIBs as growing out of the late-20th-century current of thinking that includes the new public management, neoliberal commitments to market-based institutions, and an enthusiasm for "reinventing government." They trace the specific origins of SIBs to the UK's Council on Social Action, established in 2007 by a Labour-led government; a social entrepreneur's idea to use "contingent revenue bonds" to finance infrastructure projects in developing countries, adapted by Social Finance UK to work as a financing mechanism for preventative social interventions beginning in 2008; and the concerted efforts of a number of policy and social entrepreneurs in the UK's public, private, and third sectors over a period of time that saw Labour lose its control of Parliament to a Conservative-led coalition (see Nicholls & Tomkinson, 2013, pp. 9–12 for a detailed history). According to Nicholls and Tomkinson (2013), there were at least 40 SIBs in operation or in development by mid-2013, mostly in the UK, U.S., and Australia, but with examples in countries elsewhere in Europe, North America, Africa, and Asia. Since that time, several additional U.S. states have adopted legislation to facilitate SIBs. In the U.S., SIBs have been championed by the Rockefeller Foundation, the Obama administration, the Nonprofit Finance Fund, and the Center for American Progress, among others, beginning at least as early as 2010 (Leonhardt, 2011; Liebman, 2011).

BASIC ASSUMPTIONS AND DESIGN PRINCIPLES

Advocates of the SIB approach argue that SIBs solve the problem that elected officials' policy preferences are biased by overly short time horizons and/or hyperbolic time-discount rates, by risk and uncertainty aversion, and by a tendency to focus on process rather than results (see, for example, Social Finance Limited, 2014). Thus, they say, the SIB approach makes it possible to pursue investments in preventative social services that otherwise would go unfunded due to their uncertainty, delayed payoff, and relative invisibility compared to investments in physical capital. It accomplishes this by providing incentives in the form of potential payments for documented results that can elicit and facilitate the innovative design, financing, and implementation of preventive social interventions by nongovernmental actors. SIBs in effect make it possible for motivated investors and their intermediaries to monetize the social returns to investments in human and social capital, and they therefore attract risk capital from socially and profit-oriented investors. That availability of financial capital in turn makes it possible for mission-oriented service providers to design and execute innovative programs. To the extent the intervention and its financing can be promoted to government officials and the public as substantially risk-free, and likely to pay for themselves if they are successful enough to require government payouts, it becomes possible to overcome the risk avoidance and loss aversion that otherwise make government decision makers less likely to attempt preventive social-service programs.

A further potential benefit is secondary or indirect. The need to have clear evidence of an intervention's success or failure as a way to determine payment requires the parties involved to identify measurable criteria that define policy success, and then to measure the effectiveness of interventions accordingly. Thus, the SIB model can be seen as a development that complements recent efforts to develop and promulgate the use of "evidence-based" public-policy interventions by working around the common need of political actors to build support for policy initiatives by "fuzzing up" the initiatives' purposes.

The SIB model has on the other hand been portrayed more critically as "an extreme expansion of new public management precepts into social program delivery" that relies on three staples of the New Public Management (NPM) repertoire—contracting, performance measurement, and public–private partnerships—as well as the presumption that delegating control to nongovernmental actors through an "arms-length process" can improve performance compared to a governmental process of program design and implementation (Warner, 2013, pp. 305–306). Similar to the UK's Private Finance Initiative (PFI) and other NPM-inspired models of private sector–led and –financed public improvements, the SIB structure presumes that private actors, motivated by potential profits, are more likely than government agencies to design and implement effective, innovative solutions to collective problems and that private-sector actors can do a better job of measuring and pricing financial risks than governments can.

PUBLIC–PRIVATE PARTNERSHIPS AND NETWORK STRUCTURE

The network configuration of a SIB is fairly straightforward in concept. A set of contracts ties together at least three parties: a government commissioner or purchaser, an external investor or financier, and a nongovernmental service provider. In the simplest scheme, the investor pays the service provider to implement the preventive service scheme for a fixed period of time. At the end of the period, if the contracted-for degree of improvement in a measurable condition—such as recidivism rates for a certain population of offenders—has occurred, the government commissioner will pay the investor a sum sufficient to generate a profit for the investor. Assuming that the social benefits and avoided costs that result from the intervention exceed the costs of financing and delivering the initiative, it is possible for the service provider, the financier, and the government commissioner all to earn positive returns on their respective investments (Centre for Social Impact Bonds, 2013a).

In practice, however, there are usually more than three parties involved, sometimes many more. Most SIB structures include intermediary organizations in the form of a special-purpose vehicle (SPV) that serves as the nominal project manager and as the financial intermediary connecting the commissioner, investors, and service providers, as well as the sponsoring social entrepreneur or investment manager that establishes and manages the SPV. The U.S. Department of Labor's pay-for-success pilot scheme in fact requires the inclusion of an intermediary entity between the ultimate investors and the service provider or providers, since there are often several networked service providers involved in a given SIB. In addition, an independent evaluator or "outcome validator" is usually engaged to confirm success or failure of the intervention. One result of this multi-actor implementation design is that there are often complex configurations of interdependent contracts among a large number of organizations, with multiple investors and categories of investors and often complex configurations of social-service providers all tied together by one or more intermediary or umbrella organizations. Figure 10.1 depicts a generic SIB structure that includes the most common types of direct participant.

Figure 10.1   **Generic, Ideal-type Configuration of Direct Participants in a SIB**

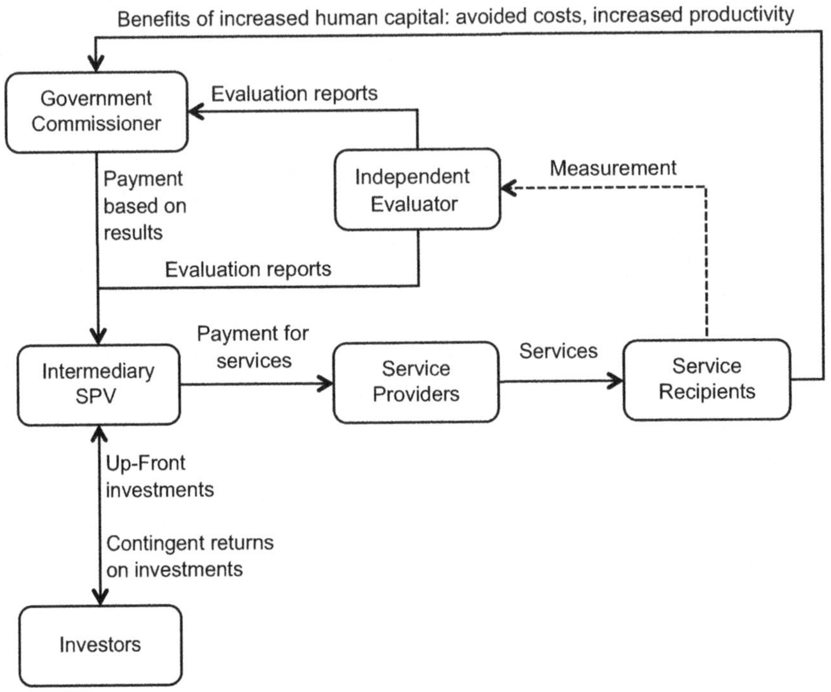

INVESTMENTS, RISKS, AND RETURNS

Investment

Although SIBs do not involve issuing conventional bonded debt, they do involve committing governments to make future payments to private parties who provide upfront funds for immediate investment. Like traditional government bonds, SIBs raise funds from nongovernmental individuals and organizations who hope to earn a positive return on their financial advances to governments, but in so doing are exposed to a variety of risks that might conceivably reduce their returns or even cause them to lose much of their initial capital if the future cash streams are smaller or later than expected (this point is articulated by Hildreth, Miller, & Sewordor, 2011; Miller & Hildreth, 2000).

There are at least three important design differences between SIBs and traditional infrastructure-financing bonds (beyond the fact that they are not legally the same type of contract). First is that SIBs are used to finance investments in "soft" human and social capital rather than "hard" infrastructure and physical capital. Second, SIBs involve using nongovernmental actors not only as sources of up-front funds for the investments, but also as the designers and managers of the human and social capital-building interventions themselves. (In this, they are analogous to the design-build-finance-operate-maintain [DBFOM] format for public–private infrastructure partnerships.) Third, SIBs involve a promise of repayment to financiers that is contingent upon the achievement of satisfactory outcomes, ostensibly transferring more of the financial risk of program design and implementation failures to the private investors than is the case with conventional infrastructure finance.

The basic cost–benefit rationale to justify debt finance is that the initial costs of designing and implementing programs to reduce recidivism, for example, will earn a return on investment in the form of long-term reductions in incarceration rates and the attendant reduction in the aggregate social costs of incarceration as well as increased productivity and well-being for the ex-offenders who succeed in staying on the outside. Also consistent with the notion of making capital investments, SIBs are often promoted as means to generate not just social benefits, but also actual net fiscal savings to governments. The rationale is that some social interventions can generate gross reductions in total government expenditure so large that even after paying the costs of the intervention and investors' profit, there will be a residual net financial savings to government/taxpayers (see Barclay and Symons, 2013, p. 18). The net-social-welfare-gains portrayal supports a basic form of the pay-as-you-use efficiency and equity rationales that economists typically cite to justify debt finance of public capital investments. The claim of net fiscal savings goes further by making SIBs seem possibly to be something of a free lunch.

Risk Transfer

A key selling point of the SIB model is that, at least in its ideal-type form, it involves some measure of risk transfer, facilitated by the focus on targeting well-defined social outcomes. The commissioning government is not required to make full payment—or any payments at all, in cases of maximal risk transfer—if the contractually stipulated improvements in social outcomes are not verifiably delivered. Thus, in theory at least, the financial risks of program failure are borne largely by the investors, who incur the certain upfront costs of paying a service provider in anticipation of the uncertain contingent payment by the commissioner. Given the ostensible risk transfer, then, SIBs seem almost magical, promising something for (almost) nothing: If the interventions fail, governments lose only the transaction costs they incurred to enter into the SIB arrangement. If the interventions succeed, governments, taxpayers, investors, and service recipients share in the gains achieved by avoiding costs of, say, incarcerating recidivists, in the fashion and to the extent provided for by the contract terms.

Less than 100% of the financial risk is transferred even in the ideal type, however, for at least two reasons. First, governments entering into SIB arrangements still have to bear the upfront costs of negotiating and documenting agreements, the operating costs incurred by the SIB arrangements themselves and by changes in operations of facilities and programs impacted by the SIB project, and the cost of the independent program evaluator's services. Second, unlike the guaranteed savings contracts sometimes used to finance energy-saving projects, SIBs are typically structured so that investors' returns are contingent upon meeting a social-performance objective, rather than a fiscal-savings objective. Thus, the commissioning governments retain the risk that the residual value of the SIB project will fail to materialize if the realized gross fiscal savings are no greater than the sum of the costs of the intervention plus the stipulated profit for investors. Further, it should be noted that some SIB projects might involve nonfinancial risks for governments and service recipients, which by their nature will resist transfer.

Risk Pricing and the Risk-Innovation Tradeoff

Risk transfer is not free. To the extent investors bear risks, they will expect to be compensated accordingly. Even in what are regarded as relatively high-risk categories of municipal finance, such as health care, conventional municipal-bond default rates are very low and so therefore are the risk premiums demanded by investors. Compared to mainstream, "plain-vanilla," municipal bonds, at least, SIBs appear to involve significantly more risk for investors if they are not supported by third-party guarantees. The technologies and effectiveness of innovative social-service intervention designs are not well understood or predictable, particularly in the policy domains to which SIBs are applied. Indeed, part of the rationale for using SIBs to tap entrepreneurial designers and implementers of innovative social interventions is precisely that conventional government programs have not succeeded. But if part of the purpose of SIBs is to innovate in the sense of attempting novel interventions or combinations of interventions that might be subject to significant uncertainty of results, the risk premium will be correspondingly large. Thus, as Warner (2013) notes, there is a certain tension in the design of SIBs. It may often be the case that the need to combine profitability for investors with acceptable pricing for governments commissioning SIBs will militate against efforts to pursue highly innovative social interventions through SIBs.

CASE STUDIES

In this section of the chapter, we present two illustrative case studies. The SIB project aimed at reducing recidivism among prisoners released from the UK's Peterborough Prison is the first SIB, and the only one for which documented results are available at this writing. It can thus be understood both as a proof-of-concept or pilot effort, organized by the inventors of the SIB structure, and as the first datum about whether SIBs are likely to deliver on their promises of innovation and value for money. The Peterborough SIB focuses on a single measured outcome objective: recidivism as measured by reconvictions of recently released prisoners. The Massachusetts case is a more recent application of the concept that, together with the Peterborough case, illustrates some of the range of variations in use for the network design, performance-evaluation methods, and financial and risk-allocation structures of SIBs. The Massachusetts SIB also targets ex-offenders, but identifies three measured pay-for-performance objectives: the extent of participant engagement with the service provider (process), increases in employment (output/outcome), and decreases in repeat incarcerations (outcome).

Proof of Concept: Peterborough Prison (UK)

The first SIB is a recidivism-reduction pilot project involving 3,000 male, short-sentence (less than a year) offenders at the UK's Peterborough Prison. Initial contractual arrangements were settled in March 2010, and the intervention itself began in September and was originally scheduled to run until 2018 (Nicholls & Tomkinson, 2013). The goal of the intervention, and the trigger for payments to the investors, was to reduce the number of convictions per service recipient for offenses committed within 12 months of their release from Peterborough,[1] compared to a control group of similar offenders that was constructed through a propensity score matching (PSM) technique (Jolliffe & Hedderman, 2014). This measurement approach had two particular advantages: the use of PSM reduced incentives for "creaming" in the selection of program participants, and the use of a count rather than binary measure of recidivism reduced incentives to abandon service recipients once they committed a first re-offense (Nicholls & Tomkinson, 2013). There were to be three cohorts of service recipients, each consisting of up to 1,000 participants (or two years' worth of participants if there are fewer than 1,000 in that time [Cave, Williams, Jolliffe, & Hedderman, 2012]), with evaluation of the first cohort's results—and a corresponding opportunity for performance payments to the SPV and investors—scheduled for 2014.

The overall Peterborough SIB structure centers on the Social Impact Partnership LP, a special purpose vehicle (SPV) operated by Social Finance UK. The SPV serves as the intermediary among a pool of 17 investors, the One Service organization created by Social Finance to manage contracts with multiple providers of direct services to the released prisoners and their families, the Ministry of Justice as commissioner, and the UK's Big Lottery Fund as a source of some of the funding to be used for contingent payments to investors. The publicly identified investors in the project appear all to be charitable trusts and foundations, as opposed to for-profit entities or individuals.

The financial logic of the intervention was grounded on the premises that re-imprisonment rates for the targeted offenders are as high as 60% and that

> It is estimated that the cost of imprisoning a single person in the UK is £40,000 plus an extra £40,000 for each year they spend incarcerated. Thus reducing recidivism amongst those most likely to re-enter the system stands to make considerable savings.(Centre for Social Impact Bonds, 2013b)

Given such large potential savings per prevented imprisonment,[2] there appeared to be an opportunity to generate large enough fiscal savings to cover the costs of delivering an effective intervention plus a profit for investors, while still leaving a residual financial benefit for the government and taxpayers.[3] According to the UK Cabinet Office (Centre for Social Impact Bonds, 2013b),

> Outcome payments will be made if there is a 10% reduction in the number of reconviction events over 12 months compared to a control group [for an individual cohort], or if the SIB's three cohorts achieve an average reduction of 7.5%. Payments are capped at £8m, which would see a rate of return of 13% for investors. The aim is to make reductions in court, police and prison costs as a result of reduced re-offending, for which reconviction events are a suitable intermediate proxy.

Outcome payments to the SPV, if any payments are triggered by the measured outcomes, will take the form of "a fixed unit payment for each reduced conviction event in a SIB cohort less than a matched baseline cohort" (Cave et al., 2012, p. 1) as calculated by the independent evaluator. If neither of the 10% individual-cohort or 7.5% overall reductions is achieved, no outcome payment is called for (p. 2).

The contractual arrangements for the Peterborough pilot program illustrate the complexity of the legal and financial arrangements required for SIBs generally, as well as the comprehensiveness of the intervention design and unique characteristics of the Peterborough pilot program. Nicholls and Tomkinson (2013) summarize the arrangements as involving six categories of contracts all told. Two sets of arrangements appear to be idiosyncratically tied to this specific implementation of a SIB. One set of contracting arrangements appears to have taken the form of amendments to an existing contract with the prison's private operator. Another case-specific contract was negotiated between the SPV and the UK's Big Lottery Fund, regarding supplemental outcome payments to be paid by the Fund.

The remaining four (sets of) contracts seem to be more inherent to the generic SIB design. First, the One Service intervention involves a broad range of services provided to prisoners and their families by multiple organizations, paid staff, and volunteers, in prison pre-release, at release, and after release.[4] This contract establishes the central parameters of the financial arrangements, performance targets, measurement, and compensation (Nicholls & Tomkinson, 2013).

Social Finance was happy to provide a redacted copy of this last document, but "[t]he detailed financial arrangements in the Peterborough SIB contract (and in other SIB contracts) remain confidential due to commercial sensitivities," according Social Finance's Director of Research and Communications (A. Helbitz, personal communication, November 11, 2014). In fact, virtually every aspect of the contract that is of interest for present purposes, including the outcome payment amounts and the non-contingent operational costs, has been redacted on grounds of commercial sensitivity.[5] Given that confidentiality, it is difficult to know precisely what the program's costs to the public purse would be under any scenario of results-measured success or failure. It does appear that the "operational costs" incurred by the SPV are to be reimbursed regardless of results. The contract stipulates, "The Fund [the SPV] shall only be paid for (i) the Fund's properly and reasonably incurred operational costs during the provision of the Interventions and (ii) the achievement of the Outcomes." Although the redactions combined with the lack of access to the agreements between investors and the SPV make it difficult to know for certain, it seems reasonable to presume that most or all of the repayments to investors are excluded from the definition of operational costs (i.e., that the investors' money truly is at risk to a significant degree, rather being covertly guaranteed).

At this writing in early 2015, some early results of the Peterborough pilot SIB are available. The independent evaluator's final analysis for the first cohort of released prisoners was released in August 2014. It confirmed the appropriateness and validity of the PSM method, and found that the intervention had reduced reconvictions for the cohort by 8.4% (Jolliffe & Hedderman, 2014). Although this reduction fell short of the 10% threshold to trigger single-cohort outcome payments, it is larger than the 7.5% difference that if maintained across all cohorts in the program would be sufficient to trigger outcome payments. The second cohort of prisoners is scheduled to receive services through June 2015, and the program will then be terminated without engaging the third cohort (Lander & Cook, 2014). The early termination of the SIB pilot program appears to reflect a larger shift in the Ministry of Justice's approach to contracting out for prisoner rehabilitation services rather than dissatisfaction with the Peterborough SIB specifically (Temple, 2014).

Lessons from the Case

As the world's first SIB, the Peterborough pilot project unquestionably presented an innovative model for social-program design, delivery, and finance. By most accounts, the One Service intervention design was innovative in its comprehensiveness and integration of multiple social supports, even if it was not innovative in the sense of inventing wholly new techniques of intervention. The intervention was designed as an investment in the sense that it aimed expressly to produce human and social capital in anticipation of future returns to that capital for the service recipients, government, and investors. In practice, the intervention generated results that were within a range deemed successful, even though not enough to trigger an immediate payout to investors. While financial details of the SIB have been kept confidential, what information has been made public does indicate that a significant proportion of the total financial risk associated with the program is in fact borne by the investors. Thus, the Peterborough SIB illustrates well the basic design features of the SIB archetype, although the financial opacity of the deal's public documentation makes it difficult to assess value for money or how the overall costs and benefits of the program are allocated among the parties to the SIB.

Massachusetts Case Study[6]

Our second illustrative case is a SIB developed in Massachusetts to increase employment and reduce recidivism for an at-risk male population of ex-offenders between the ages of 17 and 24 years, the Massachusetts Juvenile Employment and Recidivism Initiative (the Initiative). This SIB is the largest among the 20 or more SIB initiatives underway in the U.S. and the first in Massachusetts (Kresge Foundation, 2014). Like others in the Commonwealth, it was made possible by enabling legislation signed in 2012 by Governor Deval Patrick. That legislation established the Social Innovation Financing Trust Fund for the purpose of supporting "Pay for Success" (P4S) contracts in which funding is conditioned upon the following criteria:

1. "A requirement that a substantial portion of the payment be conditioned on the achievement of specific outcomes based on defined performance targets . . .
2. an objective process by which an independent evaluator will determine whether the performance targets have been achieved . . .
3. a calculation of the amount and timing of payments that would be earned by the service provider during each year of the agreement if performance targets are achieved as determined by the independent evaluator . . .
4. a sinking fund requirement under which the secretary shall request an appropriation for each fiscal year that the contract is in effect, in an amount equal to the expected payments that the commonwealth would ultimately be obligated to pay in the future based upon service provided during that fiscal year, if performance targets were achieved
5. a determination by the secretary that the contract will result in significant performance improvements and budgetary savings across all impacted agencies if the performance targets are achieved." (Section 35VV of Chapter 10 of the Massachusetts General Laws)

The Initiative is intended to reduce recidivism and increase employment among ex-offenders. To this end, the Commonwealth contracted with Roca Incorporated, a nonprofit service provider, and Youth Services Incorporated (YSI), a project manager (or intermediary) within a P4S contract. The P4S contract (the Contract) is dated January 7, 2014. The Contract reads like any other performance-based contract. The main difference is that there is no upfront money awarded by government for the services provided. The innovation of the SIB is that it leverages upfront private equity in exchange for long-term cost savings. The money flows from the lenders or philanthropies to the project intermediary and then to the service provider—Roca in this particular case. Should Roca achieve target performance, then the Commonewealth will issue payments and investors will receive a return of their principal plus a return on their investment.

Roca will provide the direct services to the target population and YSI will manage almost all aspects of the project. Roca has been providing services to youth (17–24) in the Boston region for over 25 years (Roca website). In this project they will target an at-risk population of young men with the goals of reducing recidivism and increasing employment. The SIB fact sheet describes Roca services in the following manner:

> The Roca intervention establishes transformative relationships and uses targeted life skills, education, and employment programming to support young men in developing the skills necessary to reduce violence and create positive behavioral changes. The four-year model—which consists of two years of intensive engagement and two years of follow-up—includes four basic elements: relentless outreach to young men by Roca staff; intensive case management; life skills, educational, prevocational, and employment programming; and work opportunities with community partners. Roca helps young men change their behaviors while learning how to go to work, beginning with subsidized employment opportunities and transitioning into full-time positions with employer partners. (p. 2)

In total, Roca will enroll 929 youth in their programs during the contract term. Target enrollments for Roca service provision are projected quarterly based on geographic areas. The model utilizes an experimental design in which all Roca participants receive the "treatment" (i.e., Roca services), while those who do not receive services form the control group. The model is dependent upon a designated number of enrollees necessary to establish a "test group" to determine if success has been achieved. Performance between the treatment group and the control group will be compared against historical averages.[7] If Roca reaches designated targets, then the Commonwealth will issue payments. In this contract government payments begin in Q17. Prior to government payments, YSI will draw down the loans and philanthropic funding on a quarterly basis to pay for project services (see Figure 10.2). As the project intermediary, it distributes this funding to Roca. Roca then uses this money to provide services to the target population.

In addition to the Social Innovation Financing Trust Fund, the Commonwealth received a grant from the Department of Labor (DOL) for $11.7 million, of which $800,000 is reserved for administrative costs. The DOL will not issue any payments until the end of year four and only if performance targets are reached. With the remaining $10.9 million from the DOL, the Commonwealth can save $10.9 million from the trust fund while still meeting all performance payment requirements specified in the contract. If the project proves successful, the Commonwealth will extend the project for three additional years with monetary savings. The funding schedule in Table 10.1 shows the draws on the funding sources.

Table 10.1

Funding Schedule

First Day of	Draw on Senior Loan	Draw on Junior Loans	Draw on Philanthropic Funding
Quarter 1	$450,000	$150,000	$300,000
Quarter 2	$270,000	$90,000	$180,000
Quarter 3	$360,000	$120,000	$240,000
Quarter 4	$450,000	$150,000	$300,000
Quarter 5	$450,000	$150,000	$300,000
Quarter 6	$540,000	$180,000	$360,000
Quarter 7	$540,000	$180,000	$360,000
Quarter 8	$450,000	$150,000	$300,000
Quarter 9	$540,000	$180,000	$360,000
Quarter 10	$630,000	$210,000	$420,000
Quarter 11	$630,000	$210,000	$420,000
Quarter 12	$630,000	$210,000	$420,000
Quarter 13	$630,000	$210,000	$420,000
Quarter 14	$720,000	$240,000	$480,000
Quarter 15	$630,000	$210,000	$420,000
Quarter 16	$1,080,000	$360,000	$720,000
Total	$9,000,000	$3,000,000	$6,000,000

Source: Pay for Performance Contract

Funding and Evaluation Network

The P4S contract is the primary tool that stimulates network activity. Outside of the contract signatures—The Commonwealth of Massachusetts, Roca Incorporated, and Youth Services Incorporated—the contract is contingent on a number of relationships. The additional actors include funders, evaluators, and a financial intermediary. The funders for this project are Goldman Sachs ($9 million), Living Cities ($1.5 million), Kresge Foundation ($1.5 million), Laura and John Arnold Foundation ($3.7 million), The Boston Foundation ($300 thousand), and New Profit Inc. ($2 million). Roca has also agreed to defer $3.26 million in service fees to help fund the project. The evaluators are a second group of actors engaged in this project. Sibalytics LLC is the independent evaluator hired by YSI to evaluate the performance metrics upon which the SIB is built. In addition, the Commonwealth hired an independent validator—Public Consulting Group—to review and confirm "the findings of the Independent Evaluator."

The activation of the SIB begins with the transferring of funds from the lenders to the project intermediary. The intermediary then distributes funds to the service provider which in turn, provides services. The services are then evaluated by both the independent evaluation and the validator. If performance is reached, then performance payments

Figure 10.2   **Massachusetts Juvenile Justice SIB**

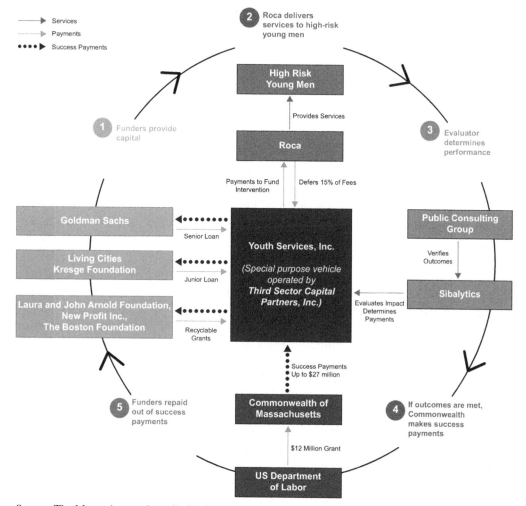

Source: The Massachusetts Juvenile Justice PFS Initiative, Third Sector Capital Partners

are distributed. The intermediary will utilize performance payments to repay both the principal and the interest to the investors (see Figure 10.2).

Performance Rewards

There are three categories in which payments can be rewarded: employment, job readiness and recidivism. Payments in the categories of job readiness and employment are distributed based on the following:

- Payments for increases in job readiness are $789 for each participant in each quarter that a Roca participant engages with a Roca youth worker nine or more times, with each engagement helping young men address barriers to employment and move toward economic independence . . .

- Payments for increases in employment are $750 for each participant in each quarter that a Roca participant is employed as compared to similar young men who are not in the program. (Contract, p. 2)

Employment is counted as any individual earning $1,000 or more in a given quarter.

Payments for reduced recidivism—measured by average bed days—are distributed based on the following:

- Payments for decreases in incarceration represent the majority of the success payments and are based on a graduated payment schedule where the Commonwealth pays increasing amounts for each day that participants avoid incarceration as compared to similar young men who are not in the program. The payment rates are based on associated savings to the Commonwealth as shown below. The minimum reduction in incarceration necessary for payments to be made is 5.2%. (Contract, p. 2)

The Commonwealth and the DOL use the same criteria for performance other than the payments category of job readiness, for which only the Commonwealth will make payments. Both the DOL and the Commonwealth will make initial payments in Quarter 17, should specified levels of performance be achieved. This will mark the end of the DOL participation in the initiative. The Commonwealth will continue payments in Quarter 19, 21, and 23. However, in the current contract period, the Commonwealth is only responsible to pay their share of performance awards less the $10.9 million committed from the DOL grant. Therefore, unless the DOL grant fails to materialize, the Commonwealth is committed to pay less than $20 million.[8] Table 10.2 shows the time period in which evaluation takes place.

Table 10.2

Evaluation Time Table

Project Quarter	Measurement Quarter	Measurement Quarter Ending	Period of Project Under Evaluation, Employment	Employment Outcomes Observed Through	Period of Project Under Evaluation Recidivism	Recidivism Outcomes Observed Through
Q16	Q14	9/30/16	Q1–11	9/30/16	Q1–12	12/31/16
Q17	Q15	6/30/17	Q1–13	12/30/16	Q1–14	3/31/17
Q19	Q17	12/31/17	Q1–15	6/30/17	Q1–16	9/30/17
Q21	Q19	6/30/18	Q1–17	12/31/17	Q1–18	3/31/18
Q23	Q21	12/31/18	Q1–19	6/30/18	Q1–20	9/30/18
Q25	Q23	6/30/19	Q1–21	12/31/18	Q1–22	3/31/19

Source: Pay for Success Contract

Government Cost Savings

According to the funding plan, a 40% reduction level in recidivism will result in a reduction of 199,293 bed days over the course of the contract. A 30% increase in employment will lead to a 1,113 increase in employment quarters over the term of the contract. The funding plan uses these medium levels of success to describe the financial outcomes of the project. The innovation of the SIB hinges on government cost savings; however, the Commonwealth notes,

> Determining which of these freed up resources are likely to result in monetizable budget savings is a complex exercise. Working with state and county officials, we have modeled these potential savings and concluded that monetizable savings primarily accrue when there is a reduction in the number of occupied prison and jail beds. The amount of savings accrued depends heavily on the scale of the bed reduction that occurs. We estimate that simply reducing the number of occupied beds in a facility, without shutting down a wing or an entire facility, saves state and county governments $12,410 per bed year in operating costs. If approximately 100 beds could be eliminated, then additional savings from closing a wing or adjusting staffing levels could occur, resulting in savings of $28,470 per bed year. If approximately 300 beds could be eliminated it would be possible to close a facility or avoid building a new one, and savings of $47,500 per bed year (or more) could be realized. (p. 20)

Important to note, the calculations behind these estimates are not released and are much more optimistic than the McKay (2013) estimates. The minimum reduction in incarceration necessary for payments to be made is 5.2% from historical averages.

Based on the Commonwealth's estimates, the government (state, county, and federal) will save on average $26,000 per participant (see Table 10.3).

Table 10.3

Savings per Participant by Level of Government

	Incarceration	Employment	Total
Federal		$680	$680
State	$16,706	$340	$17,046
County	$8,352	–	$8,352
Total	$25,058	$1,020	$26,078

Source: The Massachusetts Juvenile Employment and Recidivism Initiative Technical Narrative, the Commonwealth of Massachusetts

---

Defining Success

If Roca is successful at the most minimal levels—a 5% reduction in recidivism—government cost savings will not pay for program costs. As noted above, if Roca fails to reach a minimal threshold of 5.2% reduction in recidivism, then the Commonwealth will not make payments. However, if Roca is successful at a low-medium level—10–40% reduction in recidivism—estimated government cost savings will cover all program costs. Should Roca succeed at a high level—55–70% reduction in recidivism—the government will cover costs and make additional revenue based on the project expenditures. The lenders will receive their principal loan plus interest if the project reaches a 40% reduction in recidivism. If the project does not reach a 40% threshold, funders will receive a lower return on investment and take on the added risk of losing principal.

True Cost

The Commonwealth is overwhelmingly transparent in the provision of cost data associated with the project. There remain some figures that are not disclosed. First, it is unclear how the Commonwealth estimates cost savings. They offer an initial estimate of $12,410 per bed year as a baseline cost. The Commonwealth estimates substantial savings, ranging up to $47,000 per bed year, should a large number of clients not recidivate. This brings about a number of important questions about true cost savings.

The estimates are based on reduced staffing and facility closures. As noted above, we see these estimates as overly optimistic. They assume that the Commonwealth will readily be able to reduce their workforce and shut facilities. Ironically, it seems that the Commonwealth fails to acknowledge the same political challenges will exist in the saving estimates as existed in the initial funding streams for social innovative programs.

Table 10.4

Incarceration-Based Payment Terms

Decrease in Days of Incarceration	Incarceration-Based Success Payments	Gross Savings for Commonwealth
70.0%	$27 million	$45 million
55.0%	$26 million	$33 million
40.0%	$22 million	$22 million
25.0%	$11 million	$11 million
10.0%	$2 million	$2 million
5.0%	$0	$0.9 million

Source: Pay for Performance Contract

For example, will a legislator from a district with a prison facility simply let this facility close? Will a collective bargaining unit for prison employees simply allow for a reduction in their unit? These seem to be obstacles that were not factored into the estimated savings. Hence, the SIB is a policy solution in a vacuum—it does not consider the political reality in government savings.

Second, the Commonwealth estimates that they will reduce bed days by 199,293 over the course of the project. This is about 546 bed years. If we utilize McKay's estimated bed year savings of $4,623, the government saves $2,524,196. Even if we utilize the Commonwealth's base estimate of $12,410 per annual bed, cost savings remain substantially lower than projected at $6,775,860. The only way government cost savings pay for project costs is if we assume facility closures and staff reductions that reach $47,000 in savings per bed year. Even at this high rate, the government only saves about $26 million.

The basic costs of the project are clear. Per client service costs range from about $22,000 to $28,000 (Commonwealth of Massachusetts, 2013). The enrollments numbers have shifted slightly since the original Technical Narrative, but it remains instructive to understand true costs. For 535 participants, the total cost, including return on investment for lenders, is $16.6 million. This makes a per person cost of $31,000. The DOL grant covers 535 participants with a total contribution of $11.7 million, leaving the remaining $4.9 million the responsibility of the Commonwealth. In addition, based on the P4S contract the Commonwealth has committed to serving a total of 929 participants. Therefore, if Roca achieves all performance goals, the Commonwealth will make payments to fund 394 more participants or $12 million in additional performance payments. The sum of the performance payments for the Commonwealth in the contract term is about $16.9 million. The total return on investment for lenders increases project costs by $2.2 million for the contract term and Commonwealth administrative costs are $1.3 million.

THE EMPEROR'S NEW PUBLIC MANAGEMENT?

What can we make of SIBs so far, then, in terms of innovation, network governance, investment and finance, and risk allocation? This penultimate section will consider each dimension briefly in turn.

First, it seems clear that SIBs represent a genuinely innovative form of financial engineering, joined in an innovative combination with a model of networked third-party service delivery that is based on more familiar practice (see, for example, Provan and Milward, 1995, 2001). At the same time, there is some irony in that SIBs are likely to bias investors' search for appropriate models of social intervention toward the familiar, in order to contain risk (McKay, 2013; Warner, 2013). Proponents' depiction of the SIB structure suggests an analogy to venture capital, which invests in large numbers of individually risky companies that might be poised for dramatic growth. Venture-capital financing helps to bring promising products and services to scale, after they have already been demonstrated to have at least some potential. It relies on a portfolio model of investment, with exceptionally high returns for successful projects compensating for the larger number of failures in a portfolio, and exceptionally high targeted returns on the overall portfolio compensating for the generally high level of investment risk. For SIBs, the analogy would be that they involve taking concepts that have been to some degree proved in policy experiments or demonstration projects, and scaling them up to larger pilot programs or even full-scale implementation. To the extent gains from avoided social costs are shared in at least some measure with service clients and the broader public, high returns to financiers could be rationalized on the premise that half a loaf is better than none—relying on a satisficing rather than optimizing logic of choice.

As Warner (2013) notes, however, investors are not likely to take on extreme risks of default on any given SIB project without some kind of public guarantee or other backstop, at least not until SIB projects are as numerous as business start-ups and SIB investment portfolios correspondingly large and based on adequate risk-measurement experience. Also, investors might seek to shift risk back to governments by bailing out early from interventions that look like they won't succeed (McKay, 2013). In fact, the Massachusetts SIB expressly provides an early termination for investors.

Further, even if SIB contracts are structured in ways that maximize investors' and/or service providers' share of overall risk, governments still bear at least some share in the form of unavoidable transaction costs for negotiating agreements, monitoring the other parties to the agreements, and evaluating outcomes. An additional risk, or more properly an opportunity cost, arises for jurisdictions that—like Massachusetts—have to budget for sinking-fund payments sufficient to pay for the maximum potential payout to investors. This budgeted expenditure will necessarily displace other potential public priorities from those years' budgets.

This returns us to the bonds analogy and to a strand of reasoning that leads to the willful circumvention of popular opinion and constraints on governmental action, favoring instead what could be portrayed as a "protective" approach to democracy (see Held, 2006, for a typology of democracies) or as expertise-based paternalism (arguably adopting the stance of Friedrich [1940] rather than Finer [1941]). So, for example, executives and managers, usually aided by bankers who saw the profit opportunities involved, devised such now-ubiquitous devices as government corporations and public authorities (Doig, 1983; Mitchell, 1999), revenue bonds (Sbragia, 1996), and certificates of participation (Johnson & Mikesell, 1994) as ways to circumvent legal debt limits and bond-referendum requirements. Ostensibly, these financing mechanisms made it possible for enlightened, expert public managers to serve the needs, if not necessarily the expressed desires, of the public for physical capital, albeit at a usually higher cost compared to the legally more constrained general-obligation instruments. In short, the satisficing notion that half a loaf is better than none—or in economic terms the application of a Kaldor-Hicks rather than Pareto criterion—can be seen to justify pursuing methods for financing and implementing investments in social capital that are suboptimal but still net positive. For practitioners and scholars who (appropriately, in our view) hold dear the aspirational ideals of cost-minimization and democratic administration, this choice may well be valid although it presents a normatively ambiguous dilemma (see, for example, Miller & Justice, 2011; Justice & Miller, 2011).

Perhaps the most instructive municipal-debt analogy is to pension obligation bonds (POBs). POBs are sometimes issued by state and local governments to finance contributions to underfunded pension plans. The public rationale most often provided to support issuing POBs is that the proceeds will be invested in financial instruments that will generate returns greater than the interest payments on the bonds, thus generating arbitrage profits. Because the bonds are issued for arbitrage purposes, they are taxable, and so pay higher interest rates than tax-exempt municipal debt. Further, although it is conceivable that POBs could work as advertised under ideal conditions, in practice the costs of POBs normally exceed the returns. They thus tend to increase rather than decrease the total cost of funding pension systems. As such, POBs are often regarded by municipal-finance observers as devices that disguise risks, conceal and inflate costs, and commit future legislators and taxpayers to bear the burden of their predecessors' deferral of timely and adequate investment. This suggests that, as with social welfare and human capital, timely incremental investments would be a financially and economically preferred approach. But once governments have failed for many years to make those investments, POBs, although not pretty, do serve to get the job of political commitment done. This may be suboptimal, but sometimes it is the only politically possible approach. Similarly, by providing incentives for social and policy entrepreneurs to promote and finance investments in human capital so that they can monetize some or all of the eventual social benefits for themselves, SIBs may be the only means by which political support can be assembled for some types of human-capital investments. Indeed, this rationale is apparent, although not stated so baldly, in the references to the difficulty of pursuing preventive social services through more conventional policy-design, legitimation, and implementation processes contained in promotional materials generated by Social Finance Limited (2014, p. 1).

KEY POINTS

1. Identify the conditions under which SIBs are an acceptable choice.
2. Decide if alternatives are politically or organizationally impossible.
3. Determine the likelihood of achieving net social benefits
4. Assess how much risk government can transfer or share with private-sector partners.
5. Determine if activities can be monitored effectively.
6. Know the avoidable costs.

SIBs do not appear to be unqualified boons to the public in the way some of their proponents make them out to be. On the other hand, researchers have identified a number of the tradeoffs and potential pitfalls of SIBs in ways that, combined with thoughtful assessment of the costs and benefits of the currently extant SIBs, can facilitate informed decision making. One response to the current enthusiasm for SIBs, then, might be to think systematically about articulating a framework to *identify the conditions under which SIBs are an acceptable choice.* To do this, managers should consider the counterfactual "but for": recognizing *when lower-cost approaches to investing in human capital are truly politically and organizationally* impossible without the political and financial sleight of hand afforded by the SIB structure. Interestingly this recalls an observation made in a report recommending *against* the use of SIBs but arguing that the activities the SIBs would have financed should be pursued by other means, due to their significant potential to generate future social—although not necessarily fiscal—benefits (McKay, 2013).

In such cases, managers should consider the *likelihood of achieving net social benefits. This might compel managers to select projects that have been tested and succeeded and move* them from traditional mechanisms that have failed in the past. However, there remains the question of *whether or not government can transfer risks of programmatic failure to the profit-making financiers to a great enough degree that the expected net welfare gains might reasonably be deemed to justify the higher-than-optimal cost of the initial investment.* Lastly, we suggest two basic criteria associated with the classic contract. *Can we successfully monitor activities and what are the effective avoidable costs realized* (Sclar, 2000)? If the answer to these questions are "no, we cannot" and "we do not know," then an SIB may not be the appropriate vehicle for the project.

There is a narrative that long-term cost savings garnered in an SIB project will pay for project costs. Thus far, we have been unable to see the manner in which these cost-saving estimates have been calculated. This makes it challenging to determine the validity of any real cost savings. In our estimation it seems like the cost savings are overly optimistic and fail to consider political realities. This is especially true in the case of the Massachusetts initiative, which places a large emphasis on facility closure and staff reduction. Two important points emerge from this. First, why does it take private investment for government to scrutinize costs and suggest manners to save costs? Might a recidivism reduction program run by public correctional facilities be a perfect solution to costly and overpopulated prisons? This suggestion, while obvious, seems equally as naive as the cost-reduction estimates in the SIB project. Rarely can we align incentives. Second, why must there be government cost savings for a recidivism reduction program? Might the social benefit from such a program be deemed worthwhile by the citizenry?

Although the SIB offers some promise, our assessment suggests that at best only half of that promise will be fulfilled and at worst the promise will be broken. Political tools dressed in the clothes of management do not solve problems. From a managerial perspective, SIBs are too risky and will most likely not produce the assumed cost savings. Although they dangle shiny objects, one must remember those objects come at a high cost. The true risk transfer in an SIB is from a politician to a public manager cloaked in the cover of innovation.

NOTES

1. An offenses are counted as a re-offense if the reconviction occurs within 18 months of an individual's release (Nicholls and Tomkinson, 2013, p. 15).

2. It is worth noting that this estimated cost per prisoner-year of incarceration is larger by an order of magnitude than the estimate generated by Maryland's Department of Legislative Services of how much money can be saved by preventing a year of incarceration. The estimate of £40,000 per prisoner-year is more than $60,000 at current exchange rates and probably represents the *average* cost per prisoner-year. The estimated *marginal* fiscal savings per avoided prisoner-year in Maryland's prison system were estimated in 2013 as $4,623 (McKay, 2013). The matter of estimating marginal costs and benefits is obviously central to determining whether an effective SIB initiative that generates a profit for investors will also return benefits to governments and taxpayers. The difference between marginal and average costs is clearly one source of the large disparity between the UK and Maryland cost estimates. Another consideration in estimating costs and benefits is distinguishing between economic costs and benefits of the types included in societal cost-benefit analysis, and the subset of those costs and benefits that are financial. An analyst who wants to minimize the estimated impact of a successful SIB might focus on strictly financial, marginal savings, and bound the scope of costs and benefits narrowly, while an analyst hoping to maximize predicted savings might include monetary estimates of social benefits and try to include savings realized in the widest possible range of public and private activities affected directly or indirectly by (in this example) recidivism.

3. Note that at least some subsequent arguments in favor of SIBs in the US and UK have employed a somewhat different rationale. Rather than emphasizing financial costs and benefits, some advocates have instead suggested that net *social* benefits resulted from improved social services can justify SIBs. Although is not stated quite this baldly, the rationale appears to be that a net *increase* in public expenditure, to pay for services plus the compensation to investors, is justified by social benefits that will be greater than the financial costs. In other words, social entrepreneurs can use SIBs as a device for monetizing some of the social benefits of reducing social problems.

4. The SIB structure dictates that there will always be at least one contract for service delivery. The use of multiple specialized providers to deliver a broad range of services is not necessitated by the SIB structure, but does not appear to be unusual among SIBs. For a summary of the Peterborough service delivery arrangements and their evolution, see Nicholls and Tomkinson (2013, pp. 16–25).

5. Schedule 6 of the contract stipulates,
The following information shall constitute Commercially Sensitive Information:
- Definition of "Authority Outcome Payment"
- Definition of "BLF Outcome Payment"
- Definition of "Maximum Authority Liability" and Clause 32.5 (Indemnity and Liability)
- Clause 11 (Payment)
- Clause 34 (Warranties and Representations)
- Clauses 39 (Consequences of Expiry or Termination)
- Schedule 5 (Operational Costs Payment)
- Schedule 6 (Outcome Payment)

Although it seems inconsistent with familiar procurement and budgeting practices in the U.S., this degree of confidentiality does have a precedent in the U.K.'s NPM-inspired Private Finance Initiative for infrastructure finance. In that program, commercial confidentiality was used to facilitate price discrimination, which as one expert pointed out is not illegal (P. Watt, personal communication, November 11, 2014).

6. All information about the Massachusetts Case Study was attained from the contract which established the legal arrangement of the SIB unless otherwise noted: Pay for Success Contract. Commonwealth of Massachusetts, ROCA Incorporated, and Youth Services Incorporated. January 2014 retrieved from http://payforsuccess.org/sites/default/files/final_pay_for_success_contract_executed_1_7_2013.pdf on December 11th 2014.

7. The P4S contract is explicit as to the experimental design. While a full evaluation of the methodology is outside of the scope of this chapter it is important to note the scrutiny that must be given to an effective evaluation.

8. Section 4.02 of the contract reads (f) "Total PFS Payments Earned to Date" shall be the lesser of (i) $27,000,000 and (ii) the sum of all PFS Payments Earned to Date Due to Gains in Job Readiness, PFS Payments Earned to Date Due to Gains in Employment, and PFS Payments Earned to Date Due to Bed-Days Avoided less the Department of Labor PFS Payment Due to Gains in Employment and the Department of Labor PFS Payment Due to Bed Days Avoided remitted to YSI by the Commonwealth pursuant to this Contract.

REFERENCES

Barclay, L., & Symons, T. (2013). *A techincal guide to developing social impact bonds*. London: Social Finance Ltd.

Cave, S., WIlliams, T., Jolliffe, D., & Hedderman, C. (2012). *Peterborough social impact bond: An independent assessment. Development of the PSM methodology*. Minstry of Justice Research Series 8/12. London: Ministry of Justice.

Centre for Social Impact Bonds. (2013a, April 18). Knowledge box. *SIB knowledge box*. Retrieved May 1, 2015, from http://data.gov.uk/sib_knowledge_box/knowledge-box

Centre for Social Impact Bonds. (2013b, April 19). *Ministry of Justice: Offenders released from Peterborough prison*. Retrieved February 3, 2015, from http://data.gov.uk/sib_knowledge_box/ministry-justice-offenders-released-peterborough-prison

Commonwealth of Massachusetts. (2013). *The Massachusetts juvenile employment and recidivism initiative: Technical narrative*.

Dedeurwaerdere, T. (2005). *The contribution of network governance to sustainable development*. Idées pour le débat (ex-Les Séminaires de l'Iddri n° 13).

Doig, J. W. (1983). "If I see a murderous fellow sharpening a knife cleverly . . .": The Wilsonian dichotomy and the public authority tradition. *Public Administration Review, 43*, 292–304.

Finer, H. (1941). Administrative responsibility in democratic government. *Public Administration Review, 1*(4), 335–350.

Friedrich, C. J. (1940). Public policy and the nature of administrative responsibility. *Public Policy, 1*, 3–24.

Held, D. (2006). *Models of democracy* (3rd ed.). Palo Alto, CA: Stanford University Press.

Hildreth, W. B., Miller, G. J., & Sewordor, E. (2011). *State government catastrophe risk financing and the capital markets*. Paper presented at the National Tax Association, 2011 Conference, New Orleans. Retrieved from http://ssrn.com/abstract=2168878

Johnson, C. L., & Mikesell, J. (1994). Certificates of participation and capital markets: Lessons from Brevard County and Richmond Unified School District. *Public Budgeting & Finance, 14*(3), 41–54. doi:10.1111/1540–5850.01011

Jolliffe, D., & Hedderman, C. (2014). *Peterborough social impact bond: Final report on cohort 1 analysis*. Ministry of Justice.

Justice, J. B., & Miller, G. J. (2011). Accountability and debt management: The case of New York's Metropolitan Transportation Authority. *The American Review of Public Administration, 41*(3), 313–328.

Kresge Foundation. (2014). *Massachusetts launches landmark initiative to reduce recidivism among high-risk young men* (Press release). Retrieved from http://kresge.org/news/massachusetts-launches-landmark-initiative-reduce-recidivism-among-high-risk-young-men

Lander, E., & Cook, S. (2014). Why the social impact bond at Peterborough prison is being halted. *Third Sector*. Retrieved from www.thirdsector.co.uk/why-social-impact-bond-peterborough-prison-halted/finance/article/1294813

Leonhardt, D. (2011). For federal programs, a taste of market discipline. *New York Times*. Retrieved from www.nytimes.com/2011/02/09/business/economy/09leonhardt.html

Liebman, J. B. (2011). *Social impact bonds: A promising new financing model to accelerate social innovation and improve government performance*. Washington, DC: Center for American Progress.

Lowndes, V., & Skelcher, C. (1998). The dynamics of multi-organizational partnerships: An analysis of changing modes of governance. *Public administration, 76*(2), 313–333.

McKay, K. A. (2013). *Evaluating social impact bonds as a new reentry financing mechanism: A case study on reentry programming in Maryland.* Annapolis, MD: Department of Legislative Services.

Miller, G. J., & Hildreth, W. B. (2000, October 6). *Risk management and the capital markets.* Paper presented at the 12th Annual Conference of the Association for Budgeting and Financial Management, Kansas City, MO.

Miller, G. J., & Justice, J. B. (2011). Debt management networks and the proverbs of financial management. *Municipal Finance Journal, 31*(4), 19–40.

Mitchell, J. (1999). *The American experiment with government corporations.* Armonk, NY: M. E. Sharpe.

Nicholls, A., & Tomkinson, E. (2013). *The Peterborough pilot social impact bond.* Oxford: University of Oxford.

O'Toole Jr., L. J. (1997). Treating networks seriously: Practical and research-based agendas in public administration. *Public Administration Review, 57*(1), 45–52.

Pay for Success Contract. (2014, January). *Commonwealth of Massachusetts, ROCA Incorporated, and Youth Services Incorporated.* Retrieved December 11, 2014, from http://payforsuccess.org/sites/default/files/final_pay_for_success_contract_executed_1_7_2013.pdf

Phillips, S. D. (2004). The limits of horizontal governance. *Society and Economy, 26*(2/3), 383–405.

Provan, K. G., & Milward, H. B. (1995). A preliminary theory of network effectiveness: A comparative study of four community mental health systems. *Administrative Science Quarterly, 40*(1), 1–33.

Provan, K. G., & Milward, H. B. (2001). Do networks really work? A framework for evaluating public-sector organizational networks. *Public Administration Review, 61*(4), 414–423.

Salamon, L. M. (Ed.). (2002). *The tools of government: A guide to the new governance.* New York: Oxford University Press.

Sbragia, A. M. (1996). *Debt wish: Entrepreneurial cities, U.S. federalism, and economic development.* Pittsburgh, PA: University of Pittsburgh Press.

Sclar, E. D. (2001). *You don't always get what you pay for: The economics of privatization.* Ithaca, NY: Cornell University Press.

Social Finance Limited. (2014, July). *Introduction to social impact bonds.* Retrieved February 4, 2015, from http://socialfinance.westgatecomms.com/wp-content/uploads/2014/07/Introduction-to-Social-Impact-Bonds.pdf

Temple, N. (2014). Has the social investment flagship sailed off course? *Third Sector.* Retrieved from www.thirdsector.co.uk/social-investment-flagship-sailed-off-course/finance/article/1294822

Van Bueren, E. M., Klijn, E. H., & Koppenjan, J. F. (2003). Dealing with wicked problems in networks: Analyzing an environmental debate from a network perspective. *Journal of Public Administration Research and Theory, 13*(2), 193–212.

Warner, M. E. (2013). Private finance for public goods: Social impact bonds. *Journal of Economic Policy Reform, 16*(4), 303–319. doi:10.1080/17487870.2013.835727

About the Editor and Contributors

EDITOR

Daniel E. Bromberg is Assistant Professor of Public Administration and the MPA Director at the University of New Hampshire. His research interests include government procurement, performance management, and organizational accountability. He holds a Ph.D. from the School of Public Affairs and Administration at Rutgers-Newark.

CONTRIBUTORS

Carrie Blanchard Bush is an Assistant Professor in the Department of Government and Justice Studies at Appalachian State University in Boone, North Carolina. Her research interests include the cooperation between the public and private sectors, the use of social capital in collaborative arrangements, and local economic development. Previous to joining Appalachian State University, Bush served as the Chief of Staff to the Mayor of Tallahassee, Florida, as well as the Director of Research and Public Policy for the Florida Chamber of Commerce Foundation. Bush has been published in journals including *Economic Development Quarterly*, *Administration and Society*, *International Review of Public Administration*, and other scholarly publications.

Brian Robert Calfano is an Associate Professor of Political Science at Missouri State University and policy advisor to the City of Los Angeles Human Relations Commission (City HRC). His research focus emphasizes intergroup relations, social identity, and media effects on public behavior. Calfano's research appears in *Political Research Quarterly*, *Political Communication*, *Political Behavior*, *Politics and Religion*, *Social Science Quarterly*, and other scholarly outlets.

Sheldon Cruz is Senior Policy Analyst for the City of Los Angeles Human Relations Commission (City HRC). Cruz's work has included facilitating efforts by the Watts Gang Task Force to address needs in the South LA community and establishing City HRC's popular Youth Ambassador Program, which provides city youth with civic education and internship opportunities.

Jian Cui is a doctoral candidate of Policy Research & Analysis at the University of Pittsburgh, Graduate School of Public and International Affairs (GSPIA), with a second major in Public Administration. Her research focuses on the joint issues of energy and environmental policies, and science, technology, and society (STS), including risk communication and risk regulation of emerging and transforming technologies. In her dissertation, she studies chemical disclosure policies in shale gas development across the U.S. Her other research interests have included corporate social responsibility (CSR), disaster management, and volunteers' identify construction. She teaches an undergraduate course in Public Policy Process at the University of Pittsburgh and is consulted on collaborative projects in shale gas development between the U.S. and China.

Joshua Franzel is the Vice President of Research for the Center for State and Local Government Excellence and Director of Policy Research for the International City/County Management Association. Previously he worked for both the Delaware and Florida legislatures and was a Presidential Management Fellow with the International Trade Administration and the Office of Management and Budget. His publications and research have focused on state and local government management, public finance, public pensions and other public funds, infrastructure, health-care financing, demographics, public employee benefits and compensation, public health, and government innovation. Franzel is an adjunct professor at American University, where he teaches graduate-level courses on state and local government. He holds a Ph.D. in Public Administration and Policy from American University in Washington, DC.

Ian C. Graig is a founding partner and Chief Executive of Global Policy Group (GPG), a Washington-based research and consulting firm that he co-founded in 1995. He advises clients in such areas as legislative and regulatory trends affecting the automotive industry; environmental and climate policy; energy policy and industry developments; and international trade and investment. He is the author of numerous GPG client reports and has managed dozens of GPG research projects on such topics as climate change, automotive emissions and safety regulations, renewable energy, and federal R&D policy. He writes regularly for and is often quoted in *Automotive World* and other industry publications. He previously worked as a program manager and senior policy analyst at SRI International and for the international trade law firm of Tanaka Ritger & Middleton. He holds a Ph.D. and an M.A. in Government and Foreign Affairs from the University of Virginia, and a B.A. in Government from Hamilton College.

Ryan Gregory has worked in local government management for 15 years. His experience during this time has included economic development, planning, public/media relations, intergovernmental affairs, budget, personnel, and finance management. This experience comes from working both in a large organization (Phoenix, Arizona, population 1.3 million) and a much smaller one (Greenwood Village, Colorado, population 14,000). Gregory has a B.S. in Political Science and a Master of Public Administration, both from Arizona State University. In addition, he is a graduate of the International City/County Management Association's Leadership ICMA program and the University of Virginia's Senior Executive Institute. Gregory currently lives with his wife and two young children in Denver, Colorado.

Alexander C. Henderson is an Assistant Professor in the Department of Health Care and Public Administration at Long Island University. Henderson holds a B.A. and M.P.A. from Villanova University, and a Ph.D. in public administration from Rutgers University-Newark. His research focuses on organizational behavior, performance measurement and management, and comparative public administration.

Quintus Jett is an Assistant Professor at Rutgers University-Newark, in the School of Public Affairs and Administration, and he is a Fellow of the Rutgers Business School's Center for Urban Entrepreneurship & Economic Development (CUEED). Professor Jett is an engaged scholar focused on innovation in fields of public service and philanthropy. He has multi-disciplinary backgrounds (public and nonprofit management, business, and engineering). He has published in leading academic management journals, authored for the U.S. Department of Commerce on Minority Business Enterprises, and conducted action research in post-Katrina New Orleans. Professor Jett has a Ph.D. in Organizations from Stanford University.

Karen Jumonville is the Director of Growth Management for the City of Tallahassee, Florida. Prior to becoming the City's Growth Management Director, Jumonville served as the City's Division Director of Land Use and Environmental Services and Senior Land Use Planner. Jumonville has also served as a Senior Planner in the Growth Management Department of Leon County, Florida, as well as City Planner for the City of Quincy, Florida. Her research interests include the implementation of local government planning and land use regulations, permitting and regulatory reform, and growth management.

Jonathan B. Justice is a Professor in the School of Public Policy and Administration at the University of Delaware, where he teaches undergraduate courses in public policy and graduate courses in public/nonprofit financial management, government budgeting, and local economic development. His research focuses include public budgeting and finance, and professional accountability. Before earning his Ph.D. from Rutgers University-Newark in 2003, he worked for the City of New York and for local economic development organizations in the New York metropolitan area.

Jonathan Q. Morgan is an Associate Professor of Public Administration and Government in the School of Government at the University of North Carolina at Chapel Hill, where he teaches, advises, and conducts applied research on economic development. He directs the annual Basic Economic Development Course at UNC, which is accredited by the International Economic Development Council. Prior to joining the UNC School of Government in 2003, he worked for Regional Technology Strategies, Inc., an economic and workforce development consulting firm. Morgan has also served as Director of Economic Policy and Research for the NC Department of Commerce, as well as Research and Policy Director for the NC Institute of Minority Economic Development. He holds a B.A. in Economics from the University of Virginia, an M.P.A. from Clark Atlanta University, and a Ph.D. in Public Administration from North Carolina State University.

Lauren Bock Mullins is an Assistant Professor in the Department of Health Care and Public Administration at Long Island University. She holds an M.A. from Columbia University and a Ph.D. in Public Administration from Rutgers University-Newark. Mullins conducts research on women and family policy, performance management, and citizen participation.

Arturo E. Osorio is a faculty member in Entrepreneurship at Rutgers Business School, an international speaker, and an entrepreneurship and socioeconomic development consultant. Osorio is also a Fellow at the Cornwell Center for Metropolitan Studies and at the Center for Urban Entrepreneurship & Economic Development (CUEED). He is an associated editor for the *New England Journal of Entrepreneurship*. Osorio earned his Ph.D. and MBA in Management from the University of Massachusetts at Amherst. His research on socioeconomic development explores issues of entrepreneurship, food security, and social innovation. Osorio has participated in numerous international conferences and has published several academic and practitioner articles, as well as two book chapters.

Katharine A. Owens is an Associate Professor in the Department of Politics, Economics, and International Studies and Director of the Environmental Studies program at the University of Hartford. She works to better understand the conditions under which policy is implemented. She does this by applying the contextual interaction theory to environmental policy and program implementation scenarios. The theory evaluates the motivation, knowledge, and power of actors to recognize how they influence policy implementation. Currently, her research focuses on examining a range of policy areas, including climate change, campus sustainability, food, and marine debris.

Joumana Silyan-Saba is a Senior Policy Analyst for the City of Los Angeles Human Relations Commission (City HRC). She works with diverse communities to promote healthy intergroup relations, pluralism, and civic engagement. Her efforts include working with faith and civic leaders, civil rights organizations, policy makers, and academic institutes to bridge divides and address social justice concerns. Silyan-Saba obtained her B.S. in Criminal Justice–Law Enforcement with a minor in Business Administration Human Resources Management at California State University Long Beach. She completed her M.A. in Negotiation and Conflict Management at California State University Dominguez Hills, where she is currently an Adjunct Assistant Professor and teaches graduate courses in the Negotiations and Peace Building Program.

Linda L. Vila is a faculty member in the Department of Health Care and Public Administration at Long Island University. Professor Vila holds a B.A. in English from Hunter College of C.U.N.Y. and a J.D. from Brooklyn Law School. Her areas of expertise include health law, health-care management, and health-care ethics.

Index

Made in the USA
Coppell, TX
22 January 2021